Contents

GOTTFRIED WILHELM LEIBNIZ

Born at Leipzig on 1st July 1646. Entered the University of
Leipzig at the age of fifteen. Offered a professorship at
the University of Altdorf before he was twenty-one.
Elected F.R.S. in 1673. In 1676 went to live at the Court
of Hanover and died there on 14th November 1716.

Leibniz
Philosophical Writings

Edited by G. H. R. Parkinson
Reader in Philosophy at the University of Reading
Translated by Mary Morris
and G. H. R. Parkinson

J M Dent & Sons Ltd London

Introduction

Gottfried Wilhelm Leibniz was born in Leipzig on 1 July 1646. The son of a professor of moral philosophy, he studied at the Universities of Leipzig and Jena. Germany had been devastated by the Thirty Years' War, which ended in 1648, and the general cultural backwardness of the country was reflected in the German universities. It may have been this that decided Leibniz to reject the offer of a professorship in 1667, and to enter instead the service of the Baron of Boineburg, who had been a minister of the Elector of Mainz. This proved to be of great, perhaps of decisive importance in Leibniz's career. Whilst in Boineburg's service he was sent on a mission to Paris; this turned into a long stay, lasting from 1672 to 1676. Paris at this time was the intellectual capital of Europe, and Leibniz came into contact with such philosophers as Malebranche and Arnauld; he had access to Pascal's mathematical manuscripts; most important of all, he met the great Dutch physicist Christiaan Huygens, who in effect introduced him to higher mathematics. Leibniz could never equal Huygens as a physicist, but he was soon to outstrip him in the mathematical field; it was while he was in Paris that he discovered (independently of, but later than Newton) the differential calculus. It was in Paris, too, that he had constructed the first model of his new calculating machine, an improvement on the machine already invented by Pascal.

Boineburg died in 1672, and in 1676 Leibniz accepted a post under the Duke of Hanover. He served three successive dukes until his death in Hanover on 14 November 1716. His duties were various: he was librarian, jurist and official historian. At that time, Hanover was a small town of about 10,000 inhabitants, but Leibniz was far from being provincial in outlook. The first Duke of Hanover to employ him, Johann Friedrich, was a person of wide culture; so, too, was the Duchess Sophia, wife of the next Duke and grand-daughter of James I of England. There were journeys to Berlin to visit Sophia's daughter, Sophie Charlotte, Queen of Prussia; there was a long journey to Italy to collect historical material. Further, there was Leibniz's correspondence. During Leibniz's lifetime, learned journals were relatively few, and the private letter was still a major means of communication between scholars. Leibniz's correspondence was vast: the total number of his correspondents exceeds 1,000, and he often corresponded with more than 150 people in a single year.

In his letters, and in a large number of papers, he poured out his ideas on a great range of subjects—on mathematics, logic, science, history, law, theology and philosophy. Relatively little of this was published during his lifetime; it is symptomatic of this that of the works translated in the present volume only the *New System* and *Explanation of the New System* were published before his death. The only philosophical book of any length which he published was the *Theodicy* (1710), a semi-popular and loosely-constructed work which attempted to justify God's ways to man, and in which Leibniz's philosophy is spread somewhat thinly. Nor was any *magnum opus* left behind in his papers; instead, he left behind him a large number of short essays, which reflect his philosophy from various angles, much as (to use one of his favourite illustrations) the same town is differently represented from different points of view. It will be the aim of this introduction to provide a kind of plan of the Leibnizian philosophy, to which the various points of view presented in the papers which follow can be related.

Leibniz's philosophy is usually held to be an example of that philosophical rationalism whose other two great exponents are Descartes and Spinoza. None of the three ever called himself a rationalist, but it is true that, despite great differences, they had much in common, and it is useful to have a common name by which to refer to them. The question is what it is that marks them off from other philosophers. If the term 'rationalism' is taken to mean a philosophy which disregards sense-experience, then neither Descartes, Spinoza nor Leibniz was a rationalist. What they did have in common was the belief that sense-experience is an inferior kind of knowledge, and that genuine knowledge is provided by the reason. More precisely, it is provided by deductive reasoning; knowledge constitutes a deductive system, comparable to a system of geometry. So Descartes could write in Part II of his *Discourse on Method*, published in 1637, that 'Those long chains of reasoning, quite simple and easy, which geometricians use in order to achieve their most difficult demonstrations, had given me occasion to imagine that all things which can be known by man are mutually related in the same way'. Similarly, in his *Of Universal Synthesis and Analysis* of about 1683 Leibniz spoke of his youthful search for categories which would relate, not concepts, but propositions—not realising that what he sought was already provided by geometrical demonstrations.

Leibniz's views about the systematic character of all knowledge are linked with his plans for a universal symbolism, a *Characteristica Universalis*. This was to be a calculus which would cover all thought, and replace controversy by calculation. The ideal now seems absurdly optimistic, but it should be remembered that, in general, the philosophers and scientists of the seventeenth century were not lacking in confidence: Descartes, for example, could claim in his *Principles of Philosophy* (IV, 199) that there was no natural phenomenon not dealt with in the work. What matter here, however, are the implications that this ideal had for Leibniz.

The calculus was to cover all knowledge; it therefore presupposed as a basis an encyclopaedia which would contain, in a non-symbolic form, all that was so far known. Leibniz wrote many sketches of and introductions to such an encyclopaedia, one of which is translated in this volume, but he never completed the undertaking. However, the by-products of the plan were important. Leibniz recognised the essentially co-operative character of the enterprise, and so was led to support the foundation of new academies and of a new learned journal, the *Acta Eruditorum*. But the calculus needed more than an encyclopaedia; it was not only to cover all knowledge,

it was also to put it in a systematic form. To show the
logical dependence of one proposition on another it was
necessary, Leibniz believed, to be able to analyse the concepts which occur in propositions, reducing complex concepts to the simple concepts that are their constituents. It
must be stressed that the aim of Leibniz's analysis is not
simply the clarification of meaning, nor the solution of
puzzles, as in much modern philosophical analysis; the aim is
clarification in the service of proof. Further, the terminal
points of Leibniz's analysis, his primitive concepts, differ from
those of modern philosophers. Leibniz's analysis goes with a
metaphysics. This does not, of itself, differentiate it from all
modern philosophical analysis; Russell's philosophy of logical
atomism involves a metaphysics, and the same can be said of
Wittgenstein's. Leibniz's metaphysics, however, differs radi-
cally from that of Russell or Wittgenstein. In Leibniz's *Of an
Organum or Ars Magna of Thinking* the primitive concepts are
said to be of pure being (i.e. God) and of nothing; elsewhere,
the primitive concepts are said to be of the attributes of God.

Here, however, a gap opens in Leibniz's analysis, in that
the grasping of these primitive concepts is said to be beyond
our powers. If we could grasp them, we could show *a priori*
how everything follows from God, and this we clearly cannot
do. Leibniz therefore has to propose a more modest kind of
analysis, which terminates in concepts which are only relatively primitive, primitive for us. He gave various lists of
such concepts, one of which can be found in his *Introduction to a
Secret Encyclopaedia*. But the limitations on analysis just mentioned must not be exaggerated. What human beings cannot
do, Leibniz says, is to show *a priori* how *everything* follows from
the attributes of God. It will be seen later, however, that
Leibniz thinks that from the concept of God that we have,
imperfect as it is, it is possible to deduce something about the
nature of the universe. In short, the construction of a deductive metaphysical system is within our power; what is
not, is the construction of a metaphysical system which is
complete.

First, however, it must be explained why Leibniz should
regard the primitive concepts as being of the attributes of

God. Here it is necessary to consider the rules of his calculus—
that is, the principles of reasoning. Leibniz said many times
that reasoning is based on two great principles—that of
identity or contradiction, and that of sufficient reason. He
did not always make it clear, however, that these principles
are, as he once put it, 'contained in the definition of truth
and falsity'. This statement occurs in an appendix to the
Theodicy of 1710 ('Remarks on the book, *On the Origin of
Evil*', par. 14), but the relations between the two principles
and Leibniz's definition of truth are explored most thoroughly
in the *Discourse on Metaphysics* of 1686, and other writings of
the same period. Leibniz's view is that every proposition has a
subject and a predicate, and a true proposition is one whose
predicate is in the subject. So, for example, the proposition
'Every man is rational' is true because rationality is in man,
or, as Leibniz would also say, because the concept of rationality
is in the concept of man. Leibniz also asserts that every truth
is, implicitly or explicitly, an identical proposition. The true
proposition 'Every man is rational' is not explicitly identical,
but, Leibniz says, it can be reduced to 'A rational animal is
rational', which is. To prove something to be true is to reduce
a proposition which is only implicitly identical to one which is
explicitly identical; or, it is to show *how* the predicate is in the
subject. This is done by the analysis either of the subject, or
of the predicate, or of both. All this can now be related to
Leibniz's 'two great principles'. Leibniz's definition of
truth states that every truth is either an explicitly identical
proposition, or is reducible to such. The principle of identity
or contradiction says that every identical proposition is true
and every self-contradiction is false. The principle of sufficient
reason says that every truth can be proved; that is, that every
true proposition which is not an explicit identity can be
reduced to such a proposition.

The principle of sufficient reason provides Leibniz with an
argument for the existence of God, which he expounds in *On
the Ultimate Origination of Things* and elsewhere. There are, he
says, contingent things, things whose existence is not necessary. These must have a reason, and the reason must lie outside
them; for if it lay within them, their existence would be

self explanatory. But as long as we seek the reason for a contingent thing in some other contingent thing, so long we are left with something whose existence has in turn to be explained. Therefore the ultimate reason for contingent things must lie in that whose existence is self-explanatory; that is, in a necessary being, or God.

The validity of this argument has been called in question since the time of Kant; the point of mentioning the argument here, however, was to show how Leibniz can say that the primitive concepts are the concepts of the attributes of God. The question remains, how Leibniz viewed the dependence of contingent things on God. Spinoza would have argued that to call things 'contingent' is a mark of ignorance; such things are really modes of the one necessary being. Leibniz disagrees; for him, there is real contingency, in the sense that there are states of affairs which are not logically necessary. As this is so, contingent things cannot be modes of the necessary being, and their dependence must be of another sort. Their dependence is that of creatures on their creator; in other words, the ultimate reason for contingent things is not only a necessary being, but is also a creative deity.

God chooses between various possible states of affairs, various 'possible worlds', and he chooses, and creates, the best possible. This is why Leibniz says that contingent things owe their existence to the 'principle of the best' (e.g. to Clarke, Paper 5, par. 9). The principle of the best is an easy target for the satirist; but Leibniz is no Dr. Pangloss, for whom legs exist in order that we may wear stockings. To an important extent, to say that Leibniz's God acts for the best is to say that he acts in accordance with the principles that the scientist follows in explaining the universe—or, as Leibniz would prefer to say, that scientific explanation is a kind of copying of the thought-processes of God, a re-tracing of the rational pattern which God follows in creating the universe. 'God', as Leibniz says in *A Specimen of Discoveries*, 'acts like the greatest geometer, who prefers the best constructions of problems'. What this means is that the creation of the best is the production of the maximum effect with the least expenditure, much as a geometer, in constructing a deductive system, prefers that axiom set which is the most economical and from which most consequences can be derived. From this, Leibniz claims to prove a number of scientific and metaphysical propositions, the most important of which is the thesis that there are no atoms and there is no vacuum, but that an infinity of substances exists. Leibniz insists, however, that the principle of the best is not merely quantitative; the substances that God has created also constitute an order which is morally the best.

The principle of the best, which God follows in creating this world in preference to other possible worlds, serves to differentiate the truths of physics from those of mathematics, which are true of all possible worlds. Leibniz also states the distinction between these two sorts of truths by saying that physics, unlike mathematics, requires the principle of sufficient reason (*A Specimen of Discoveries*; cf. to Clarke, Paper 2, par. 1). Here he can hardly mean the principle that every truth can be proved, for this is of universal application, and is presupposed by the mathematician as much as by the physicist. Sometimes he seems to be referring to the principle of the best; sometimes, however, he seems to mean simply that the truths of physics imply a reference to God's choice, and God never chooses without a reason. This principle plays an important part in Leibniz's attack, in his correspondence with Clarke (1715–16), on the Newtonian concept of absolute space, Leibniz's argument being that this concept implies that God must choose something without a reason.

In an earlier paragraph, mention was made of substances. Leibniz's theory of substance contains some of his most characteristic doctrines, and in this theory his views about the nature of truth again play an important part. Aristotle and his followers, Leibniz says, have regarded a substance as a subject to which predicates can truly be ascribed, but which is not in turn a predicate of anything else; and this is true as far as it goes (*Discourse on Metaphysics*, art. 8). However, it fails to make clear what it is for something to be truly ascribed to a subject. The answer has already been given: something is predicated truly of a subject when the concept of that something is contained in the concept of the subject. This means that everything that can truly be said of a substance is contained in the concept of that substance; so, for example, anyone who could grasp fully the concept of Alexander the Great would know *a priori*, and not simply by experience, that he is the conqueror of Darius. Leibniz puts this by saying that every substance has a 'complete' concept.

Leibniz was aware of the fact that he might seem to be abolishing the distinction between contingent and necessary truths, and to be falling into a kind of Spinozism. For example, the concept of the equality of its radii is contained in the concept of a sphere, and the proposition that the radii of a sphere are equal is logically necessary; why, then, is the true proposition that Gottfried Wilhelm Leibniz was born in 1646 not logically necessary? Leibniz's answer is two-fold. First, a logically necessary truth is not to be defined simply as one whose predicate is in its subject; rather, it is a proposition such that the inclusion of its predicate in its subject can be demonstrated in a finite number of steps. In the case of a contingent truth, too, the predicate is in the subject, but here the demonstration of its inclusion would require an infinite number of steps. Second, a contingent truth, unlike a necessary truth, involves a reference to the free decrees of God. God does not decide to make the radii of a sphere equal; that its radii are equal is an eternal truth. God does decide to create a Leibniz who is born in 1646, and the proposition that Leibniz was born in 1646 is therefore a contingent truth.

The idea that a substance has a complete concept involves obvious difficulties for someone who believes that human beings are free, as Leibniz did. In his correspondence with Leibniz, Arnauld pointed out that since, for example, his own complete concept included that of being a bachelor, it seemed to follow that he could not be other than a bachelor. Yet he chose freely to be a bachelor, he *could have* married. Leibniz replied to this and to similar objections by distinguishing between absolute and hypothetical necessity. A proposition is absolutely necessary when it would be self-contradictory to deny it, and in this sense there is no necessity for Arnauld to be a bachelor. However, his being a bachelor is hypothetically necessary; it is necessary given that his being a bachelor is part of the best possible world, and given that there is a God who creates such a world. Against this, it may be argued that all that Leibniz has shown is that when a man chooses something, some other choice is logically possible, and that this is not enough for freedom. The man's choice may, for example, be causally determined, and given the cause, the effect follows necessarily, though (as Hume and Kant showed) it does not follow with logical necessity. Again, in creating Arnauld, in actualising his complete concept, God created an Arnauld who will choose to be a bachelor; how, then, can Arnauld be free in this respect? Leibniz grappled with such problems in many papers, but it cannot be said that he found a satisfactory solution.

Leibniz argues that although determinism is only an apparent consequence of his doctrine of the completeness of the concept of a substance, many important consequences really follow from it. One of these is the identity of indiscernibles. According to Leibniz the complete concept of a substance, such as Alexander, differs from the concept of an abstraction, such as kingship, in that the former and the former alone is sufficient to identify an individual (*Discourse on Metaphysics*, art. 8). This means that no complete concept of a substance can have more than one instance; that is, there cannot be two substances which are exactly alike, differing in number alone. The point of calling this doctrine the 'identity of indiscernibles' may be brought out by the following example. Suppose that there is a substance called 'Jacob', and suppose that there is a substance called 'Israel'; suppose, also, that what is predicated of each is exactly alike. Then 'Jacob' and 'Israel' do not refer to two substances, but are two names for the same substance. Here it may be objected that although 'Jacob' and 'Israel' are indeed two names for the same person, what is predicated of Jacob and Israel is not exactly alike; for example, one has a name beginning with 'J', the other a name beginning with 'I'. Leibniz would probably reply that in his account of the identity of indiscernibles, predicates that relate to names (as opposed to the predicates of what is named) have to be excluded. This may be part of what he has in mind in his discussion of 'reduplicative' propositions in a paper on the nature of truth (*c.* 1686).

There are other consequences of Leibniz's views about the complete concept of a substance. Such a concept, he has said, includes all that can truly be said about the substance. But all things are interrelated, therefore each substance must 'express' the whole universe. The concept of expression is an important one in Leibniz. One thing expresses another, Leibniz says, when there is a constant and ordered relation between what can be said of the one and of the other (to Arnauld, 9 October 1687); in this sense, an ellipse expresses a circle. In effect, then, to say that A expresses B is to say that the one is what would now be called a function of the other (and in fact Leibniz, in his later mathematical writings, uses the term 'function' in something approaching its modern sense: cf. J. E. Hofmann, in *Leibniz*, ed. Totok and Haase, p. 455, n. 231). To say that each substance 'expresses' the whole universe, therefore, is to say that from the predicates of each substance the predicates of all the others can be inferred. This is what Leibniz means when he says that a substance is a 'mirror' of the universe, and (since it expresses past and future states as well as present ones) is 'big with the future and laden with the past' (*New Essays*, Preface).

Not only is a substance a mirror of the universe; it is also 'like a world apart' (*Discourse on Metaphysics*, art. 14). Leibniz argues that since all the states of a substance are simply the consequences of the complete concept of that substance— since, in other words, all its states are the consequences of its own being, and of that alone—then no other substance in the universe can affect it. Strictly, therefore, no substance (with the exception of God, the creator of all contingent things) acts on any other. From this it follows that, in a sense, all our ideas are innate. In another sense, however, Leibniz asserts that only some ideas are innate, and that others are acquired. This is when he argues in the *New Essays*, against Locke, that a purely empiricist epistemology, according to which all ideas are acquired and none are innate, can account for *a posteriori* but not for *a priori* knowledge.

Though Leibniz has argued that no thing really acts on

another, yet it is a fact that people commonly say that they do, that A is cause and B effect, and this has to be explained. Here the notion of expression enters again. Leibniz has said that each substance expresses all others; he adds that it sometimes happens that, for us, substance A expresses substance B 'more distinctly' than B expresses A—that is, it is easier to infer from the states of A to those of B than conversely. When this is the case, we say that A is the cause of changes in B. This leaves the question, how it is that the states of A and B are so correlated that it is possible to infer from the one to the other, even though one does not really act on the other. Leibniz's answer is that they are correlated by God, who 'pre-establishes' a harmony between substances; that is, creates substances which are such that, although independent of each other, they also harmonise. This may seem a metaphysical fantasy; but it is important to realise that Leibniz is making two points which have nothing to do with theism as such, and which are far from fantastic. First, he is saying that when some effect is brought about, no causal agency, no 'influx' is transmitted from one thing to another. Here he agrees with Hume, though he reaches his conclusion by a different route. Second, he is saying in effect that the concept of a cause is a crude one, which (if one wishes to be precise) has to be replaced by the concept of a function—much as Bertrand Russell was to say in 1912 in his essay 'On the Notion of Cause'.

This account of causality provides Leibniz with an answer to the problem of the relations between mind and matter. Descartes had found no problem in the causal connexions between bodies, or within a mind, but he found it hard to understand how such different substances as mind and body could act on each other, as they clearly seemed to do. For Leibniz, the problem of mind-body interaction is no more and no less puzzling than the problem of the action of one body on another. All substances, he argues, harmonise with each other; but what happens in a man's mind corresponds more perfectly to what happens in his body, and it is therefore said that the one acts on the other (*Discourse on Metaphysics*, art. 33; *Monadology*, par. 62). It may be objected that this view (like Descartes' account of mind and body) destroys the unity of a human being; each of us, it may be said, is one individual and not two. In his correspondence with Arnauld (1686–7) and later in his correspondence with des Bosses (1709–12) Leibniz struggled hard, but not very successfully, to find a reply.

But although Leibniz may not have explained the unity of mind and body, he is insistent that every substance must be one, a unit, a 'monad' (the word for a unit which he applied to substances after 1695). What is not genuinely *one* being, he wrote to Arnauld (30 April 1687), cannot be genuinely one *being*; an aggregate, such as an army, or a machine, is not a substance. Leibniz applies this to the notion of extension. Descartes and Spinoza seemed to regard extension as something indefinable, but Leibniz denies that this is so. To speak of something extended, he says, is to speak of an aggregate; a plurality, continuity and co-existence of parts. It follows from this that no substance can properly be called extended, since 'extended' is a predicate that can be ascribed only to a class, and no substance is a class.

This is part of what Leibniz means when he says that every substance is either a soul or (since not all substances are conscious beings like ourselves) soul-like. But he means more than this. He has said that a substance is 'big with the future' and this, he argues, means that it must have a tendency to other states. He therefore says that a substance has to be viewed in teleological terms; it must have what Aristotle and the Scholastics called a 'form', towards which it strives. The connexion between form and soul is again Aristotelian; for Aristotle, to speak of the human soul is to speak of a form, the form of the human body. Leibniz knew that in rehabilitating forms he was opposing an important thesis of seventeenth-century science. That science was mechanistic, and rejected the idea that nature must be viewed as a kind of organism. Leibniz's view was that to a certain extent it was right in doing so. One may not, he says, use souls or forms to explain particular physical events; such events must be explained in mechanistic terms. He insists, however, that the principles of mechanics themselves cannot be stated adequately without a reference to forms.

What, in conclusion, has Leibniz to offer to the modern reader? Deductive metaphysics of the kind defended in the seventeenth and eighteenth centuries has never recovered from Kant's attacks, and since Kant's time serious criticisms have been brought against Leibniz's philosophy in particular. In *The Philosophy of Leibniz*, Bertrand Russell presented Leibniz as an example of the dangers of over-estimating the importance of subject-predicate propositions and failing to give relational propositions their due. It would generally be agreed that Russell is right on the whole, though he is less than convincing in his thesis that a subject-predicate logic should have led Leibniz to monism. More recently, the theory of monads has been attacked by J. L. Austin, on the grounds that Leibniz makes the mistake of regarding demonstrative expressions (expressions which 'refer') as if they were descriptive (*Philosophical Papers*, Oxford, 1961, p. 90n.). But even if these are errors, they are errors of a deep kind, whose rectification takes one into fundamental issues of philosophy. Again, no one is now likely to defend the theory of the pre-established harmony; yet by regarding the notion of the action of one substance on another as incoherent, Leibniz makes one think about the nature of such action. The idea that all substances are souls or soul-like finds little response today; but the idea that things are essentially dynamic lives on in the Hegelian tradition. As to Leibniz's account of the problem, or rather problems of human freedom, it may fairly be said that despite its shortcomings it belongs to the classical literature on the subject. Finally, something may be said about the relation between Leibniz's metaphysics and his science. Collingwood's thesis that metaphysics is a historical science, the 'science of absolute presuppositions', has not won wide acceptance; nevertheless, it is true that a man's metaphysics shows what he regards as the fundamental constituents of the universe. The principle of the best does not enable Leibniz to establish the timeless truth of certain scientific propositions; but by his use of it he does at any rate show what he regards as the basic concepts and principles of the science of his time.

1972   G. H. R. PARKINSON

Select Bibliography

1 LEIBNIZ'S WORKS

(A) COLLECTED EDITIONS

There is at present no complete edition of Leibniz's works. The task of compiling such an edition was begun in 1923, initially under the auspices of the Prussian Academy of Sciences and then (after an interruption due to the Second World War) under the German Academy of Sciences. This edition—*Gottfried Wilhelm Leibniz, Sämtliche Schriften und Briefe*—is divided into seven series. The first comprises the general political and historical correspondence; the second, the philosophical correspondence; the third, the mathematical, scientific and technical correspondence; the fourth, political writings; the fifth, historical writings; the sixth, philosophical writings; the seventh, mathematical, scientific and technical writings. The edition is to consist of some 40 volumes in all; by 1972, 8 volumes of Series 1 had appeared, 1 of Series 2, 2 of Series 4, and 3 (vols. 1, 2 and 6) of Series 6. Until the edition is complete, reference must be made to the various partial editions that exist. The following three editions are probably the most useful for the student of Leibniz's philosophy:

Die philosophischen Schriften von G. W. Leibniz, ed. by C. I. Gerhardt, 7 vols. (Berlin, 1875–90).

Opuscules et fragments inédits de Leibniz, ed. by L. Couturat (Paris, 1903). (Of particular importance to the student of Leibniz's logic, and of his philosophy as influenced by logic.)

G. W. Leibniz: Textes inédits, ed. by G. Grua, 2 vols. (Paris, 1948). (Concentrates on Leibniz's theology and moral philosophy.)

Mention may also be made of the following:

G. G. Leibnitii Opera Omnia, ed. by L. Dutens, 6 vols. (Geneva, 1768).

Leibniz, Deutsche Schriften, ed. by G. E. Guhrauer, 2 vols. (Berlin, 1838–40).

G. C. Leibnitii Opera Philosophica, ed. by J. E. Erdmann (Berlin, 1840).

Leibniz, Gesammelte Werke, Folge I, Geschichte, ed. by G. H. Pertz, 4 vols. (Hanover, 1843–7).

Leibnizens mathematische Schriften, ed. by C. I. Gerhardt, 7 vols. (Berlin and Halle, 1849–63).

Nouvelles Lettres et Opuscules inédits de Leibniz, ed. by Foucher de Careil (Paris, 1857).

Die Werke von Leibniz. Reihe I: Historisch-politische und staatswissenschaftliche Schriften, ed. by O. Klopp, 11 vols. (Hanover, 1864–84).

A valuable guide to editions of Leibniz published before 1937 is:
E. Ravier, *Bibliographie des Oeuvres de Leibniz* (Paris, 1937).

Another important reference work is:
E. Bodemann, *Die Leibniz-Handschriften der Königlichen öffentlichen Bibliothek zu Hannover* (Hanover, 1895).

(B) EDITIONS OF SEPARATE WORKS

Confessio Philosophi, ed. by O. Saame (Frankfurt a.M., 1967).

Correspondance Leibniz-Clarke, ed. by A. Robinet (Paris, 1957).

Discours de Métaphysique, ed. by H. Lestienne (Paris, 1907 and 1952).

Discours de Métaphysique et Correspondance avec Arnauld, ed. by G. Le Roy (Paris, 1957).

Lettres de Leibniz à Arnauld d'après un manuscrit inédit, ed. by G. Lewis (Paris, 1952).

Principes de la Nature et de la Grace; Principes de la Philosophie ou Monadologie, ed. by A. Robinet (Paris, 1954).

(C) ENGLISH TRANSLATIONS

Discourse on Metaphysics, trans. by P. G. Lucas and L. Grint (Manchester, 1953).

The Leibniz-Arnauld Correspondence, trans. by H. T. Mason (Manchester, 1967).

The Leibniz-Clarke Correspondence (Clarke's translation, ed. by H. G. Alexander, Manchester, 1956).

Logical Papers: A Selection, trans. by G. H. R. Parkinson (Oxford, 1966).

Monadology and other Philosophical Essays, trans. by P. and A. M. Schrecker (New York, 1965).

Monadology and other Philosophical Writings, trans. by R. Latta (Oxford, 1898).

Philosophical Papers and Letters, trans. by L. E. Loemker (Chicago, 1956; Dordrecht, 1969).

Theodicy, trans. by E. M. Huggard (London, 1952).

2 WORKS ON LEIBNIZ

A valuable guide to the literature on Leibniz is provided by K. Müller, *Leibniz Bibliographie* (Frankfurt a.M., 1967).

Bibliographical surveys, as well as articles on Leibniz and on seventeenth-century philosophy in general, are contained in *Studia Leibnitiana,* the journal of the *Gottfried-Wilhelm-Leibniz-Gesellschaft.*

(A) LEIBNIZ'S LIFE

G. E. Guhrauer, *Gottfried Wilhelm, Freiherr von Leibniz* (Breslau, 1842).

K. Fischer, *Gottfried Wilhelm von Leibniz* (5th ed., revised by W. Kabitz, Heidelberg, 1920).

K. Müller and G. Krönert, *Leben und Werk von G. W. Leibniz: eine Chronik* (Frankfurt a.M., 1969).

(B) LEIBNIZ'S THOUGHT

L. Couturat, *La Logique de Leibniz* (Paris, 1901).

G. Grua, *Jurisprudence universelle et théodicée selon Leibniz* (Paris, 1953).

R. Kauppi, *Über die Leibnizsche Logik* (Helsinki, 1960).

G. H. R. Parkinson, *Logic and Reality in Leibniz's Metaphysics* (Oxford, 1965).

G. H. R. Parkinson, *Leibniz on Human Freedom* (Wiesbaden, 1970: *Studia Leibnitiana*, Sonderheft 2).

N. Rescher, *The Philosophy of Leibniz* (Englewood Cliffs, 1967).

Bertrand Russell, *The Philosophy of Leibniz* (2nd ed., London, 1937).

W. Totok and C. Haase (eds.), *Leibniz: sein Leben, sein Wirken, seine Welt* (Hanover, 1966).

See also chapters relating to Leibniz in the following general works:

G. Buchdahl, *Metaphysics and the Philosophy of Science* (Oxford, 1969).

W. von Leyden, *Seventeenth Century Metaphysics* (London, 1968).

W. Risse, *Die Logik der Neuzeit, Vol. II, 1640–1780* (Stuttgart, 1970).

Notes on Translation

Mrs. Morris's translations from Leibniz were first published in Everyman's Library in 1934, and have been reprinted several times. For this new edition a number of the works translated by her which are of less than major importance have been omitted; those that have been retained are the *Monadology*, *Principles of Nature and of Grace*, *On the Ultimate Origination of Things*, the selections from the correspondence with Arnauld, the *New System* and *Explanation of the New System*, the Preface to the *New Essays*, the selections from the correspondence with Clarke, and a letter on human freedom (1934 edition, pp. 3–41, 57–87, 97–116, 141–67, 192–229, 250–3). I have revised these transalations, comparing them with the original French or Latin, and I have revised Mrs. Morris's footnotes and added supplementary notes at the end of the volume. Footnotes are indicated by numbers; references to the supplementary notes are by letters—a, b, c, d, e, f, g, h, j, k, etc., and (where necessary) aa, ab, ac, etc.

To replace the works that have been excluded, I have made the following translations: (1) *Of an Organum or Ars Magna of Thinking*, (2) *An Introduction to a Secret Encyclopaedia*, (3) *Of Universal Synthesis and Analysis*, (4) Selections from the *Discourse on Metaphysics*, (5) *A Specimen of Discoveries*, (6) *Primary Truths*, (7) *The Nature of Truth*, (8) *Necessary and Contingent Truths*, (9) *On Freedom*, (10) *On the Principle of Indiscernibles*, (11) *A Résumé of Metaphysics*, (12) *Metaphysical Consequences of the Principle of Reason*. Of these, numbers (1), (2), (5), (7), (10), (11) and (12) have not appeared in English before, and there has previously been no complete English translation of (8). Of the works retained from Mrs. Morris's original translations, the letter on freedom is not available elsewhere in English.

In making the new translations and revising those of Mrs. Morris I have tried to provide equivalents of Leibniz's technical terms which are consistent throughout. The aim has been to produce a version of Leibniz which will convey clearly the meaning of what he wrote, whilst keeping as close to the text as is consistent with this.

1972

G. H. R. P.

Of an Organum or Ars Magna[a] of Thinking (c. 1679)

The supreme happiness of man consists in the greatest possible increase of his perfection.

Vigour, or the state of increased perfection, is as much above *health* as *disease* is below health. For *perfection* is a more excellent degree of health. Just as *disease* consists in an impaired functioning of the *faculties*, so *perfection* consists in an increase of one's power or faculties.

The most powerful of human faculties is the *power of thinking*.

The power of thinking can be assisted either by remedies of the body or by remedies of the mind.

The remedies of the body are bodies which are applied to the corporeal organs themselves, by which torpor is shaken off, the imagination is strengthened and the senses sharpened. But these are not our concern here.

The remedies prescribed for the mind consist of certain modes of thinking, by which other thoughts are made easier.

It is the greatest remedy for the mind if a few thoughts can be found from which infinite others arise in order, just as from the assumption of a few numbers, from one to ten, all the other numbers can be derived in order.

Whatever is thought by us is either conceived through itself, or involves the concept of another.

Whatever is involved in the concept of another is again either conceived through itself or involves the concept of another; and so on.

So one must either proceed to infinity, or all thoughts are resolved into those which are conceived through themselves.

If nothing is conceived through itself, nothing will be conceived at all. For what is conceived only through others will be conceived in so far as those others are conceived, and so on; so that we may only be said to conceive something in actuality when we arrive at those things which are conceived through themselves.

I will illustrate this by a simile. I give you a hundred crowns, to be received from Titus; Titus will send you to Caius, Caius to Maevius; but if you are perpetually sent on in this way you will never be said to have received anything.

It is necessary that those things which are perceived through themselves are several. For let there be a, which is conceived through b, i.e. which involves b; I assert that a necessarily involves not only b, but something else also. For if it is conceived through b alone, then nothing can be conceived in a which could not be conceived in b, and so there will be no distinction between a and b. But this is contrary to the hypothesis, for we assumed that a is conceived through something else, namely b. So it is necessary that a should be conceived through two things at least, e.g. b and c.

Although the things which are conceived are infinite, yet it is possible that those conceived through themselves are few; for infinite things can be compounded out of the combination of a few.

Indeed, this is not only possible, but even credible or probable; for nature usually does as many things as possible with the smallest possible number of assumptions, that is, it operates in the simplest way.[b]

It may be that there is only one thing which is conceived through itself, namely God himself, and besides this there is nothing, or privation. This is made clear by an admirable simile. When we count, we commonly use the decimal system, so that when we arrive at ten, we start again from unity. That this is convenient, I do not now dispute; meanwhile, I will show that it is possible to use in its place a binary system,[c] so that as soon as we have reached two we start again from unity, in this way:

(0)	(1)	(2)	(3)	(4)	(5)	(6)	(7)	(8)
0	1	10	11	100	101	110	111	1000

(9)	(10)	(11)	(12)	(13)	(14)	(15)	(16)
1001	1010	1011	1100	1101	1110	1111	10000

The immense advantages of this system I do not touch on at present; it is enough to have noted in what a wonderful way all numbers are thus expressed by unity and by nothing.

Although there is no hope that men can, in this life, reach this hidden series of things, by which it will appear in what way everything comes from pure being and from nothing, it is sufficient to carry the analysis of ideas as far as the demonstrations of truths require.

Every idea is analysed perfectly only when it is demonstrated *a priori* that it is possible. For if we give some definition from which it does not appear that the idea which we ascribe to the thing is possible, we cannot trust the demonstrations which we have derived from the definition. For if that idea should happen to involve a contradiction, it can be the case that contradictories are true of it simultaneously, and so our demonstrations will be useless.[d] From this it is evident that definitions are not arbitrary—a secret to which hardly anyone has paid sufficient attention.

Since, however, it is not in our power to demonstrate the possibility of things in a perfectly *a priori* way, that is, to analyse them into God and nothing, it will be sufficient for us to reduce their immense multitude to a few, whose possibility can either be supposed and postulated, or proved by experience. Thus all the lines of motion in the whole of geometry are reduced to two motions only, one in a straight line and the other in a circle. For when these two have been assumed it can be demonstrated that all other lines—e.g. the parabola, hyperbola, conchoid and spiral—are possible. Euclid, however, did not show that a straight line can be drawn and a circle described, but thought it sufficient to postulate this. Though, granted space, body, a straight line, and continuous motion, one could also demonstrate the possibility of a circle; further, even a straight line can be demonstrated, granted space, body and continuous motion. But what is to be thought of these three continua seems to depend on a consideration of the divine perfection. However, it is not necessary for geometry to rise as high as this. For even if there were not, and could not be, any straight lines and circles in nature, it would be enough that it is possible for there to be figures which differ from straight lines and circles so little that the error is less than anything given. This is sufficient both for the certainty of a demonstration and for its use. That there can be figures of this kind is proved without difficulty, provided that it is simply admitted that there are some lines.

To have at the outset perfect definitions of these ideas (i.e. definitions which show the possibility of the thing *a priori*) is difficult. In the mean time we shall employ nominal definitions of them; that is, we shall analyse the idea of a thing into other ideas through which it can be conceived, even though we cannot proceed as far as the primary ideas. And this will be enough, when it is established by experience that the thing is possible. For example, we can define fire as a hot, bright vapour, and the rainbow as a coloured bow in the clouds; for it is established by experience that concepts of this kind are possible, though we cannot at once show their possibility *a priori* by explaining their generation or cause.

There are some things of which there are no nominal definitions. Thus, there are no nominal definitions of heat and light themselves, for if a man is ignorant of what is signified by the name of heat, he cannot be helped except either by exhibiting the thing under consideration, or by mentioning equivalent names in a language known to him, or by exciting his memory in some other way, if he felt heat at some earlier time. But no one doubts that there is some cause of heat, and if this were known perfectly, there would be a definition of heat.

An Introduction to a Secret Encyclopædia

or, foundations and specimens of the General Science,
of the renewal and increase of the sciences,
of the perfection of the mind, and of discoveries,
for the public happiness.

It will be necessary to speak both of what pertains to this book, and of what pertains to the argument of the book.

As to the book, it will be necessary to speak of its author, its scope, argument and form; its occasions; its diction, and the judgements that others are to form about it. Should the author be anonymous? First, however, one must speak about its fruits and the method of using it, and to these two the others are to be reduced. Its fruits are rendered probable by what is said about the author and his aids, and by the scope and form of the work; the method of use appears from the argument and form alone.

The argument of the book is the General Science itself; we must treat both of its principles and its precepts.

The principles of science are those of reason and of fact; or, they are dogmatic and historical.

The dogmatic principles are: the definition of science, its names, object, method or division, and its utility or end.

The General Science is simply the science of what is universally thinkable in so far as it is such. This includes not only what has hitherto been regarded as logic, but also the art of discovery, together with method or the means of arrangement, synthesis and analysis, didactics, or the science of teaching, Gnostologia (the so-called Noologia), the art of reminiscence or mnemonics, the art of characters or of symbols, the Art of Combination, the *Art of Subtlety,* and philosophical grammar; the Art of Lull, the Cabbala of the wise, and natural magic. Perhaps it also includes Ontology, or the science of something and nothing, being and not being, the thing and its mode, and substance and accident. It does not make much difference how you divide the sciences, for they are one continuous body, like the ocean.

The object of this science is what is universally thinkable, in so far as it is such through our mode of considering it.[1] We therefore exclude a name without a notion, i.e. that which is nameable but not thinkable, such as 'Blitiri', which the Scholastics use as an example.

That which is thinkable is either simple or complex. That which is simple is called a 'notion' or 'concept'.

That which is complex is that which involves in itself a proposition, i.e. an affirmation or negation, truth or falsity.

A concept is either distinct or confused, and clear or obscure; either simple (i.e. primitive) or composite (i.e. derivative); and either adequate or inadequate.[a]

A concept is clear when it is such that we can recognise a thing when it is presented to us, such as the concept of horse, light, colour, circle. If anything less, the concept is obscure, such as the one I have of a man whose face I do not represent to myself sufficiently well, or such as those unskilled in geometry have of an elliptical figure which they call an oval; not distinguishing the true one, described by drawing from two foci, from that which is described by the arcs of circles.

A concept is distinct when I can consider separately and distinguish between the marks which I have for recognising a thing. Thus an assayer has a distinct concept of gold; he does not only recognise it by its sight, sound and weight, but he can also state and describe the marks of gold.

A concept is adequate when it is so distinct that it contains nothing confused, whether it be that the marks themselves are known by a distinct concept, or through other marks, up to simple or primitive notions.[2]

---

[1] Note by Leibniz: We conceive many things, not as they are in themselves, but according to the way in which they are conceived by us and affect us.

[2] Note by Leibniz: Here we should remove abstract concepts as un-

A concept is primitive when it cannot be analysed into others; that is, when the thing has no marks, but is its own sign. But it can be doubted whether any concept of this kind appears distinctly to men, namely, in such a way that they know that they have it. And indeed, such a concept can only be of the thing which is conceived through itself, namely the supreme substance, that is, God. But we can have no derivative concepts except by the aid of a primitive concept, so that in reality nothing exists in things except through the influence of God, and nothing is thought in the mind except through the idea of God, even though we do not understand distinctly enough the way in which the natures of things flow from God, nor the ideas of things from the idea of God. This would constitute ultimate analysis, i.e. the adequate knowledge of all things through their cause.[1]

That which is complex is either a proposition or is composed of propositions. This again is either an argument or it is composed of several arguments having a common conclusion, or it is a discussion. The matter could also be reduced to questions: for either a question is one, or it is composed of several questions.

Every proposition is affirmative or negative, true or false, pure or modal, categorical or hypothetical, full or contracted.

The nature of the negative is simply that one negative cancels another, and that if it is true then the affirmative is false, and conversely.

A proposition is held to be true by us when our mind is ready to follow it and no reason for doubting it can be found. But absolutely and in itself, that proposition is true which is either identical or is reducible to identical propositions; that is, which can be demonstrated *a priori*, or, the connexion of whose predicate with its subject can be exhibited in such a way that its reason always appears. And indeed, nothing at all

---

necessary, especially as there may be abstractions of abstractions. In place of heat, we shall consider what is hot, since one can again suppose some 'caloreity', and so ad infinitum.

[1] Note by Leibniz: A concept is either apt or inept. An apt concept is one of which it is agreed that it is possible, i.e. that it does not imply a contradiction.

happens without some reason, i.e. there is no proposition, except identical ones, in which the connexion between subject and predicate cannot be displayed distinctly. (In identical propositions the subject and predicate coincide, or come to the same.) This is one of the first principles of all human reasoning, and after the principle of contradiction it has the greatest use in all the sciences. Thus the axioms of Euclid, 'If equals are added to equals, etc.', are corollaries of this principle alone, for no reason can be given for their diversity. Similarly, the axiom which Archimedes uses at the beginning of his treatise on equilibrium[b] is a corollary of this principle of ours, that nothing is without a reason. Since, however, it is not granted to us always to discover the reasons for everything *a priori*, we are therefore compelled to trust our senses and authorities, and especially our inmost perceptions and various perceptions which agree with one another. There is given to us a natural propensity to trust the senses, and to count as the same those things in which we find no difference, and also to believe all appearances unless there is a reason against this; for otherwise we should never do anything. In matters of fact, those things are sufficiently true which are as certain as my thoughts and perceptions of myself. Here we must dispute with the Sceptics.[c]

An analysis of concepts by which we are enabled to arrive at primitive notions, i.e. at those which are conceived through themselves, does not seem to be in the power of man. But the analysis of truths is more in human power, for we can demonstrate many truths absolutely and reduce them to primitive indemonstrable truths; let us therefore pay particular attention to this.

Categories: i.e. a catalogue of concepts set out in order, and of conceivable things, i.e. of simple terms. The concepts are: possible; entity; substance; accident or adjunct; absolute substance; limited substance, or that which can be passive; living substance, which has in itself a principle of operation, or soul; *thinking substance*, which acts on itself—this is also called *mind*.[1]

---

[1] In the margin, Leibniz has added the following list: Possible; entity; existent; potent; knowing; willing; enduring; what is changed; suffering; perceiving; having location; extended; bounded; shaped; touching; close; distant.

Every soul is immortal; the mind, however, is not only immortal, but also always has some knowledge of itself, or memory of what has preceded, and therefore is capable of reward and punishment.

The body is a living or sentient substance, which, however, lacks reason or reflexion. The substantial form of the body is the soul. The soul is a substance, active and passive. Matter is that which is passive only and never acts, but is acted on at any moment, even when it seems to act. Consequently, matter is only an instrument of a form, or soul.

Principles of metaphysical certainty[1]

First principles a priori

Nothing can at the same time be and not be, but everything either is or is not.

Nothing is without a reason.

First principles of a posteriori *knowledge* (or, of logical certainty)

Every perception of my present thinking is true.

Principle of moral certainty

Everything which is confirmed by many indications, which can hardly concur except in the truth, is morally certain, i.e. incomparably more probable than its opposite.

Principle of physical certainty

Everything which men have experienced always and in many ways will still happen: e.g. that iron sinks in water.

Principles of topical[d] knowledge

Everything is presumed to remain in the state in which it is. The more probable is that which has fewer requisites, or, which is easier.

---

[1] These principles were written by Leibniz as a marginal note.

Of Universal Synthesis and Analysis; or, of the Art of Discovery and of Judgement (c. 1683)

When I studied logic as a boy, and was even then in the habit of inquiring rather deeply into the reasons for what was propounded to me, I used to raise the following objection to my teachers: in the case of simple terms, there are categories by which concepts[a] are ordered—why, then should there not be categories for complex terms, by which truths might be ordered? I was, of course, ignorant of the fact that this is just what geometers do when they demonstrate, and arrange propositions in accordance with their dependence on one another. However, it seemed to me that we should in general be able to do this if first we possessed the true categories for simple terms and if something new was established to obtain these. This would be a kind of alphabet of human thoughts, i.e. a catalogue of summa genera (or of what are assumed to be summa genera), such as *a*, *b*, *c*, *d*, *e*, *f*, out of whose combination inferior concepts would be formed. For it must be known that genera afford the differences to one another, and that every difference can be conceived as a genus and every genus as a difference, and that it is as right to say 'rational animal' as (if one may coin a phrase) 'animal rational'. But as what are commonly accepted as genera do not exhibit their species by their combination, I concluded that they are not rightly formed, and that the genera immediately below the summa genera should be groups of two, such as *ab*, *ac*, *bd*, *cf*; the genera of the third grade should be groups of three, such as *abc*, *bdf*, and so on. It may be that the summa genera, or those assumed to be the summa genera, are infinite, as in the case of numbers; for here the prime numbers can be taken as the summa genera, and all numbers divisible by two can be called binary, all numbers divisible by three can be called ternary, and so on, and a derived number can be expressed through the primes as its genera; thus, every senary is a binary ternary. If this should be the case, at any rate the order of the summa genera should be established, as in the case of numbers, and an order would also appear in the lower genera. Further, given any species, there could be enumerated in order the propositions which are demonstrable of it, i.e. its predicates, both those which are wider than it and those which are convertible, of which the more memorable could be selected. Suppose, for example, that there is a species y, whose concept is $abcd$, and suppose that for ab there is substituted l; for ac, m; for ad, n; for bc, p; for bd, q; and for cd, r, all of which are groups of two; and suppose that for abc there is substituted s; for abd, v; for acd, w; and for bcd, x, which are groups of three. All of these will be predicates of y, but the convertible predicates of y will be the following only: ax, bw, cv, ds, lr, mq, np. I have said more of this in my little treatise *On the Art of Combinations*, which I published when I had scarcely entered on manhood, and when the long-promised work of the same title by Kircher[b] had not yet appeared. I hoped that, in this work, matters of this sort would be settled; but later, when it did appear, I found that it merely revived the doctrines of Lull, or something like them, and that the true analysis of human thoughts had not so much as been dreamed of by the author, any more than by others who have thought about the restoration of philosophy. The primary concepts, by the combination of which the rest are formed, are either distinct or confused. Those are distinct which are understood through themselves, such as 'being'. Those are confused, and yet clear, which are perceived through themselves, such as 'coloured', which we cannot explain to another except by pointing. For though its nature is analysable, since it has a cause, it cannot be sufficiently described and recognised by us by means of any marks which can be explained separately, but is only known confusedly, and therefore cannot be given a *nominal definition*. A nominal definition consists of the enumeration of the marks or requisites which are sufficient to distinguish a thing from all others; where, if we continue to seek the requisites of requisites, we shall finally arrive at primitive concepts, which are either absolutely without requisites, or are without requisites which we can explain sufficiently. This is the art of handling distinct concepts. To the art of handling confused concepts there belongs the indication of the distinct concepts, either understood through themselves or at any rate analysable into such, which accompany the confused ones. By means of these we can sometimes arrive at the cause of confused concepts, i.e. at some analysis of them.

All derivative concepts arise from a combination of primitive ones, and those which are composite in a higher degree arise from a combination of composite concepts. However, care must be taken that no useless combinations are made, by joining together what are mutually incompatible. This can be decided only by experience, or else by analysis into distinct simple concepts. In forming real definitions, one must take great care to establish that they are possible; that is, that the concepts of which they consist can be joined together. Consequently, although every convertible property of a thing can be counted as a nominal definition, since all the other attributes of the thing can always be demonstrated from it, it is not always suitable for a real definition. For I have noted that there are certain properties, which I call 'paradoxical', whose possibility can be doubted. For example, it can be doubted whether there is a curve such that any point on each segment of it makes the same angle with the two ends of the segment.[c] For let us assume that we have fitted the points to a curve in this way for one segment. This may seem to have occurred by a lucky chance in one place only, and we cannot foresee whether the same points falling on another segment will again satisfy this condition; for they are now determinate, and can no longer be freely assumed. Yet we know that this is the nature of a circle; so even if someone could give the name to the curve having this property, its possibility would still not be established, nor, therefore, would it be established whether the definition is real. But the concept of a circle put forward by Euclid—namely, that it is the figure described by the motion of a straight line in a plane about one fixed end—does afford a real definition, for it is clear that such a figure is possible. It is useful, therefore, to have definitions which involve the generation of a thing, or failing that, at least its constitution, i.e. a way in which it appears to be either producible or at least possible. I used this observation some time ago in examining an imperfect demonstration of the existence of God advanced by Descartes, and I have often argued about this in correspondence with the most learned Cartesians.[d] Descartes argues in this way. Whatever can be demonstrated from the definition of a thing can be predicated of that thing. But from the definition of God (namely, that he is the most perfect being, or, as some Scholastics used to say, that than which nothing greater can be thought) existence follows; for existence is a perfection, and that which involves existence as well will be greater or more perfect. Therefore existence can be predicated of God, i.e. God exists. This argument, which was renewed by Descartes, was defended by one of the old Scholastics in a peculiar book called *Against the fool*.[e] But St. Thomas,[f] following others, replied that this presupposes that God exists; or, as I understand him, that God has an essence, at any rate in the sense that a rose has an essence in winter—i.e. that such a concept is possible. This, then, is the privilege of the most perfect being: that granted that it is possible, it at once exists—i.e. that from its essence, that is, its possible concept, existence follows. But if this demonstration is to be rigorous, the possibility must be demonstrated beforehand.[g] Clearly, we cannot safely devise demonstrations about any concept, unless we know that it is possible; for of what is impossible, i.e. involves a contradiction, contradictories can also be demonstrated. This is the *a priori* reason why possibility is required for a real definition. From this we can also answer a difficulty raised by Hobbes.[h] Hobbes saw that all truths can be demonstrated from definitions, but he believed that all definitions are arbitrary and nominal, since the imposition of names on things is arbitrary. He therefore wanted truths to consist in names, and to be arbitrary. But it must be known that concepts cannot be combined in an arbitrary fashion, but a possible concept must be formed from them, so that one has a real definition. From this it is evident that every real

definition contains some affirmation of at least possibility.
Further, even if names are arbitrary, yet once they have been
imposed their consequences are necessary and certain truths
arise which, though they depend on the symbols imposed,
are nevertheless real. For example, the rule of nine depends
on symbols imposed by the decimal system, and yet it contains
a real truth. Again, to form a hypothesis, i.e. to explain a
way of producing something, is simply to demonstrate the
possibility of the thing; and this is useful, even though the
thing in question has often not been generated in such a way.
Thus, the same ellipse can be understood either as described
in a plane by a thread tied round two foci, or as cut from a
cone or a cylinder. When one hypothesis, i.e. one mode of
generation, has been found, then one has a real definition
from which others can be deduced; of these there may be
selected those which agree more with other things, when one
seeks the way in which the thing was actually produced.
Further, those real definitions are the most perfect which are
common to all hypotheses or modes of generation and involve a proximate cause, and from which, finally, the possibility of the thing is immediately evident without presupposing any experience, or even supposing the demonstration
of the possibility of another thing; that is, when a thing is
analysed into nothing but primitive concepts, understood
through themselves. Such knowledge I am accustomed to call
'adequate' or 'intuitive'; for if there should be any in-
consistency anywhere, it would appear at once, since no
further analysis can be carried out.

From such ideas or definitions all truths can be demonstrated, with the exception of identical propositions; these,
it is evident, are by their very nature indemonstrable, and
can truly be called axioms. But what are commonly regarded
as axioms are reduced to identities, i.e. are demonstrated, by
the analysis either of the subject or of the predicate, or of
both, so that if one supposes the contrary they appear at the
same time to be and not to be. It is evident, therefore, that in
the last analysis direct and indirect proof[j] coincide, and that
it was rightly observed by the Scholastics that all axioms,
once their terms have been understood, are reduced to the

principle of contradiction. And so a reason can be given for each truth; for the connexion of the predicate with the subject is either self-evident, as in the case of identities, or it has to be displayed, which is done by the analysis of the terms. This is the unique and the highest criterion of truth in the case of abstractions, which do not depend on experience: namely, that it should either be an identity or reducible to identities. From this there can also be derived the elements of eternal truth, and a method of proceeding in all things (provided that they are understood) in a way which is as demonstrative as that of geometry. In this way, all things are understood by God *a priori*, as eternal truths; for he does not need experience, and yet all things are known by him adequately. We, on the other hand, know scarcely anything adequately, and only a few things *a priori*; most things we know by experience, in the case of which other principles and other criteria must be applied. So in matters of fact, i.e. contingent matters, which do not depend on reason but on observation or experience, the truths which are primary for us are whatever we perceive immediately within ourselves, i.e. of which we are conscious in ourselves concerning ourselves. For it is impossible for these to be proved through other experiences which are closer and more intrinsic to us. But I perceive within myself, not only I myself who am thinking, but also many differences in my thoughts; from which I gather that there are other things besides myself and, as against the Sceptics, gradually put trust in my senses. For in the case of what is not of metaphysical necessity, we must count as the truth the agreement of phenomena amongst themselves, which will not occur by chance but will have a cause. At all events, we do not distinguish dreams from waking except by this agreement of phenomena, and we predict that the sun will rise tomorrow only because it has fulfilled our trust so often. To this one may add the great weight of authority and of public testimony, since it is not credible that many should conspire to deceive; one may also add what St. Augustine has said about the usefulness of believing.[k] Now that the authority of the senses and of other witnesses has been established, we must compile a record of phenomena; and if with these we combine the truths abstracted from experience, mixed sciences are formed. But we need a special art both to make, arrange and combine our experiences, so that useful inductions may be made from these, causes discovered, and definitions and axioms[1] established. But one must marvel at the carelessness of men, wasting their time on trifles and neglecting those things by which they might provide for their health and well-being, when they might perhaps have in their power the remedies for a great part of their ills if they would use rightly the copious observations of this century which are already available, and also the true analysis. But as things are, man's knowledge of nature seems to me like a shop, well stocked with goods of all kinds, but lacking any order or inventory.

From the above, the nature of the distinction between synthesis and analysis is also apparent. Synthesis is when, beginning from principles and running through truths in order, we discover certain progressions and form tables, as it were, or sometimes even general formulae, in which the answers to what arises later can be discovered. Analysis, however, goes back to principles solely for the sake of a given problem, just as if nothing had been discovered previously, by ourselves or by others. It is better to produce a synthesis, since that work is of permanent value, whereas when we begin an analysis on account of particular problems we often do what has been done before. However, to use a synthesis which has been established by others, and theorems which have already been discovered, is less of an art than to do everything by oneself by carrying out an analysis; especially as what has been discovered by others, or even by ourselves, does not always occur to us or come to hand. There are two kinds of analysis: one is the common type proceeding by leaps, which is used in algebra, and the other is a special kind which I call 'reductive'.[m] This is much more elegant, but is less well-known. In practice, analysis is more necessary, so that we may solve the problems which are presented to us; but the man who can indulge in theorising will be content to practise analysis just far enough to master the art. For the rest, he will rather practise synthesis, and will apply himself readily only to those questions to which order itself leads him. For in this way he will always progress pleasantly and easily, and will never feel any difficulties, nor be disappointed of success, and in a short time he will achieve much more than he would ever have hoped for at the outset. Usually, however, people spoil the fruits of meditation by haste, leaping to attack problems which are too difficult, and with great labour they achieve nothing. It must be understood that a method of inquiry is finally perfect when we can foresee whether it will lead us to a solution. It is a mistake to think that one proceeds analytically when one discloses, synthetically when one suppresses the origin of a discovery.[n] I have often noted, of the minds able to make discoveries, that some are more analytic, others more combinatory. It is more combinatory or synthetic to discover the use and application of something; as, for example, given a magnetic needle, to think of its application to the compass. On the other hand it is more analytic, given the name of an invention, i.e. the proposed end, to discover the means to it. However, pure analysis is rare; for when we look for means we often come across devices which have already been discovered either by others or by ourselves, whether by chance or by reason. These we find, whether in our own memory or in the accounts of others, as in a table or inventory, and we apply them to the matter in hand; and this is a synthetic procedure. For the rest, the art of combinations in particular is, in my opinion, the science which treats of the forms of things or of formulae in general (it could also be called generally the science of symbols, or of forms[o]). That is, it is the science of *quality* in general, or, of the like and the unlike, according as various formulae arise from the combination of *a*, *b*, *c* etc., whether they represent quantities or something else. It is distinguished from algebra, which is concerned with formulae applied to *quantity*, i.e. with the equal and the unequal. Consequently, algebra is subordinate to the art of combinations, and constantly uses its rules. These rules, however, are much more general and can be applied not only in algebra but also in cryptography, in various kinds of games, in geometry itself, treated in linear fashion in the old style, and finally in all matters where similarity is involved.[p]

Discourse on Metaphysics (1686)
(Selections)

8. To distinguish between the actions of God and the actions of creatures, an explanation is given of what constitutes the notion of an individual substance.

It is somewhat difficult to distinguish the actions of God from those of creatures.[a] There are those who believe that God does everything; others imagine that he merely conserves the force which he has given to creatures.[b] The sequel will show to what extent either of these can be said. Now, since actions and passions belong, strictly speaking, to individual substances (*actiones sunt suppositorum*), it will be necessary to explain what such a substance is. It is very true that when several predicates are attributed to one and the same subject, and this subject is not attributed to any other, one calls this subject an individual substance.[c] But this is not enough, and such an explanation is only nominal. It is necessary, therefore, to consider what it is to be truly attributed to a certain subject. Now, it is agreed that every true predication has some basis in the nature of things, and when a proposition is not identical—that is, when the predicate is not contained expressly in the subject—it must be contained in it virtually. This is what philosophers call '*in-esse*',[d] when they say that the predicate is 'in' the subject. The subject-term, therefore, must always include the predicate-term, in such a way that a man who understood the notion of the subject perfectly would also judge that the predicate belongs to it. That being so, we can say that it is the nature of an individual substance, or complete being, to have a notion so complete that it is sufficient to contain, and render deducible from itself, all the predicates of the subject to which this notion is attributed. On the other hand, an accident is a being whose notion does not include all that can be attributed to the subject to which this notion is attributed. Take, for example, the quality of being a king, which belongs to Alexander the Great. This quality, when abstracted from its subject, is not sufficiently determinate for an individual and does not contain the other qualities of the same subject, nor everything that the notion of this prince contains. God, on the other hand, seeing the individual notion or *haecceitas*[e] of Alexander, sees in it at the same time the foundation of and reason for all the predicates which can truly be stated of him—as, for example, that he is the conqueror of Darius and Porus—even to the extent of knowing *a priori*, and not by experience, whether he died a natural death or died by poison, which we can know only from history. Therefore, when one considers properly the connexion between things, one can say that there are in the soul of Alexander, from all time, traces of all that has happened to him, and marks of everything that will happen to him—and even traces of everything that happens in the universe—though no one but God can know all of them.

9. That every individual substance expresses the entire universe in its way, and that there are contained in its notion all the things that happen to it, together with all their circumstances and the entire series of external things.

From this, several notable paradoxes follow. One of these is that it is not true that two substances resemble each other entirely and are different in number alone (*solo numero*), and that what St. Thomas[f] asserts in this connexion about angels or intelligences, namely, that in these cases every individual is an *infima species* (*quod ibi omne individuum sit species infima*) is true of all substances, provided that one takes the specific difference in the way that geometers take it with respect to their figures. Another paradox is that a substance can begin only by creation, and perish only by annihilation; that one substance is not divided into two, nor is one made out of two, and that therefore the number of substances is neither increased nor diminished naturally, though substances are often transformed. Further, every substance is like an entire world and like a mirror of God, or of the whole universe, which each one expresses in its own way, very much as one and the same town is variously represented in accordance with different positions of the observer. Thus the universe is in a way multiplied as many times as there are substances, and in the same way the glory of God is redoubled by so many wholly different representations of his work. It can even be said that every substance bears in some way the stamp of the infinite wisdom and omnipotence of God, and imitates him as far as it is able. For it expresses, although confusedly, everything that happens in the universe, past, present and future, and this has some resemblance to infinite perception or knowledge. And as all other substances express that substance in their turn and agree with it, it can be said that it extends its power over all others, imitating the omnipotence of the Creator.

10. That the view that there are substantial forms has some solidity, but that these forms change nothing in phenomena, and must not be used to explain particular effects.

It seems that some knowledge of what we have just said was possessed by the ancients, and also by many able men, accustomed to profound meditation—some of them also praiseworthy for their holiness—who taught theology and philosophy several centuries ago. This knowledge made them introduce, and uphold, substantial forms, which are so decried today. But they are not so far from the truth, or so ridiculous, as the common run of our modern philosophers imagine. I agree that the consideration of these forms is of no value in the detail of physics, and must not be used in the explanation of particular phenomena. It is in this respect that our scholastics failed, and (following their example) the doctors of a past age. For they thought that they could explain the properties of bodies by mentioning forms and qualities, without going to the trouble of examining their method of operation—as if someone thought it sufficient to say that a timepiece has a time-indicative quality which comes from its form, without considering what all that consists in. That can indeed be sufficient for the man who buys the timepiece—provided that he abandon the care of it to another. But this shortcoming, and this misuse of forms, must not make us reject something the knowledge of which is so necessary in metaphysics that I maintain that without it first principles cannot be known properly, nor can the mind be raised high enough to know incorporeal natures and the wonders of God. However, we may make a comparison here. A geometer has no need to trouble his mind with the famous labyrinth of the composition of the continuum,g and no moral philosopher, and still less a jurist or a politician, needs to trouble himself with the great difficulties which are found in reconciling free will with the providence of God. For the geometer can carry out all his demonstrations, and the politician can bring his deliberations to an end, without entering into these discussions—which are none the less necessary and important in philosophy and theology. In the same way, the physicist can explain his experiments by the use of simpler experiments that he has already made, or by demonstrations in geometry and mechanics, without the need of general considerations which belong to a different sphere. And if he uses the concourse of God,h or some soul, archaeusj or other thing of that nature, he is straying outside his proper limits,k just as much as a man who, in the case of an important deliberation about what to do, tried to go into the great arguments about the nature of destiny and our freedom. Indeed, men make this mistake often enough without realising it, when they trouble their mind with thoughts about fate, and often are even turned away by this from some good resolution, or necessary concern.

11. That the meditations of the so-called Scholastic philosophers and theologians are not to be entirely despised.

I know that I am putting forward a great paradox in claiming to rehabilitate ancient philosophy to some extent, and to restore the rights of citizenship to substantial forms, which have practically been banished. But perhaps I shall not readily be condemned when it is known that I have thought carefully about modern philosophy, and that I have devoted much time to physical experiments and to geometrical demonstrations. I was for a long time persuaded of the emptiness of these entities, and was finally obliged to take them up again despite myself, and as it were by force. This was after I had myself conducted some researches which made me recognise that our modern philosophers do not do enough justice to St. Thomas and to other great men of that era, and that the views of the Scholastic philosophers and theologians have much more soundness than is imagined, provided that one uses them in a proper way and in their right place. I am even persuaded that if some precise and thoughtful mind were to take the trouble of clarifying and setting in order their thoughts, in the manner of analytic geometry, he would find in them a treasury of truths which are extremely important and wholly demonstrative.

12. That the notions which consist in extension include something imaginary, and cannot constitute the substance of a body.

But to take up again the thread of our discussion: I believe that anyone who will meditate on the nature of substance, as I have explained it above, will find that the entire nature of body does not consist in extension alone, that is to say in size, shape and motion. Rather, he will find that it is necessary to recognise in it something which has some relation to souls, and which is commonly called a substantial form, although this changes nothing in phenomena, any more than the soul of the lower animals does, if they have one. It can even be demonstrated that the notion of size, shape and motion is not as distinct as is imagined, and that it contains something that is imaginary and relative to our perceptions, just as is the case (though even more so) with colour, heat and other similar qualities, of which it may be doubted whether they are really found in the nature of things outside us. This is why qualities of these kinds cannot constitute any substance. And if there is no other principle of identity in bodies besides that which we have just mentioned, no body will ever last longer than a moment. However, the souls and substantial forms of other bodies are very different from intelligent souls. Only the latter know their actions, and not only do not perish naturally, but even retain perpetually the basis of the knowedge of what they are. It is this which brings it about that they alone are capable of punishment and reward, and makes them citizens of the commonwealth of the universe, of which God is the monarch. It also follows that all other creatures must serve them, of which we shall speak at greater length presently.

13. Since the individual notion of each person includes, once and for all, everything that will ever happen to him, there are seen in this notion the *a priori* proofs of or reasons for the truth of each event, or why the one has occurred rather than the other. But these truths, though certain, are none the less contingent, being based on the free will of God and of creatures. It is true that their choice always has its reasons, but these incline without necessitating.

But before we go any further, it is necessary to try to answer a great difficulty which can be raised on the foundations that we have just laid. We have said that the notion of an individual substance contains, once and for all, everything that can ever happen to it, and that in considering this notion one can see in it everything that can truly be stated of it, as we can see in the nature of the circle all the properties that can be deduced from it. But it seems that this will destroy the difference between contingent and necessary truths, that human freedom will no longer hold, and that an absolute fatality will rule over all our actions as well as over all the rest of what happens in the world. To this I reply that one must distinguish between what is certain and what is necessary. Everyone agrees that future contingents are certain, since God foresees them, but it is not thereby admitted that they are necessary. But, it will be said, if some conclusion can be deduced infallibly from a definition or notion, it will be necessary. Now, we maintain that everything that is to happen to some person is already contained virtually in his nature or notion, as the properties of a circle are contained in its definition. So the difficulty still remains. To give a satisfactory answer to it, I assert that connexion or sequence is of two kinds. The one is absolutely necessary, whose contrary implies a contradiction; this kind of deduction holds in the case of eternal truths, such as those of geometry. The other is only necessary by hypothesis (*ex hypothesi*),[1] and so to speak by accident; it is contingent in itself, since its contrary does not imply a contradiction. This connexion is based, not on ideas pure and simple, and on the simple understanding of God, but on his free decrees and on the sequence of the universe. Let us give an example. Since Julius Caesar will become perpetual dictator and master of the republic, and will destroy the liberty of the Romans, this action is contained in his notion; for we are assuming that it is the nature of such a perfect notion of a subject to contain everything, so that the predicate is included in it, *ut possit inesse subjecto*.[m] It could be said that it is not by virtue of this notion or idea that he must perform this action, since it belongs to him only because God knows everything. But it will be replied that his nature or form corresponds to this notion, and since God has imposed this personality on him, it is henceforth necessary for him to satisfy it. I could answer this by instancing future contingents; for they have no reality except in the understanding and will of God, and since God has given them this form in advance, they must correspond to it. However, I prefer to satisfy difficulties, rather than to excuse them by citing similar difficulties, and what I am about to say will throw light on both. This is where it is necessary to apply the distinction between connexions. I assert that that which happens in conformity with its antecedents is certain, but that it is not necessary, and that if someone were to do the opposite he would do nothing that is impossible in itself, although it is impossible by hypothesis (*ex hypothesi*) that that should happen. For if some human being could complete the whole demonstration by virtue of which he could prove the connexion between the subject who is Caesar, and the predicate which is his successful undertaking, he would indeed show that the future dictatorship of Caesar has its basis in his notion or nature, that one sees in it a reason why he decided to cross the Rubicon rather than halt there, why he won rather than lost the battle of Pharsalus, and that it was reasonable, and therefore certain, that that would happen. But he would not show that it is necessary in itself, or that the contrary implies a contradiction. (In much the same way it is reasonable, and certain, that God will always do the best, though the less perfect does not imply a contradiction.) For it will be found that this demonstration of this predicate of Caesar is not as absolute as those of arithmetic or geometry, but that it presupposes the sequence of things that God has chosen freely, which is based on the primary free decree of God, namely, always to do that which is the most perfect, and on the decree which God has made (consequentially upon the first) with regard to human nature, which is that man will always do—but do freely—that which appears the best. Now, every truth which is based on decrees of these sorts is contingent, although it is certain. For these decrees do not alter the possibility of things and, as I have already said, although God's choice of the best is certain, that does not prevent the less perfect from being and remaining possible in itself, although it will not occur; for it is not its impossibility but its imperfection which makes God reject it. Now, nothing is necessary whose opposite is possible. One is therefore in a position to satisfy difficulties of these kinds, however great they may appear (and indeed they are no less urgent for all others who have ever discussed this matter) provided that one bears this in mind: that all contingent propositions have reasons for being thus rather than otherwise, or (what is the same thing) that they have *a priori* proofs of their truth which make them certain, and which show that the connexion between the subject and the predicate of these propositions has its basis in the nature of the one and of the other. But these proofs are not necessary demonstrations, for these reasons are based only on the principle of contingency or of the existence of things—that is, on that which is or appears the best among several things which are equally possible— whereas necessary truths are based on the principle of contradiction and on the possibility or impossibility of essences themselves, with no relation to the free will of God or of creatures.

14. God produces various substances according to the different views that he has of the universe, and through God's intervention the individual nature of each substance is such that what happens to one corresponds to what happens to all others, without any one acting immediately on any other.

Now that we have got to know in some way what the nature of substances consists in, it is necessary to try to explain the dependence they have on each other, and the way they act and are acted on. Now in the first place it is very clear that created substances depend on God, who conserves them and even produces them continually by a kind of emanation, as we produce our thoughts. For God, as it were, turns on all sides and in all ways the general system of phenomena which he finds it good to produce in order to manifest his glory, and regards all aspects of the world in all possible ways, since there is no relation which escapes his omniscience. The result of each view of the universe, as seen from a certain position, is a substance which expresses the universe in conformity with this view, if God finds it good to render his thought effective and to produce this substance. And as God's view is always a true one, our perceptions are true also; it is our judgements which come from us and deceive us. Now we have said above, and it follows from what we have just said, that each substance is like a world apart, independent of every other thing, except for God. Therefore all our phenomena, that is to say all the things that can ever happen to us, are only consequences of our being. These phenomena preserve a certain order, which conforms to our nature, or so to speak to the world which is in us, which means that we are able to make observations which are useful for regulating our conduct, which are justified by the success of future phenomena, and in this way we are often able to judge accurately about the future by means of the past. This would be enough for us to say that these phenomena are true, without our troubling ourselves as to whether they exist outside us, or whether others apperceive[n] them too. However, it is very true that the perceptions or expressions of all substances correspond to one another, in such a way that each one, following with care certain reasons or laws which it has observed, agrees with another which does the same; it is just as when several men, who have agreed to meet together in some place on a certain prearranged day, can in fact do so if they wish. Now although all express the same phenomena, this is not to say that all their expressions are perfectly alike, but it is sufficient that they should be proportional; just as several spectators believe that they see the same thing, and do indeed understand one another, although each one sees and speaks in accordance with his point of view. Now it is God alone (from whom all individuals emanate continually and who sees the universe, not only as they see it, but also in quite a different way from all of them) who is the cause of this correspondence between their phenomena, and who brings it about that what is particular to one should be public to all; otherwise there would be no interconnexion. It could therefore be said in a way, and in a perfectly good sense (although remote from ordinary usage), that one particular substance never acts on another particular substance, nor is acted on by another, if one considers the fact that what happens to each is simply a consequence of its complete idea or notion alone, for this idea already contains all its predicates or events and expresses the entire universe. Really, nothing can happen to us apart from thoughts and perceptions, and all our future thoughts and perceptions are only consequences (although contingent consequences) of our preceding thoughts and perceptions, such that if I were able to consider distinctly everything that happens to or appears to me at the moment, I could see in it everything that will ever happen to or ever appear to me. This would not fail to occur, but would happen to me just the same, if everything outside me were destroyed, provided that there remained only God and myself. But as we attribute what we apperceive in a certain way to other things, as to causes acting on us, it is necessary to consider the basis of this judgement, and how much truth it has.

15. The action of one finite substance on another consists only in the increase of the degree of its expression, joined to the diminution of that of the other, in so far as God has formed them in advance in such a way that they agree with one another.

But without entering into a long discussion, it is sufficient for the moment, to reconcile metaphysical language with practice, to note that we attribute to ourselves (and rightly) the phenomena which we express more perfectly, and that we

attribute to other substances what each one expresses best
Thus a substance which is of an infinite extent, in so far as i
expresses everything, becomes limited by the more or less
perfect manner of its expression. It is in this fashion that one
can conceive the way in which substances hinder or limit one
another, and consequently it can be said in this sense that
they act on one another and are, so to speak, obliged to
harmonise with one another. For it can happen that a change
which increases the expression of one diminishes that of another. Now the virtue of a particular substance is to express
well the glory of God, and it is through this that it is less
limited. And when each thing exercises its virtue or power,
that is to say when it acts, it changes for the better and extends itself in so far as it acts. When, therefore, a change
occurs by which several substances are affected (and indeed
every change concerns all substances) I believe that one can
say that the one which, by this, immediately passes to a
greater degree of perfection or a more perfect expression
exercises its power and *acts*, and that which passes to a lesser
degree of perfection displays its weakness and *is acted on*. I
also maintain that every action of a substance which has
perception involves some *pleasure* and every passion some *pain*,
and vice versa. However, it can happen that a present advantage is destroyed by a greater evil which follows, from
which arises the fact that one can sin in acting or exercising
one's power and finding pleasure in it.

16. God's extraordinary concourse is comprised in that which our essence
expresses, for this expression extends to everything, but it surpasses the
forces of our nature or our distinct expression, which is limited and follows
certain subordinate maxims.

It now only remains to explain how it is possible for God
sometimes to have influence on men or on other substances
by an extraordinary and miraculous concourse;[o] for it seems
that nothing can happen to them which is extraordinary or
supernatural, in view of the fact that all the things that
happen to them are only consequences of their nature. But it
is necessary to recall what we said above[p] about miracles in the

universe: namely, that these are always in conformity with the universal law of general order, although they are above subordinate maxims. In so far as each person or substance is like a little world which expresses the great world, it can also be said that this extraordinary action of God on this substance does not cease to be miraculous, even though it is contained in the general order of the universe in so far as it is expressed by the essence or individual notion of the substance. This is why, if we include in our nature everything which it expresses, nothing is supernatural to it, for it extends to everything; for an effect always expresses its cause, and God is the true cause of substances. But as what our nature expresses more perfectly belongs to it in a special way (for, as I have just explained, it is that which constitutes its power, and the fact that it is limited) there are many things that surpass the forces of our nature, and even those of all limited natures. Consequently, to speak more clearly, I assert that miracles and the acts of God's extraordinary concourse have this special feature: they cannot be foreseen by the reasoning of any created mind, however enlightened it may be, for the distinct comprehension of the general order surpasses all of them. On the other hand, all that one calls 'natural' depends on less general maxims, which creatures can understand. So that our words may be as unobjectionable as our meaning, it would be advantageous to link certain ways of speaking with certain thoughts. One could call our 'essence' or 'idea' that which contains all that we express, and as it expresses our union with God himself, it has no limits, and nothing surpasses it. But that which is limited in us could be called our 'nature' or our 'power', and in this respect what surpasses the natures of all created substances is supernatural.

17. An example of a subordinate maxim or law of nature, where it is shown that God always regularly conserves the same force, but not the same quantity of motion—contrary to the Cartesians and several others.

I have often mentioned subordinate maxims or laws of nature, and it seems advisable to give an example. Our modern philosophers[q] commonly make use of the famous rule that

God always conserves the same quantity of motion in th
world. This is indeed very plausible, and in the past I regarde
it as indubitable. Since then, however, I have recognise
the nature of the error. Descartes, and many other abl
mathematicians, have believed that the quantity of motion—
that is, the speed multiplied by the size of that which moves—
agrees perfectly with the motive force, or, to speak geo
metrically, that forces are in a compound ratio of speeds an
of bodies. Now, it is reasonable that the same force shoul
always be conserved in the universe. Thus, when one pay
attention to phenomena, one sees clearly that perpetua
mechanical motion cannot occur; for if it were to do so
then the force of a machine (which is always diminishe
slightly by friction and must soon come to an end) woul
restore itself, and consequently would increase of itsel
without any new impulse from outside. One notes also tha
the force of a body is diminished only to the extent that i
gives some of it to some contiguous bodies, or to its ow
parts in so far as they have a separate motion. Thus it ha
been believed that what can be said of force could also b
said of the quantity of motion. To show the difference be
tween these, *I assume* that a body, falling from a certai
height, acquires the force to rise again to that height if it
direction takes it that way, at any rate if there are no ob
stacles. For example, a pendulum would rise again to th
exact height from which it has descended, if the resistance o
the air and some other slight obstacles did not diminish a
little the force that it has acquired. *I assume* also that a
much force is needed to raise a body *A*, of one pound, to th
height *CD* of four fathoms, as to raise a body *B* of four pound
to a height of one fathom. All this is granted by our moder
philosophers. It is therefore evident that the body *A*, havin
fallen from the height *CD*, has acquired exactly as much forc
as the body *B*, having fallen from the height *EF*. For the body
(*B*), having arrived at *F*, and having (by the first supposition
the force to rise again as far as *E*, has in consequence the forc
to raise a body of four pounds (i.e. its own body) to th
height *EF* of one fathom. Similarly the body (*A*), having
arrived at *D*, and having the force to rise again as far as *C*

has the force to raise a body of one pound (i.e. its own body) to the height *CD* of four fathoms. Therefore (by the second supposition) the force of these two bodies is equal. Let us now see if the quantity of motion is also the same on both sides. Here, however, we shall be surprised to find a very great difference. It has been demonstrated by Galileo that the speed acquired by the fall *CD* is twice the speed acquired by the fall *EF*, although the height is quadruple. Let us therefore multiply the body *A*, which is as 1, by its speed, which is as 2; the product or quantity of motion will be as 2. On the other hand let us multiply the body *B*, which is as 4, by its speed,

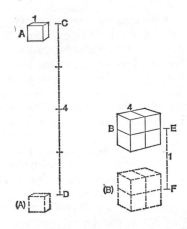

which is as 1; the product or quantity of motion will be as 4. Therefore the quantity of motion of the body (*A*) at the point *D* is half the quantity of motion of the body (*B*) at the point *F*; and yet their forces are equal. There is, therefore, a great difference between quantity of motion and force; which is what was to be shown. By this one sees how force must be measured by the quantity of the effect which it can produce; for example, by the height to which a heavy body of a certain size and kind can be raised, which is very different from the speed which can be given to it. And to give it double the speed, more than double the force is needed. Nothing is simpler than this proof, and Descartes only fell into error

here because he trusted his thoughts too much, when they
were not yet sufficiently mature. But I am amazed that his
followers have not noticed this error. I am afraid that they
are gradually beginning to imitate some of the Aristotelians
whom they mock, and, like them, are falling into the habit
of consulting the books of their master rather than reason and
nature.[1]

23. To return to immaterial substances: it is explained how God acts on
the understanding of minds, and whether we always have the idea of that
of which we think.

I have found it relevant, in connexion with bodies, to lay
some stress on these considerations about final causes, incorporeal natures and an intelligent cause, to make known
their use in physics and in mathematics, both to rid mechanical philosophy of the irreligious nature which is ascribed
to it, and to raise the minds of our philosophers from exclusively material considerations to nobler meditations. Now
it will be timely to return from bodies to immaterial natures,
and in particular to minds, and to say something about the
method that God uses to enlighten them and to act on them.
There is no room for doubt that certain laws of nature also
exist here, about which I could speak more fully elsewhere.
For the moment it will be sufficient to touch on the question
of ideas, and whether we see everything in God, and how
God is our light. Now it will be relevant to remark that the
faulty employment of ideas is the occasion of many errors.
For when one reasons about something, one imagines that one
has an idea of that thing, and on this basis several philosophers,
ancient and modern, have constructed a certain demonstration of the existence of God, a demonstration which is very
imperfect. They say that I must have an idea of God or a
perfect being, since I think of such a being and one cannot
think without an idea. Now, the idea of this being includes all
perfections, and existence is one of them; consequently this
being exists. But this argument is insufficient, for we often
think of impossible chimeras—for example, of the highest
degree of speed, of the greatest number, of the meeting of the

conchoid with its base or axis. It is therefore in this sense that it can be said that there are true and false ideas, as the thing in question is possible or not. One can only claim that one has an idea of a thing when one is sure of its possibility. Thus, the argument just mentioned proves at least that God exists necessarily, if he is possible. Indeed, this is an excellent privilege of the divine nature—that it needs only its possibility or essence in order to exist actually—and it is precisely this that one calls an *Ens a se*.[8]

24. The nature of knowledge: clear or obscure, distinct or confused, adequate or inadequate, intuitive or suppositive. Of definitions: nominal, real, causal, essential.

In order to understand better the nature of ideas it is necessary to touch on the varieties of knowledge. When I can recognise one thing amongst others, without being able to say in what its differences or properties consist, my knowledge is *confused*. It is in this way that we sometimes know *clearly*, without being in any kind of doubt, if a poem or a picture is good or bad, because there is a *je ne sais quoi* which satisfies us or displeases us. But when I can explain the marks which I have, my knowledge is called *distinct*. Such is the knowledge possessed by an assayer, who distinguishes true from false gold by means of certain tests or marks which constitute the definition of gold. Distinct knowledge has degrees; for normally the notions which enter into the definition are themselves in need of definition and are known only confusedly. But when everything which enters into a definition or into distinct knowledge is itself known distinctly, right up to primitive notions, I call this knowledge *adequate*. When my mind understands distinctly and at the same time all the primitive ingredients of a notion, it has *intuitive* knowledge of it. This is very rare, the bulk of human knowledge being only confused or *suppositive*. There is also a distinction to be drawn between nominal and real definitions. I call a definition *nominal* when it is still possible to doubt whether the notion defined is possible. For example, if I say that an endless screw is a solid line whose parts are congruent, or can be superimposed

on one another, someone who did not know from othe
sources what an endless screw is could doubt whether such a
line is possible—though this is in fact a reciprocal property
of the endless screw, for the other lines whose parts are con
gruent (and these are only the circumference of the circle
and the straight line) are plane, that is to say can be described
in a plane (*in plano*). This shows that every reciprocal pro
perty can serve as a nominal definition, but when the property
enables us to know the possibility of the thing, it makes the
definition real. Further, as long as one has only a nomina
definition one cannot be certain of the consequences which
one derives from it, for if it concealed some contradiction o
impossibility, one could derive opposite conclusions from it
This is why truths do not depend on names and are not
arbitrary, as some modern philosophers have believed.[t] It
must be added that there is a considerable difference between
kinds of real definitions. When the possibility is proved only
by experience, as in the definition of quick-silver—whose
possibility one knows because one knows that there is indeed
such a body, namely one which is a fluid, extremely heavy
and yet very volatile—the definition is only real, and no
more. But when the proof of possibility is *a priori*, the definition is both *real* and *causal*, as when it contains the possible
generation of the thing. When the definition pushes the
analysis to the end, right up to primitive notions, without
presupposing anything which needs an *a priori* proof of its
possibility, the definition is perfect or *essential*.

25. In what case our knowledge is joined with the contemplation of the
idea.

Now it is evident that we have no idea of a notion when that
notion is impossible. When the knowledge is only *suppositive*,
then even when we have the idea we do not contemplate it.
For such a notion is known only in the same way as notions
which conceal an impossibility, and if it is possible, it is not
by this manner of knowing that one learns of its possibility.
For example, when I think of a thousand, or of a thousand-
sided figure, I often do this without contemplating its idea

(as when I say that a thousand is ten times a hundred) without giving myself the trouble of thinking what ten and a hundred are, because I *suppose* that I know this and I do not believe that I need to stop to conceive it at the moment. So it can very well happen, and indeed it very often does happen, that I deceive myself with regard to a notion which I suppose or believe myself to understand, although in reality it is impossible, or at any rate incompatible with the other notions with which I join it. And whether I deceive myself or not, this suppositive manner of conception remains the same. It is, therefore, only when our knowledge is *clear* in the case of confused notions, or *intuitive* in the case of distinct notions, that we see the entire idea.

26. We have in us all ideas; and of Plato's reminiscence.

In order to conceive properly what an idea is, we must forestall an equivocation. Several take the idea to be the form or difference of our thoughts, and in this way we have an idea in our mind only in so far as we think of it, and every time we think of it afresh, we have other ideas (though like the ones which have preceded them) of the same thing. Others, however, seem to take the idea to be an immediate object of thought or some permanent form which remains even when we do not contemplate it. And indeed our soul always has in it the quality of representing to itself any nature or form whatever, when the occasion for thinking of it presents itself. I believe that this quality of our soul, in so far as it expresses some nature, form or essence, is properly the idea of the thing, which is in us, and is always in us, whether we think of it or not. For our soul expresses God, the universe and all essences as well as all existences. This agrees with my principles; for nothing enters our mind naturally from outside, and our habit of thinking as if our soul received some messenger species[u] and as if it had doors and windows is a bad one. We have in our mind all forms, and, indeed, we have them from all time; for the mind always expresses all its future thoughts and already thinks confusedly of all that it will ever think distinctly. We could never be informed of anything whose idea we do not already have in the mind—an idea which is like the matter from which this thought forms itself. Plato had an excellent appreciation of this when he put forward his theory of 'reminiscence', a theory which has much solidity provided that one takes it in the right way, that one rids it of the error of pre-existence, and does not imagine that the soul must at some previous time have known and thought distinctly what it learns and thinks now. He also confirmed his opinion by a fine experiment, introducing[v] a little boy whom he leads imperceptibly to some very difficult geometrical truths regarding incommensurables, without teaching him anything, but simply asking relevant questions in an orderly way. This shows that our soul knows all this virtually, and only needs *attention* to know truths, and consequently that it has at least the ideas on which these truths depend. One can even say that it already possesses these truths, if one takes them as the relations of ideas.

27. How our soul can be compared to blank tablets, and how our notions come from the senses.

Aristotle[w] preferred to compare our soul to tablets that are still blank, where there is space for writing, and he maintained that there is nothing in our understanding that does not come from the senses. This agrees more with popular notions, as is Aristotle's manner, whereas Plato is more profound. However, expressions of this kind, based on opinion or on practice,[x] can pass into ordinary usage, much as we see that those who follow Copernicus do not cease saying that the sun rises and sets. I even find that one can often give them a good sense, according to which they have no falsity, as I have noted already that there is a way in which it can be said truly that particular substances act on each other. In the same sense it can be said that we receive knowledge from outside through the medium of our senses, because certain external things contain or express more particularly the reasons which determine our soul to certain thoughts. But when it is a matter of the precision of metaphysical truths, it is important to recognise the extent and the independence of our soul.

This goes infinitely further than is commonly supposed, although in the ordinary usage of everyday life one attributes to it only that which one apperceives more clearly, and which belongs to us in a more particular way, for there is no point in going any further. However, it would be useful to choose terms which are proper to each sense, to avoid equivocation. Therefore those expressions which are in our soul, whether we conceive them or not, can be called *ideas*, but those which we conceive or form can be called *notions, conceptus*. But in whatever way one takes it, it is always false to say that all our notions come from the so-called external senses, for the notion that I have of myself and my thoughts, and consequently of being, substance, action, identity and many others, come from an internal experience.

28. God alone is the immediate object, existing outside us, of our perceptions, and he alone is our light.

Now, in strict metaphysical truth there is no external cause which acts on us except God alone, and it is God alone who communicates himself to us immediately by virtue of our continual dependence. From this it follows that there is no other external object which affects our soul and excites our perception immediately. Therefore we have in our soul the ideas of all things only by virtue of the continual action of God upon us, that is to say because every effect expresses its cause, and that thus the essence of our soul is a certain expression, imitation or image of the divine essence, thought and will, and of all the ideas that are contained therein. It can therefore be said that God alone is our immediate external object, and that we see all things by means of him. For example, when we see the sun and the stars, it is God who has given us and conserves for us the ideas of them, and who determines us by his ordinary concourse actually to think of them at the time when our senses are disposed in a certain way, following the laws that he has established. God is the sun and the light of souls, 'the Light which lighteth every man that cometh into the world'ʸ (*lumen illuminans omnem hominem venientem in hunc mundum*); and this view is not just

held at the present day. After Holy Scripture and the Father
of the Church, who have always been in favour of Plate
rather than of Aristotle, I recall having previously remarked
that from the time of the Scholastics several have believed
that God is the light of the soul and, in their terminology, the
active intellect of the rational soul (*intellectus agens anima
rationalis*)[z]. The Averroists have interpreted this in a bad
sense, but others—among whom, I believe, are Guillaume de
St. Amour[aa] and several mystical theologians—have taken
it in a way which is worthy of God and capable of elevating
the soul to the knowledge of its good.

29. However, we think immediately by means of our own ideas, and not
by those of God.

However, I do not share the opinion of some able philo
sophers,[ab] who seem to maintain that our ideas themselves
are in God, and not at all in us. In my view, this springs from
the fact that they have not yet considered sufficiently what
we have just explained here about substances, nor all the
extent and independence of our soul, as a result of which it
contains all that happens to it, and that it expresses God and
with him, all possible and actual beings, as an effect expresses
its cause. It is therefore inconceivable that I should think by
means of somebody else's ideas. The soul must also be affected
actually in a certain way when it thinks of something, and
there must be in it in advance not only the passive power of
being able to be affected in this way, which is already entirely
determined, but also an active power, by virtue of which it
has always had in its nature marks of the future production of
this thought and dispositions to produce it at its time. And all
this already includes the idea contained in this thought.

30. How God inclines our soul without necessitating it; that we have no
right to complain; that it must not be asked why Judas sins, since this free
act is contained in his notion, but only why Judas the sinner is admitted
to existence in preference to some other possible persons. Of imperfection or
original limitation before sin, and of the degrees of grace.

The question of the action of God on the human will involves

many very difficult considerations, which it would be tedious
to pursue here. Roughly speaking, however, what can be
said is as follows. God, in his ordinary concourse with our
actions, does no more than follow the laws which he has
established; that is to say, he conserves and continually produces our being in such a way that thoughts arise in us
spontaneously or freely in the order implied by the notion
of our individual substance, in which one could foresee them
from all eternity. Further, God has decreed that the will shall
always tend to the apparent good, expressing or imitating the
will of God in certain particular respects, in regard to which
this apparent good always has something of the genuine
good in it. By virtue of this decree God determines our will
to the choice of that which appears the best, without necessitating it in the least. For absolutely speaking it is in a state
of indifference, in so far as this is opposed to necessity, and has
the power of acting differently or even suspending its action
entirely, both choices being and remaining possible. It therefore rests with the mind to take precautions against the surprises which come from appearances by means of a firm will
to reflect, and only to act or judge in certain situations after
thorough and mature deliberation. Nevertheless it is true, and
even certain from all eternity, that a certain soul will not
make use of this power in such and such a situation. But
whose fault is that? Can the soul complain of anything but
itself? For all such complaints made after the fact are unjust
if they would have been unjust before the fact. Now could this
soul, a little before sinning, fairly complain of God, as if he
were determining it to sin? The determinations of God in
these matters are things that cannot be foreseen; how, then,
does it know that it is determined to sin, unless it is already
actually sinning? It is only a matter of not willing, and God
could not propose a condition which is easier or more just.
Similarly, no judge seeks the reasons which have disposed a
man to have an evil will; the judge only stops to consider how
evil this will is. But perhaps it is certain, from all eternity, that
I shall sin? Answer this yourself: perhaps it is not certain;
and, without dreaming about that which you cannot know
and which cannot bring you any kind of enlightenment, act

according to your duty, which you do know. But someone
else will say: how is it that this man will certainly commit
this sin? The reply is easy: namely, that otherwise he would
not be this man. For God sees from all time that there will be
a certain Judas, whose notion or idea, which God has, contains this future free action. There therefore remains only this
question: why such a Judas, the betrayer, who in God's idea
is only possible, exists actually. But no reply may be ex-
pected to this question here on earth, apart from this general
observation that must be made: that since God has found it
good that he should exist, despite the sin which he foresaw, it
is necessary that this evil is recompensed with interest in the
universe at large, that God will draw out of it a greater good,
and that it will be found that in sum this sequence of things,
in which the existence of this sinner is contained, is the most
perfect among all other possible kinds. But we cannot always
explain the admirable economy of this choice whilst we are
travellers in this world; it is enough for us to know it without
understanding it. And it is here that it is time to recognise the
'depth of the riches'[ac] (*altitudo divitiarum*), the depth and the
abyss of the divine wisdom, without seeking a detail which
involves infinite considerations. However, it is clear that God
is not the cause of evil. For not only did original sin seize hold
of the soul after man's fall from innocence, but even before
this there was an original limitation or imperfection, natural
to all creatures, which makes them liable to sin, or capable of
going wrong. So there is no more difficulty with regard to
the supralapsarians[ad] than there is with regard to the others.
And it is to this, in my view, that one must reduce the opinion
of St. Augustine and others,[ae] that the root of evil is in
nothingness, that is, in the privation or limitation of creatures,
which God in his grace remedies by the degree of perfection
which it pleases him to bestow. This grace of God, whether
ordinary or extraordinary, has its degrees and its measures;
in itself it is always efficacious in producing a certain proportionate effect; further, it is always sufficient, not only to
guarantee us against sin, but even to produce salvation,
assuming that man joins himself to it by that which comes
from him. But it is not always sufficient to surmount the in-

clinations of man, for otherwise he would be without fault, and that is reserved for absolutely efficacious grace which is always victorious, whether by itself, or by the suitability of the circumstances.[af]

32. The utility of these principles in matters of piety and religion.

For the rest, it seems that the thoughts that we have just expounded—and especially the great principle of the perfection of God's operations, and that of the notion of a substance which includes all that happens to it together with all their circumstances—are far from harming religion, but serve rather to strengthen it, to dispel great difficulties, to inflame souls with a divine love, and to elevate minds to the knowledge of incorporeal substances, much more than the hypotheses which have been seen hitherto. For it is seen clearly that all other substances depend on God, as thoughts emanate from our substance, that God is all in all, that he is united intimately with all creatures, though in proportion to their perfection, and that it is God alone who determines them from outside by his influence. Further, if to act is to determine immediately, it can be said in this sense, in the language of metaphysics, that God alone acts on me, and that God alone can do good or evil to me, other substances only contributing to the reason of these determinations, since God, having regard to them all, distributes his bounty and obliges them to harmonise with one another. Again, God alone brings about the liaison or communication between substances, and it is by him that the phenomena of any one tally with and agree with the phenomena of others, with the result that there is reality in our perceptions. In practice, however, one attributes action to particular reasons, in the sense which I have explained above, since it is not always necessary to mention the universal cause in particular cases. It is also seen that every substance has a perfect spontaneity (which becomes freedom in the case of intelligent substances), that everything which happens to it is a consequence of its idea or being, and that nothing determines it, apart from God alone. It is for this reason that a person of lofty mind and

revered sanctity[ag] used to say that the soul ought often to
think as if there were nothing but God and itself in the world.
Now, nothing gives us a better understanding of immortality
than this independence and extent of the soul, which gives it
absolute protection from all external things; for it alone constitutes all its world and, together with God, is self-sufficient.
It is as impossible that it should perish, except by annihilation, as it is impossible that the world, of which it is a living
and perpetual expression, should destroy itself. It is therefore
impossible that changes in that extended mass which is called
our body should do anything to the soul, or that the dissolution
of this body should destroy what is indivisible.

33. An explanation of the communication between soul and body, which
has hitherto been regarded as inexplicable or miraculous, and of the origin
of confused perceptions.

We see also an unexpected elucidation of that great mystery,
the union of the soul and the body; that is to say, how it happens
that the passions and actions of the one are accompanied by
the actions and passions, or the corresponding phenomena, of
the other. For it is inconceivable that the one should have any
influence on the other, and it is unreasonable simply to have
recourse to the extraordinary operation of the universal
cause in a matter which is ordinary and particular. But here
is the real reason. We have said that everything that happens
to the soul, and to each substance, is a consequence of its
notion; therefore the very idea or essence of the soul implies
that all that appears to it, all its perceptions, must arise in it
spontaneously (*sponte*) from its own nature, and precisely
in such a way that, of themselves, they correspond to what
happens in the whole universe, but more particularly and
more perfectly to what happens in the body which is assigned
to it; for in some way and for a time the soul expresses the
state of the universe, in accordance with the relation of other
bodies to its own. This also explains how our body belongs
to us, without being attached to our essence. And I believe
that people who are capable of meditation will judge favour-
ably of our principles for this very reason: that they can

easily see the nature of the connexion between soul and body, which seems inexplicable in any other way. It is also seen that our sense-perceptions, even when they are clear, must necessarily contain some confused sensation. For as all bodies in the universe are in sympathy, our own receives the impression of all the others, and although our senses are related to everything, it is not possible for our soul to be able to attend to everything in particular. This is why our confused sensations are the result of an absolutely infinite variety of perceptions. This is very like the way in which the confused murmur which is heard by those who approach the sea-shore comes from the accumulation of the repercussions of innumerable waves. Now if, of several perceptions (which do not agree together, to make one) there is none which surpasses the others, and if they produce impressions which are almost equally strong, or equally capable of determining the attention of the soul, it can perceive them only confusedly.

Express the Universe?

34. Of the difference between minds and other substances, souls or substantial forms, and that the immortality which is demanded implies memory.

Assuming that the bodies which constitute an essential unity (*unum per se*), such as man, are substances and that they have substantial forms; assuming, too, that the beasts have souls, one has to admit that these souls and these substantial forms cannot entirely perish, any more than the atoms or ultimate particles of matter that are believed in by other philosophers. For no substance perishes, though it can become quite different. Further, they express the entire universe, though in a less perfect way than minds do. But the chief difference is that they know neither what they are nor what they do; consequently, being unable to reflect, they cannot discover necessary and universal truths. It is also for lack of reflexion on themselves that they have no moral quality; the result is that as they pass through a thousand transformations—much as we see a caterpillar change into a butterfly—it is morally or practically the same as if they were said to perish, and we can even say the same in terms of natural science, as when we say that bodies perish by their corruption. But the intelligent soul, knowing what it is and being able to say this 'I' which says so much, does not merely remain and subsist metaphysically (which it does more fully than the others), but also remains morally the same and constitutes the same personality. For it is the memory or knowledge of this 'I' which makes it capable of reward and punishment. Therefore the immortality which is demanded in morals and in religion does not consist solely in that perpetual subsistence, which belongs to all substances, for without the memory of what one has been it would be in no way desirable. Let us suppose that some individual were suddenly to become King of China, but on condition of forgetting what he has been, as if he had just been born anew. Is not this practically the same, or the same as far as the effects which can be apperceived, as if he were to be annihilated and a King of China were to be created in his place at the same moment? And this particular individual has no reason to desire this.

35. The excellence of minds; that God considers them in preference to other creatures; that minds express God rather than the world, and that other simple substances express the world rather than God.

But so that it can be judged by natural reasons that God will always conserve, not only our substance but also our personality, that is to say the memory and knowledge of what we are (though the distinct knowledge of this is sometimes suspended in sleep and in fainting fits) it is necessary to join morals to metaphysics. That is, it is necessary to consider God, not only as the principle and the cause of all substances and of all beings, but also as the chief of all persons or intelligent substances, and as the absolute monarch of the most perfect city or commonwealth, such as is that of the universe which is composed of all minds taken together, God himself being the most perfect of all minds, as he is the greatest of all beings. For it is certain that minds are the most perfect substances, and that they express the divinity best. And as the whole nature, end, virtue and function of substances is only to express God and the universe (as has been sufficiently explained), there is no room for doubt that the substances who express him with a knowledge of what they are doing, and are capable of knowing great truths that concern God and the universe, express him incomparably better than those natures which are merely animal or incapable of knowing truths, or are wholly without sensation and knowledge; and the difference between the substances which are intelligent and those which are not is as great as the difference between the mirror and the man who sees. And as God himself is the greatest and wisest of minds, it is easy to form the opinion that the beings with whom he can, so to speak, enter into conversation and even into social relations—communicating to them his opinions and his volitions in a particular way, such that they can know and love their benefactor—must concern him infinitely more than all other things, which can be considered only as the instruments of minds. In the same way, we see that all wise men have an infinitely higher regard for a human being than for any other thing, however precious it may be; and it seems that the greatest satisfaction which can be had by a soul which is in other respects content, is to see itself loved by others. In the case of God, however, there is this difference: that his glory and our worship can add nothing to his satisfaction, the knowledge that creatures have of him being only a consequence of his sovereign and perfect happiness, far from contributing to it or being its partial cause. However, that which is good and rational in finite minds is found eminently[ah] in him, and as we would praise a king who preferred to preserve the life of a man rather than that of the most precious and rare of his animals, we may not doubt that the most enlightened and most just of all monarchs shares the same opinion.

36. God is the monarch of the most perfect commonwealth composed of all minds, and the happiness of this city of God is his chief purpose.

Minds, indeed, are the substances that are most capable of perfection, and their perfections have this peculiarity: that they hinder each other the least—or rather, they help each other, for only the most virtuous can be the most perfect friends. From this it clearly follows that God, who always aims at the greatest perfections in general, will take the greatest care of minds, and will not only give to them in general but also to each one in particular the greatest perfection that the universal harmony can permit. It can even be said that God, in so far as he is a mind, is the origin of existences; otherwise, if he lacked the will to choose the best, there would be no reason why one possible being should exist in preference to others. Thus the quality that God has of being himself a mind precedes all the other considerations which he can have with reference to creatures; minds alone are made in his image, and are as it were of his family, or like the children of his house, for they alone can serve him freely and act knowingly in imitation of the divine nature. One single mind is worth a whole world, for it does not merely express the world, but it also knows it and manages its affairs there after the fashion of God. It seems, then, that although every substance expresses the whole universe, other substances express the world rather than God, whereas minds express God rather than the world. This great nobility of the nature of minds, which approximates them to the divinity as much as is possible for mere creatures, means that God derives from them infinitely more glory than from all other beings; or rather, the other beings only provide an occasion for minds to glorify him. This is why this moral quality of God, which makes him the lord or monarch of minds, concerns him as it were personally, in a quite unique manner. It is in this that he humanises himself, that he is prepared to tolerate anthropomorphisms, and that he enters into a society with us, as a prince with his subjects. This consideration is so dear to him that the happy and flourishing state of his empire, which consists in the greatest possible happiness of its inhabitants, becomes his supreme law. For happiness is to persons what perfection is to beings. And if the first principle of the existence of the physical world is the decree to give it as much perfection as is possible, the first aim of the moral world, or of the city of God which is the most noble part of the universe, must be to spread in it as much happiness as is possible. It must not therefore be doubted that God has ordained everything in such a way that minds can not only live for ever—which is certain—but also that they will preserve for ever their moral quality, so that his city may not lose any person, just as the world does not lose any substance. Consequently, they will always know what they are, otherwise they would not be capable of reward or punishment; but that is the essence of a commonwealth, and above all of the most perfect commonwealth, where nothing can be neglected. Finally, as God is at once the most just and the most mild of monarchs, and demands nothing but a good will, provided that it is sincere and serious, his subjects could not wish for a better condition, and to make them perfectly happy God only requires them to love him.[aj]

Correspondence with Arnauld
(Selections) (1686–7)

To Landgraf Ernst von Hessen-Rheinfels. 12 April 1686

... I said in the thirteenth article of my Summary[a] that the individual notion of each person includes once for all everything which will ever happen to him. He[1] draws from this the consequence that everything which happens to a person, and even to the whole human race, must happen by a more than fatalistic necessity—as if notions or previsions rendered things necessary, and as if a free action could not be contained in the notion or perfect vision which God has of the person to whom it will belong. He adds that perhaps I shall find nothing to trouble me in the conclusion he draws. And yet I had expressly protested in the very same article that I did not admit such a conclusion. So either he must doubt my sincerity, for which I have given him no reason, or else he has not sufficiently examined the view he is rejecting. Still I will not reproach him for this, as it seems I have a right to do, since I bear in mind that he was writing at a time when some indisposition did not allow him the free use of all his mind, as is witnessed by his letter itself.[2]

---

[1] Arnauld.

[2] Arnauld had complained of a bad cold in the previous letter; and he had added, 'All that I can now do is to say in two words to Your Highness that I find in these meditations so many things which frighten me, and which, unless I am much mistaken, all mankind will find so shocking, that I do not see that any purpose would be served by a piece of writing which will manifestly be rejected by the whole world. ... Would it not be better for him to abandon these metaphysical speculations, which can be of no value either to him or to any one else, and to apply himself earnestly to the matter which is of the greatest importance of all to him, namely to assure his own salvation by returning to the Church ...?' Arnauld afterwards sincerely apologised for this rather off-hand treatment of Leibniz.

48

And I wish to have it known how much respect I feel for him. I come now to the proof of his inference, and to answer it better, I shall give M. Arnauld's own words.[b]

If that is the case, he says (namely that the individual notion of each person includes once for all everything which will ever happen to him), *God was not free to create all that has happened to the human race, and all that will ever happen to it had to happen, and must happen by a more than fatalistic necessity* (there is some fault in the copy but I think I have succeeded in restoring it as above). *For the individual notion of Adam included his having so many children, and the individual notion of each of these children included everything that they would do and all the children they would have, and so on. God had, then, no more freedom in all this, supposing that he had once willed to create Adam, than he had freedom not to create a being capable of thought supposing that he had willed to create me.*[1] These last words should strictly contain the proof of the consequence; but it is very clear that they confuse *necessitatem ex hypothesi*[2] with absolute necessity. A distinction has always been drawn between what God is absolutely free to do and what he is obliged to do by virtue of certain resolutions already taken (and he does not take any without previous regard to all). It is not worthy of God to conceive of him (under pretext of vindicating his liberty), in the manner of some Socinians,[c] as being like a human being who takes his resolutions in consideration of circumstances, and as now being no longer free to create what he considers good, if his earliest resolutions in regard to Adam or others already include a relation with what concerns their posterity. On the contrary every one is agreed that God has ordered from all eternity the whole succession of the universe, without its diminishing his freedom in any way.

It is evident also that this objection separates off from one another acts of will on the part of God, which are really connected together. We must not consider God's will to create a particular Adam as separated from all his other

---

[1] Gerhardt's text is very confused at this point. The sense can be restored with the help of a copy of the letter that Arnauld actually received (*Lettres de Leibniz à Arnauld*, ed. Geneviève Lewis, p. 29).

[2] i.e. that which necessarily follows from a given hypothesis.

acts of will in regard to the children of Adam and all the human race; as if God first made the decision to create Adam without any relation to his posterity, and none the less by that decision, according to my view, deprived himself of the freedom to create the posterity of Adam, as seemed to him good. This would be a strange way of reasoning. Rather we should think of God as choosing, not just any Adam vaguely, but a particular Adam, of whom there exists among the possible beings in the ideas of God a perfect representation, accompanied by certain individual circumstances, and possessing among other predicates that of having in the course of time certain posterity; we must think of God, I say, as choosing him with an eye to his posterity, and so as equally at the same time choosing the one and the other. I cannot see what harm there is in that. If he acted otherwise, he would not be acting like God. Let me suggest a comparison. A wise prince, when he chooses a general whose connexions he knows, in effect chooses at the time same a number of colonels and captains, whom he well knows the general will recommend, and whom he will not want to reject for reasons of prudence; yet they do not in any way destroy his absolute power, nor his freedom. *A fortiori*, the case is exactly the same with God. Therefore, to be exact, we must recognise in God a certain more general and comprehensive will, in which he has an eye to the whole order of the universe, since the universe is like a whole which God apprehends in a single view. This will virtually includes all the other acts of will about what enters into this universe, and among the rest it includes that of creating a particular Adam, who is connected with the whole succession of his posterity, which God has also chosen as such. We might even say that these particular acts of willing the details only differ from the willing of the whole general purpose by a simple relation, very much as the situation of a town considered from a particular point of view differs from its ground-plan.[1] For these particular acts of will all of them express the whole universe in the same way as each situation

---

[1] *Plan géométral*: a plan drawn to scale, showing the true measurements in proportion, i.e. having no regard to perspective. Cf. p. 72.

expresses the town. In fact the wiser a man is, the less does he have *detached acts of will*, and the more do his views and his acts of will become comprehensive and *connected*. And each particular act of will includes a relation to all the others, so that they are as well harmonised as possible. Far from finding in all this something shocking, I should have thought that the contrary would destroy the perfection of God. And in my opinion it must have been a matter of great difficulty, or else of great prejudice, to find in opinions so innocent, or rather so reasonable, an occasion for such strange exaggerations as those which were sent to Your Serene Highness.

Moreover, some slight consideration of what I have said will show that it is evident *ex terminis*.[1] For by the individual notion of Adam I undoubtedly mean a perfect representation of a particular Adam, with given individual conditions and distinguished thereby from an infinity of other possible persons very much like him, but yet different from him (just as every ellipse is different from the circle, however closely it approaches to it). God preferred him to all these others, because it pleased him to choose just this particular order of the universe; and all that follows from this decision of his is necessary only by a hypothetical necessity, and in no way derogates from the freedom of God nor from that of created minds. There is one possible Adam whose posterity is such and such, and an infinity of others whose posterity would be different; is it not the case that these possible Adams (if I may so speak of them) are different from one another, and that God has chosen only one of them, who is exactly our Adam? There are so many reasons which prove the impossibility, not to say the absurdity and even impiety, of the contrary, that I think that at bottom all men are of the same opinion, when they give a little thought to what they say. Perhaps, too, if M. Arnauld had not held about me the prejudiced view with which he started, he would not have found my propositions so strange and would not have drawn from them the consequences which he did. . . .

---

[1] 'from the terms themselves', i.e. from an analysis of the meaning of the terms.

To Landgraf Ernst von Hessen-Rheinfels. 12 April 1686

... Every man who acts wisely considers all the circumstances and connexions of the decision he is taking, and the
more so in proportion to his capacity. Will God, who sees
everything perfectly and with a single glance, fail to have taken
decisions in conformity with everything he sees? Can he
have chosen a particular Adam without considering and deciding as well everything which has any connexion with him?
Consequently it is ridiculous to say that this free decision of
God's takes away his liberty. Otherwise, to be free it would
be necessary to be for ever undecided. . . .

*Remarks on M. Arnauld's letter about my proposition that the in-
dividual notion of each person includes once for all everything that
will ever happen to him.* May 1686

... He admits in good faith that he understood my opinion
to be that everything that happens to an individual can be
deduced from his individual notion in the same way and with
the same necessity as the properties of a sphere can be deduced from its specific notion or definition; and that he
supposed I had been considering the notion of the individual
in itself, without regarding the manner in which it exists in
the understanding or will of God. *For* (he says) *it appears to
me that we are not accustomed to consider the specific notion of a
sphere in relation to what it is as represented in the Divine understanding, but in relation to what it is in itself, and I supposed it was
the same with the individual notion of each person;* but he adds
that, *now that he knows what my view is, that is enough to enable
him to grant it sufficiently to try and find out whether it removes all the
difficulties;* a matter of which he is still in doubt.

I see that M. Arnauld has not remembered, or at least has
not concerned himself about, the opinion of the Cartesians,
who hold that God establishes by his will the eternal truths,
like those regarding the properties of the sphere. But as I
am not of their opinion any more than M. Arnauld, I will
simply explain why I hold that we must philosophise differently about the notion of an individual substance than we do
about the specific notion of a sphere. This is because the notion
of a *species* includes eternal or necessary truths only, whereas

the notion of an individual includes *sub ratione possibilitatis*[1] what is fact, or what is related to the existence of things and to time; and consequently it depends on certain free decisions of God, considered as possible. For truths of fact or of existence depend upon God's decisions. Thus, the notion of a sphere in general is incomplete or abstract; that is to say we only consider the essence of a sphere in general or in theory, without regard to individual circumstances. Consequently the notion does not include in any way what is required for the existence of a certain sphere. But the notion of the sphere which Archimedes had placed upon his tomb is a complete notion, and is bound to include everything which belongs to the subject of that form. This is why in the case of individual considerations, or considerations of practice, *quae versantur circa singularia*,[2] besides the form of the sphere there enter in the matter of which it is made, the place, the time, and the other circumstances, which by a continual chain would in the end cover the whole series of the universe, if it were possible to follow out all that these notions include. For the notion of this piece of matter, of which this sphere is made, involves all the changes which have ever happened or will ever happen to it. According to my view, every individual substance always contains traces of all that has ever happened to it and marks of all that ever will ever happen to it for all time. What I have just said may suffice to explain my train of thought.

... As regards the objection that possibles are independent of the decisions of God, I grant that they are so of actual decisions (though the Cartesians do not agree with this); but I hold that possible individual notions include a number of possible free decisions. For example, if this world were possible only, the individual notion of some body in this world, which includes certain movements as possible, would include our laws of motion (which are free decisions of God), but it would include them as possible only. For as there is an

---

[1] 'considered as possible'.
[2] 'which are concerned with individuals', what is individual being opposed to what is general.

infinity of possible worlds, there is also an infinity of laws, some proper to one world, others to another; and each possible individual of any world includes in its notion the laws of its world.

The same thing can be said of miracles or the extraordinary operations of God, which none the less belong within the general order; they are in conformity with the principal designs of God, and consequently are included in the notion of this universe, which is a result of those designs. Just as the idea of a building results from the ends and designs of the builder, so the idea or notion of this world is a result of these designs of God, considered as possible. For everything must be explained by its cause; and the cause of the universe is the ends of God. Now each individual substance, according to my view, expresses the whole universe from a certain point of view, and consequently it also expresses the said miracles. All this must be understood of the general order, of the designs of God, of the series of this universe, of individual substance, and of miracles, whether they are taken in their actual state or are considered *sub ratione possibilitatis*.[1] For another possible world will have all those things too in its own manner, though the designs of our own world have been preferred.

It will be seen too, from what I have just said about the designs of God and about the primary laws, that this universe has a certain principal or primary notion, of which particular happenings are merely consequences—without, however, eliminating freedom and contingency, to which certainty is in no way inimical, since the certainty of events is partly based on free actions. ... To speak exactly, it should be said that it is not so much because God decided to create this Adam that he decided on all the rest; the truth is rather that both his decision regarding Adam and his decision about other particular things are a consequence of his decision in regard to the whole universe and of the principal designs which determine its primary notion and establish in it this general inviolable order, with which everything is in conformity, without even excepting miracles, which are

[1] i.e. not as facts, but as possibilities.

without doubt in conformity with the principal designs of
God, although they do not always observe the particular
maxims which are called laws of nature.

I said before that the supposition from which all human
events can be deduced is not simply that of the creation of a
vague Adam, but that of the creation of a particular Adam
determinate in respect to all these circumstances[d] and chosen
from among an infinity of possible Adams. This has given M.
Arnauld occasion to object, not without reason, that it is as
impossible to conceive of several Adams, taking Adam as an
individual nature, as it would be to conceive of several *I*s. I
agree; but I must add that in speaking of several Adams, I
was not taking Adam as a determinate individual. I must
explain myself; this is what I meant. When in considering
Adam we consider a part of his predicates, as for instance
that he is the first man, set in a pleasure garden, from out of
whose side God took a woman, and similar things conceived
sub ratione generalitatis[1] (i.e. without naming Eve, Paradise,
or other circumstances which fix individuality), and we give
the name Adam to the person to whom these predicates are
attributed, all this is not sufficient to determine the individual; for there might be an infinity of Adams, that is to say
of possible persons, different from one another, to whom all
that is appropriate. Far from disagreeing with what M.
Arnauld says against such a plurality of one and the same
individual, I used the same argument myself to make it clear
that the nature of an individual must be complete and determinate. I am indeed entirely persuaded of what St. Thomas
had already taught in regard to intelligences and, which I hold
to be of general application, namely that it is not possible
that there should be two individuals entirely alike, or differing
solo numero.[2] We must not then conceive of a vague Adam,
that is to say a person to whom certain of Adam's attributes
belong, when it is a question of determining whether all
human happenings follow from the supposition of him; we
must attribute to him a notion so complete that everything

---

[1] i.e. considered in general, as opposed to considered in respect of its
unique, individual character.
[2] 'numerically only'. *Cf. Discourse on Metaphysics*, art. 9.

that can be attributed to him can be deduced from it. Now there is no room for doubt but that God could form such a notion of him, or rather that he finds it ready made in the country of possibles, that is, in his understanding.

It follows also that he would not have been our Adam, but another, if different things had happened to him; for nothing prevents us from saying that he would be another. Therefore he is another. It appears evident to us that this square of marble brought from Genoa would have been in all respects the same, if it had been left there, because our senses only make us judge superficially; but at bottom, because of the interconnexion of things, the whole universe with all its parts would be quite different, and would have been a quite different universe from the beginning, if the least thing went differently from the way it does go. This does not mean that all that happens is necessary; rather everything that happens is certain after God made choice of this possible universe, whose notion contains this series of things. I hope that what I am going to say will make even M. Arnauld agree with me.

Let there be a straight line *ABC* representing a certain time. And let a certain individual substance, for instance myself, remain or exist throughout the given time. Let us first take the *I* which exists during the time *AB*, and then the *I* which exists during the time *BC*. Since then the assumption is that it is the same individual substance enduring throughout, or rather that it is I who exist in the time *AB*, being then in Paris, and that it is still I who exist in the time *BC*, being then in Germany, it follows necessarily that there is a reason which makes us say truly that we endure, that is, that I who was in Paris am now in Germany. For if there is no reason, we should have as much right to say that it is another person. It is true that my internal experience convinces me *a posteriori* of this identicalness, but there must be a reason *a priori*. Now it is not possible to find any other except that both my attributes in the preceding time and state and my attributes in the later time and state are predicates of one and the same subject: *insunt eidem subjecto*.[1] Now what is meant by saying

---

[1] 'they are included in the same subject'.

that a predicate is in a subject, except that the notion of the predicate is in some way included in the notion of the subject? And since from the time when I began to exist it was possible to say of me truly that this or that would happen to me, it must be acknowledged that these predicates were laws included in the subject, or in the complete notion of me which makes that which is called *I*, which is the foundation of the interconnexion of all my different states, and which was perfectly known to God from all eternity.

After this I think that all doubts should disappear, for when I say that the individual notion of Adam includes everything that will ever happen to him, I do not mean anything other than what all philosophers mean when they say *praedicatum inesse subjecto verae propositionis*.[1] It is true that the consequences of so evident a doctrine are paradoxical; but that is the fault of the philosophers, who do not follow up sufficiently the clearest notions.

I think that M. Arnauld, being as penetrating and fair-minded as he is, will now no longer find my proposition so strange, even if he is not yet able to approve of it entirely (though I almost persuade myself that he will approve). I agree with what he says so judiciously about the circumspection that is necessary in attempting to use the Divine knowledge[2] to find out what we ought to judge about the notions of things. But, rightly understood, what I have just said must be allowed, since God would only be brought in as much as is necessary. For we should not need to assert that God, in considering the Adam whom he is deciding to create, sees in him everything that will happen to him; it is enough that we can always prove that there must be a complete notion of this Adam which contains them. For all the predicates of Adam either depend upon other predicates of the same Adam, or they do not so depend. Putting on one side, then, those which do not depend on others, we have only to

---

[1] 'in a true proposition the predicate is included in the subject'.

[2] Arnauld had written: 'I find it hard to believe that the right way of philosophising would be to seek, in the way in which God knows things, what we are to think either of their specific or of their individual notions. . . . For what do we know at present of God's knowledge?'

take together the primary predicates in order to form the complete notion of Adam, which is sufficient to make it possible to deduce from it everything which must happen to him, as far as is necessary to give an explanation of it. It is evident that God can invent, and even does in fact conceive, such a notion, which is sufficient to account for all the phenomena which belong to Adam; but it is no less evident that it is possible in itself. It is true that we must not, unless it is necessary, involve ourselves in the investigation of Divine knowledge and Divine will because of the great difficulties therein; still, we can explain what we have derived from this for our question without entering into the difficulties mentioned by M. Arnauld—for example, how the simplicity of God is reconcilable with the distinctions we are obliged to make with regard to him. It is also extremely difficult to explain perfectly how God has a knowledge which he might not have had, namely the knowledge of *vision*, for if future contingents did not exist, God would have no vision of them. It is true that he would have simple knowledge, which became vision when his will was joined to it;[e] so that this difficulty perhaps reduces itself to such difficulty as there is about his will, that is, how God is free to will. This is without doubt beyond us, but it is not so necessary to understand it in order to solve our problem.

As for the manner in which we conceive that God acts in choosing the best among several possibles, M. Arnauld is right in finding some obscurity there. Yet he seems to recognise that we are led to conceive that there is an infinity of possible first men, each with a great following of persons and events, and that God chose the one who together with his following pleased him. All that is not as strange as it had first appeared to him. It is true that M. Arnauld testifies that he is very much inclined to think that substances that are purely possible are nothing but chimeras. About this I do not want to enter into dispute: but I hope that in spite of that he will grant me what I need. I agree that there is no other reality in pure possibilities but that which they have in the Divine understanding; and from this it can be seen that M. Arnauld himself will be obliged to fall back on the Divine knowledge to explain them, whereas he seemed to mean just now that they ought to be looked for in themselves. Since I should admit also the proposition, of which M. Arnauld is convinced and which I do not deny, namely that we do not conceive of any possibility except through ideas which are to be found in the things which God has created, this objection does not affect my argument. For when I speak of possibilities, I am quite satisfied that it should be possible to form true propositions about them. For example, if there were no perfect square in the world, we should still see that it does not involve any contradiction. And if we absolutely reject pure possibilities, this means that there is no contingency; for if nothing is possible except what God has in fact created, what God has created would be necessary, supposing he had once decided to create anything.

Finally, I agree that in order to judge of the notion of an individual substance it is a good thing to consider that which I have of myself, just as it is necessary to consider the specific notion of a sphere in order to judge of its properties. And yet there is a considerable difference; for the notion of *me* and of every other individual substance is infinitely more extended and more difficult to understand than a specific notion like that of a sphere, which is incomplete only. It is not enough that I feel myself a substance which thinks, it would be necessary to conceive distinctly what distinguishes me from all other minds; but of this I have only a confused experience. The result is that, though it is easy to determine that the number of feet in the diameter is not included in the notion of the sphere in general, it is not so easy to determine whether the journey which I intend to make is included in my notion; otherwise it would be as easy for us to be prophets as to be geometers. I am uncertain whether I shall go on the journey; but I am not uncertain that, whether I go or not, I shall still be the same *I*. It is an unreflective conviction,[1] which must not be confused with a distinct notion or item of knowledge. These things only seem to us to be undetermined because the foreshadowings or marks which are there in our substance

---

[1] *Prévention*. There is not, I think, a sufficiently exact English equivalent; and this cumbrous phrase seems to be unavoidable.

are not recognisable by us. In the same way those who take
no account of anything but the senses will treat with ridicule
any one who says that the least movement communicates
itself on and on as far as matter extends, because this could
not be learnt from experience alone;[1] but when we consider
the nature of motion and of matter, we are convinced. It is
the same here: when I consider the confused experience I
have of the individual notion of *me* in particular, I am far
from perceiving this connexion of events; but when I consider
the general, distinct notions which enter into the notion of
me, I come upon that connexion. In fact, in considering the
notion that I have of every true proposition, I find that every
predicate, necessary or contingent, past, present, or future,
is contained in the notion of the subject; and I ask no more.

Indeed, I think that this will open up to us a way of reconciliation; for I imagine that M. Arnauld felt a repugnance
against assenting to my proposition only because he took the
connexion, which I am maintaining, to be intrinsic and necessary at the same time, whereas I hold it to be intrinsic, but
in no way necessary; for I have now sufficiently explained
that it is founded on free decisions and actions. I do not
mean any other connexion between subject and predicate
than that which is to be found in the most contingent truths;
that is to say, there is always something to be conceived in the
subject which provides the explanation why this predicate or
this event belongs to it, or why a particular event happened
rather than not. But the reasons of these contingent truths
incline without necessitating. It is true then that I could fail
to go on this journey, but it is certain that I shall go. This
predicate or event is not certainly connected with my other
predicates conceived incompletely or *sub ratione generalitatis*,[1]
but it is connected certainly with my complete individual
notion, since I suppose that this notion was expressly so
constructed that it might be possible to deduce from it
everything which happens to me. This notion is without
doubt *a parte rei*;[2] and it properly is the notion of *me*, who

---

[1] Cf. p. 55, note 1.

[2] 'from the side of the thing itself'; i.e. the notion is of something really
existing, and not of an imaginary or merely possible object.

ind myself in a number of different states, since it is this
notion alone which is capable of including them all. . . .

To Arnauld. Hanover, 14 July 1686

... I agree that the connexion of events, although it is
certain, is not necessary, and that it is open to me to go or
not to go on this journey; for although it is included in my
notion that I shall go, it is also included that I shall go freely.
And of all that in me which can be conceived *sub ratione
generalitatis seu essentiae seu notionis specificae sive incompletae*[1]
there is nothing from which it can be inferred that I shall go
necessarily; whereas from the fact that I am a man it can be
concluded that I am capable of thinking. Consequently, if I
do not go on this journey, it will not violate any eternal or
necessary truth. Nevertheless, since it is certain that I shall
go, there is bound to be some connexion between me, who
am the subject, and the accomplishment of the journey,
which is the predicate; *semper enim notio praedicati inest subjecto
in propositione vera.*[2] Thus if I did not go there would be a
falsity which would destroy my individual or complete
notion, or that which God conceives of me, or did conceive
even before he decided to create me. For this notion involves
sub ratione possibilitatis[3] existences, or truths of fact, or decisions
of God, on which facts depend. . . .

... You approve, sir, the interconnexions of God's decisions; you recognise as certain my principal proposition, in
the sense which I gave to it in my reply. You are simply in
doubt whether I made the interconnexion independent of
the free decisions of God; and this quite rightly troubles you.
But I have made it clear that according to my view it depends
on these decisions, and that it is not necessary though it is
intrinsic. You insisted on the difficulty that would be involved in saying that if I do not go on this journey as I am
bound to do, I shall not be I; and I explained how it may be

[1] 'in general terms, or in terms of its essence or of its specific or incomplete notion'.
[2] 'for in a true proposition the notion of the predicate is always included
in the subject'.
[3] Cf. p. 54, note.

said or may not. Finally I gave a decisive reason, which i
my opinion has the force of demonstration; namely, that i
every affirmative true proposition, necessary or contingen
universal or singular, the notion of the predicate is containe
in some way in that of the subject, *praedicatum inest subjecto*.[1]
Or else I do not know what truth is.

Now I ask no more connexion here than that which exist
a parte rei[2] between the terms of a true proposition; and it i
in this sense only that I say that the individual substanc
includes all its events and all its denominations, even thos
which are commonly called extrinsic[g] (that is, they belong t
it only by virtue of the general interconnexion of things an
because it expresses the whole universe in its own way)
*since there must always be some foundation of the connexion of th
terms of a proposition, which foundation must lie in their notions*
This is my chief principle, on which I hold that all philo
sophers ought to be agreed. And one of its corollaries is th
common axiom that nothing happens without a reason
which can always be given to explain why the thing turne
out thus rather than otherwise, though this reason often in
clines without necessitating, a perfect indifference being
chimerical or incomplete supposition. It will be seen tha
from the aforesaid principle I draw surprising consequences
but this is only because people are not accustomed to thinkin
out sufficiently the clearest items of knowledge. . . .

You may perhaps be surprised that I deny the action o
one bodily substance on another, when it seems to be s
evident. But besides the fact that others have denied it befor
me, we must bear in mind that it is rather a play of th
imagination than a distinct conception. If a body is a sub
stance, and not a mere phenomenon like the rainbow, nor a
entity united by accident or by aggregation like a heap c
stones, it cannot consist of extension; and it must necessaril
be conceived as something which is called substantial form
and which corresponds in some way to a soul. I became con
vinced of this in the end, as it were in spite of myself, afte

[1] 'the predicate is included in the subject'.
[2] Cf. p. 60, note 2.

having held a very different opinion in earlier days. Still, approve as I may of the Schoolmen in this general and, if I may so put it, metaphysical explanation of theirs of the principles of bodies, I still subscribe fully to the corpuscular theory in the explanation of particular phenomena; in this sphere it is of no value to speak of forms or qualities. Nature must always be explained mathematically and mechanically, provided it is remembered that the very principles or laws of mechanics or of force do not depend on mathematical extension alone, but on certain metaphysical reasons. . . .

To Arnauld. Hanover, 14 July 1686

. . . Also I do not much approve of the behaviour of those who are always appealing to their ideas, when they have exhausted their proofs, and who misuse the principle that every clear and distinct conception is valid.[1] I hold that we must always look for the marks of distinct knowledge; and as we often think without ideas, by using ciphers (in place of the ideas in question) whose signification we falsely suppose ourselves to know, and make up for ourselves impossible chimeras, I hold that the mark of a genuine idea is that its possibility can be proved, either *a priori* by conceiving its cause or reason, or *a posteriori* when experience teaches us that it in fact exists in nature. For this reason definitions, in my view, are real when it is known that the thing defined is possible; otherwise they are nominal only, and should not be trusted, since if by chance the thing defined implied a contradiction, two contradictory consequences might be inferred from one and the same definition. Hence you were absolutely right to inform Fr. Malebranche and others[h] that a distinction must be made between true and false ideas, and that too much rein must not be given to a man's imagination under pretext of its being a clear and distinct intellection.

Draft of a letter to Arnauld. 8th December 1686

. . . Action is attributed to that substance, whose expression is more distinct, and one calls this the cause. For instance,

---

[1] Leibniz is here attacking the Cartesian doctrine that every clear and distinct idea is known to be true; he is in effect saying that we need to know *when* an idea is clear and distinct.

when a floating body moves through water, there is an infinity of movements of the parts of the water, such as are
necessary so that the place which the body leaves may always
be filled by the shortest way. Hence we say that the body is
the cause of these movements; because by its means we can
explain distinctly what happens. But if we examine what is
physical and real in the motion, we can as well suppose
that the body is at rest, and that everything else moves in
conformity with this hypothesis, since all motion is in itself
nothing but a relative thing, namely a change of situation,
such that we cannot know to what to attribute it with mathematical precision. Actually we attribute it to a body by whose
means everything is explained distinctly. . . .

Thus, in strict metaphysical precision, we have no more
reason to say that the ship pushes the water to produce this
large number of circles which serve to fill up the place of the
ship, than to say that the water is caused to produce all these
circles and that it causes the ship to move accordingly. But
short of saying that God has expressly willed to produce this
large number of movements in this co-ordinated manner, we
cannot give the reason for them; and as it is not reasonable to
have recourse to God in matter of detail, we fall back on the
ship, although as a matter of fact in the last analysis the
agreement of all the phenomena of the different substances
comes simply from the fact that they are all the products of
one and the same cause, namely God, who arranges that each
individual substance expresses the decision which God has
taken in regard to the whole universe.

I do not know whether the body, when the soul or substantial form is put aside, can be called a substance. It might
well be a machine, an aggregate of several substances, so
that, if I am asked what I should say *de forma cadaveris*[1] or
about a square of marble, my reply is that they are perhaps
unities *per aggregationem*[2] like a heap of stones, and are not
substances. The same might be said of the sun, of the earth,
of machines; and with the exception of man there is no body

[1] 'about the form of a corpse'.
[2] 'by aggregation'.

of which I can be assured that it is a substance rather than an aggregate of several substances, or perhaps a phenomenon. Nevertheless it seems to me certain that, if there are any corporeal substances, man is not the only one; and it appears probable that the brutes have souls, though they are without consciousness.

Finally, although I agree that the consideration of forms or souls is useless in particular physics, it is for all that of importance in metaphysics. In much the same way geometers do not trouble themselves *de compositione continui*,[1] and physicists do not concern themselves whether one ball impels another, or whether it is God who does this.[j]

It would be unworthy of a philosopher to admit such souls or forms unless there were a reason for it; but without them the fact that bodies are substances is not intelligible.

To Arnauld. Göttingen, 30 April 1687

. . . You suppose that I will not say that a body can move itself; and so, since the soul is not the real cause of the movement of the arm, nor is the body, the cause will therefore be God. But I am of a different opinion. I hold that all that is real in the state which is called motion proceeds as much from the corporeal substance as thought and will proceed from the mind. Everything happens in each substance in consequence of the first state which God gave to it in creating it, and, extraordinary concourse apart, his ordinary concourse consists simply in the conservation of the substance itself, in conformity with its precedent state and with the changes which it carries within it. Nevertheless, it is quite right to say that one body impels another; that is to say that the fact is that one body never begins to have a given tendency except when another body which is touching it has a proportionate loss, in accordance with the constant laws which we observe in phenomena. And in fact, motions being real phenomena rather than entities, a movement as phenomenon is in my mind the immediate consequence or effect of another phenomenon, and similarly in the minds of others.

[1] 'about the composition of a continuum'; i.e. how that which is continuous can have parts and yet be continuous, etc.

But the state of a substance is not the immediate consequence of the state of another particular substance. . . .

If my opinion that substance requires a true unity were only founded on a definition that I had myself made up contrary to common usage, then *the dispute would be simply one of words*. But in the first place philosophers have understood this term in much the same manner, *distinguendo unum per se et unum per accidens, formamque substantialem et accidentalem, mixta imperfecta et perfecta, naturalia et artificialia*.[1] In the second place, I approach the matter from a higher ground also, and, waiving the analysis of terms, *I hold that where there are only entities by aggregation, there will not be any real entities*. For every entity by aggregation presupposes entities endowed with a true unity, for it only takes its reality from the reality of those of which it is composed, so that it will not have any at all, if each entity of which it is composed is itself an entity by aggregation; or else it is necessary to look further for a different foundation of its reality, which, if it is at every stage necessary to go further in looking for it, can never be found. I agree, sir, that in all corporeal nature there are nothing but machines (which are often animated); but I do not agree that *there are nothing but aggregates of substances*; and if there are aggregates there must also be some true substances of which the aggregates are made up. We must then come down to either the mathematical points, out of which some authors compound extension, or to the atoms of Epicurus and M. Cordemoy[k] (which are things that you and I alike reject), or else we must acknowledge that no reality can be found in bodies; or finally we must recognise some substances as having a genuine unity. I have already said in another letter that a combination of the Grand Duke's diamond and the Great Mogul's diamond may be called a pair of diamonds, but that is only an entity of reason; when they are put side by side, that will be an entity of imagination or of perception, that is to say a phenomenon; for their contact, their common movement, and their co-ordination to carry out one and the

[1] 'by distinguishing between that which is a unity of itself and that which is a unity adventitiously, between substantial and accidental form, and between imperfect and perfect, natural and artificial compounds'.

same design, make no difference as regards substantial unity. It is true that there is sometimes more, sometimes less foundation for our supposition, when we suppose that several things are combining to make one single thing, according as the things have more or less connexion; but this is only a way of abbreviating our thoughts and of representing phenomena.

It appears, too, that what constitutes the essence of an entity by aggregation is nothing but a manner of existence of the things of which it is composed; for example, what constitutes the essence of an army is simply a manner of existence of the men who compose it. This manner of existence, then, presupposes a substance, whose essence is not the manner of existence of a substance. Every machine, too, presupposes some substance in the pieces of which it is made; and there can be no plurality without true unities. To put it shortly, I maintain as axiomatic this identical proposition, whose differentiation can only be marked by the accentuation —namely, that that which is not truly *one* entity is not truly one *entity* either. It has always been held that unity and entity are reciprocal things. An entity is one thing, entities are quite another thing: but the plural presupposes the singular, and where there is no entity still less are there several entities. What could be more clearly stated? I therefore thought that I might be allowed to distinguish entities by aggregation from substances, since such entities have their unity in our mind only; which unity is based upon the relations or modes of genuine substances. If a machine is a substance, a circle of men holding one another's hands will be a substance too; so will an army, and so will every plurality of substances.

I do not mean that there is nothing substantial, or nothing but appearance, in the things which have no genuine unity; for I agree that they have always as much reality or substantiality as there is genuine unity in that of which they are composed.

You object, sir, that it may perhaps be of the essence of

body not to have a true unity. But in that case it will be of the essence of body to be a phenomenon, deprived of all reality, like an ordered dream; for phenomena themselves, like a rainbow or a heap of stones, would be wholly imaginary, if they were not composed of entities with a genuine unity.

You say that you do not see what leads me to admit that there are such substantial terms, or rather corporeal substances, endowed with a genuine unity. It is because I do not conceive of any reality at all as without genuine unity. According to my view the notion of singular substance involves consequences which are incompatible with its being an entity by aggregation. I conceive of there being properties in substance which cannot be explained by extension, shape, and motion, besides the fact that there is no exact and fixed shape in bodies because of the actual subdivision of the continuum *ad infinitum*. Moreover, motion inasmuch as it is only a modification of extension and a change of neighbourhood, involves an imaginary element, so that it is not possible to determine to which of the subjects that change it belongs, unless we have recourse to the force in corporeal substance which is the cause of the motion. I admit that there is no need to mention these substances and qualities in order to explain particular phenomena, but neither is there any need to mention the concourse of God, the composition of the continuum, the plenum, and countless other things. We can explain mechanically, I fully admit, the particularities of nature; but this is after having discovered or presupposed the principles of mechanics themselves, which we cannot establish *a priori* except by metaphysical arguments; and even the difficulties *de compositione continui*[1] will never be resolved so long as extension is regarded as constituting the substance of bodies, and we go on embarrassing ourselves by our own chimeras.

I think, too, that to allow genuine unity or substance to man almost alone is to be as limited in metaphysics as those people were in physics who confined the world within a ball. And as genuine substances are so many expressions of the

[1] Cf. p. 65, note 1.

whole universe taken in a certain sense, and so many reproductions of Divine works, it is in agreement with the greatness and beauty of these works of God, since these substances do not hinder one another from accomplishing as much in this universe as is possible and as much as superior reasons allow. . . .

I agree that there are degrees of accidental unity; that an ordered society has more unity than a confused mob, and that an organised body or a machine has more unity than a society—that is to say there is more point in conceiving them as one single thing, because there is more relation between the constituent parts. But in the end all these unities only receive their existence from thoughts and appearances, like colours and other phenomena, which for all that are called real. The tangibility of a heap of stones or of a block of marble does not any the more prove its substantial reality than the visibility of a rainbow proves the substantial reality of the rainbow; and as there is nothing so solid that it has not some degree of fluidity, perhaps this block of marble is only a heap made of an infinity of living bodies, or is like a lake full of fish, although these living creatures cannot ordinarily be distinguished by the eye except in the case of bodies that are half rotted. We may say then of these composites and of similar things what Democritus so well said of them, namely *esse opinione, lege,* νόμῳ.[1] Plato held the same view about everything which is purely material. Our mind notices or conceives a number of genuine substances which have certain modes; these modes involve relations to other substances, and so the mind takes occasion to join them together in thought and to give an inclusive name to all the things together. This is a convenience for reasoning; but we must not allow ourselves to be misled into making of them so many substances or genuinely real entities. This only befits those people who go no further than appearances, or else those who make realities of all the abstractions of the mind, and who conceive of number, time, place, motion, figure, and sensible qualities as so many separate entities.

[1] 'they depend for their existence on opinion or custom'.[1]

Whereas I hold that philosophy cannot be better established, and reduced to some degree of precision, than by learning to recognise the only substances or complete entities, endowed as they are with a genuine unity in their different states following one another, all the rest being nothing but phenomena, abstractions, or relations.

No kind of arrangement will ever be found which can make a genuine substance out of a number of entities by aggregation. For example, if the parts which fit together into one and the same design are more competent to produce a genuine unity than are parts which are in contact, then all the officials of the Dutch East India Company will make a real substance far better than a heap of stones. But what else is a common design but a resemblance, or rather an ordered arrangement of actions and passions, which our mind notices in different things? If on the other hand we prefer the unity based on contact, we are faced by other difficulties. Hard bodies have perhaps nothing uniting their parts except the pressure of surrounding bodies and of themselves, and in their substance are no more united than a heap of sand, *arena sine calce*.[1] Or, consider a number of rings interlaced to make a chain: why should they compose a genuine substance thus any more than if they had openings in them through which they could be separated? It may be that one of the parts of the chain does not touch another and even does not enclose it, and yet they are so interlaced that unless they are taken in a certain manner they cannot be separated, as in the figure here given. Are we to say in that case that the

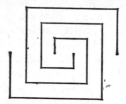

substance of the compound of these things is as it were in suspense and depends on the future skill of whoever may wish

[1] 'sand without lime', i.e. without anything to bind it into mortar.

to disentangle them? These are all fictions of the mind; and so long as we do not distinguish what is genuinely a complete entity, or substance, we shall never have any fixed point at which we can stop; and such a fixed point is the one and only means of establishing solid and real principles.

In conclusion, nothing should be taken as certain without foundations; it is therefore for those who manufacture entities and substances without a genuine unity to prove that there is more reality than I have just said; and I am waiting for the notion of a substance, or of an entity, which successfully comprehends all these things; after which mock-suns[m] and perhaps even dreams will be able one day to lay claim to reality, unless very precise limits are set to this *droit de bourgeoisie*[1] which is to be accorded to entities formed by aggregation.

I have written at some length on these matters, so that you may be able to form some opinion not only of my views, but also of the reasons which have driven me to adopt them. . . .

To Arnauld. 9 October 1687

. . . You reply that you have no clear idea of what I mean by the word *express*. If I mean by it a thought, you say, you do not agree that the soul has any more thought and knowledge of the movement of the lymph in its lymphatic ducts than of the movements of the satellites of Saturn; if I mean something else, you do not know what I mean, and consequently (supposing that I cannot explain myself distinctly) this term will be of no use to make clear how the soul can give itself the sensation of pain, since for that it would be necessary (so you say) for it to know beforehand that I am being stung, instead of learning of the sting by feeling the pain. In reply to your objection, I will first explain the term which you find obscure, and then apply it to the difficulty you raise. One thing *expresses* another (in my language) when there is a constant and ordered relation between what can be asserted of the one and what can be asserted of the other. In this

---

[1] Leibniz seems to mean a kind of inferior citizenship. A *bourgeois* was originally a member of a small township who had certain rights akin to those of a citizen in a city.

sense a projection in perspective expresses its ground plan.[1]
Expression is common to all forms, and is a genus of which
natural perception, animal sensation, and intellectual knowledge are species. In natural perception and in sensation it is
sufficient that what is divisible and material, and is to be
found dispersed in a number of entities, should be expressed
or represented in a single indivisible entity, or in a substance
possessing a genuine unity. There can be absolutely no doubt
of the possibility of a good representation of several things in
one single thing; for our soul presents us with an example.
This representation is accompanied by consciousness in a
rational soul, and it is then that it is called thought.

Now such expression is to be found on all sides, because
every substance sympathises with every other and receives
some proportionate change, corresponding to the least
change which occurs in the universe; though this change is
more or less noticeable in proportion as the other bodies or
their activities have more or less relation to ours. On this
point I think M. Descartes himself would have agreed; for
he would certainly grant that because of the continuity and
divisibility of all matter the effect of the least movement is
extended over all the neighbouring bodies, and consequently
from body to body *ad infinitum*, though diminishing pro-
portionately. Thus our body must be affected to some extent
by the changes in all the others.

Now to all the movements of our body there correspond
certain perceptions or thoughts of our soul, more or less
confused; so the soul in turn will have some thought of all
the movements of the universe, and according to my opinion
every other soul or substance will have some perception or
expression of them. It is true that we do not perceive distinctly all the movements of our body, as for example the
movement of the lymph; but (to make use of an example
which I have employed previously)[n] it is like this. It must
be the case that I have some perception of the movement
of each wave on the shore if I am to be able to apperceive
that which results from the movements of all the waves put
together, namely the mighty roar which we hear by the sea.

[1] *son géométral.* Cf. p. 50, note.

similarly we feel some confused result of all the movements which take place in us, but, being accustomed to this internal movement, we do not apperceive it distinctly and reflectively except when there is a considerable change, as at the beginning of an illness. And it would be an excellent thing if physicians devoted themselves to distinguishing more exactly these kinds of confused sensations which we have of our bodies. Now since we do not apperceive the other bodies except by the relation which they bear to ours, I was quite right in saying that the soul expresses better what belongs to our body, and that we only know of the satellites of Saturn or of Jupiter in consequence of a movement occurring within our eyes. . . .

With regard to minds, that is to say substances which think, and are capable of knowing God and of discovering eternal truths, I hold that God governs them by laws different from those by which he governs the rest of substances. All forms of substances express the whole universe; but it may be said that brute substances express the world rather than God, while minds express God rather than the world. Moreover God governs brute substances by the material laws of force, or of the communication of motion, whereas he governs minds by the spiritual laws of justice, of which the other substances are incapable. It is for this reason that brute substances may be called material, because the economy which God observes in regard to them is that of a Workman or a Machine-maker; whereas in regard to minds, God fulfils the function of Prince or Legislator, which is infinitely more exalted. And whereas God is nothing in regard to these material substances but that which he is in regard to everything, namely the general Author of entities, he takes on, in regard to minds, a different character, such that he must be conceived as invested with will and moral qualities; since he is himself a mind, and as it were One among us, even to the point of entering with us into a social community of which he is the chief. It is this society or general Commonwealth of Minds under this sovereign Monarch which is the noblest part of the universe, composed of so many little gods under

this great God. For it can be said that created minds differ
from God only as less from greater, as finite from infinite.
And we may be truly assured that the whole universe was
created only to contribute to the adornment and to the
happiness of this City of God. This is why everything is so
disposed that the laws of force, or purely material laws,
conspire in all the universe to execute the laws of justice or of
love, and that nothing can hurt the souls that are in the hand
of God, and that all things must work together for the
greatest good of those who love him. This is why, since minds
must keep their personality and their moral qualities, to the
end that the City of God may not lose any person, it must be
that in particular they should keep some manner of reminiscence or consciousness, or the power of knowing what they
are; on this depends all their morality, punishments, and
chastenings. Consequently it is necessary that every mind
should be immune from those revolutions of the universe
which would render it entirely unrecognisable to itself, and
would make of it, morally speaking, a different person.
Whereas for brute substances it is sufficient that each should
simply remain the same individual in the strict metaphysical
sense, even though it is subjected to all imaginable changes,
since in any case it is without consciousness or reflection. . . .

A Specimen of Discoveries About Marvellous Secrets of a General Nature (*c.* 1686)

In every universal affirmative truth the predicate is in the subject: expressly in the case of primitive or identical truths, which are the only truths which are known *per se*, but implicitly in the case of all the rest. This implicit inclusion is shown by the analysis of terms, by substituting for one another definitions and what is defined.[a]

So there are two first principles of all reasonings: a principle of contradiction, to the effect that every identical proposition is true and its contradictory is false; and a principle of the need for giving a reason, to the effect that every true proposition which is not known *per se* has an *a priori* proof, or, that a reason can be given for every truth, or as is commonly said, that nothing happens without a cause. Arithmetic and geometry do not need this principle, but physics and mechanics do, and Archimedes used it.

There is an essential distinction between necessary or eternal truths, and truths of fact or contingent truths; they differ from one another very much in the way that rational numbers and surds differ. For necessary truths can be reduced to identical truths, just as commensurable quantities can be reduced to a common measure; but in the case of contingent truths, as in the case of surds, the reduction proceeds to infinity and is never terminated. So the certitude and perfect reason of contingent truths is known only to God, who grasps the infinite with one intuition. Once this secret is known the difficulty about the absolute necessity of all things is removed, and the difference between the infallible and the necessary is clear.[1]

---

[1] Note by Leibniz. The true cause of the fact that these things exist rather than those is to be derived from the free decrees of the divine will, of

75

A real definition is one by which it is established that that which is defined is possible and does not involve a contradiction. For if this is not established of something, no reasoning can safely be undertaken about it; for if it involves a contradiction, perhaps the opposite could with equal right be concluded of it. This was the fault in the proof of Anselm, revived by Descartes, that a most perfect or greatest being must exist, since it involves existence. For it is assumed without proof that a most perfect being does not involve a contradiction, and this gave me the occasion to recognise the nature of a real definition. Therefore causal definitions, which contain the generation of a thing, are also real; again, we do not think of the ideas of things except in so far as we contemplate their possibility.

A necessary being, if it is possible, exists. This is the pinnacle of modal theory, and makes a transition from essences to existences, from hypothetical truths to absolute truths, from ideas to the world.

If there were no necessary being, there would be no contingent being; for a reason must be given why contingent things should exist rather than not exist. But there would be no such reason unless there were a being which is in itself,[b]

---

which the primary one is the will to do everything in the best manner possible, as is fitting for the most wise. And so, though it may sometimes happen that the more perfect is excluded by the more imperfect, all in all that method of creating a world is chosen which involves more reality or perfection, and God acts like the greatest geometer, who prefers the best constructions of problems. Therefore all beings, in so far as they are involved in the first being, have, besides bare possibility, some propensity to exist in proportion to their goodness; and, if God wills, they do exist, unless they are incompatible with things which are more perfect. The latter occurs if they have too much volume in proportion to their power, so that they occupy more space than they fill, such as angular things, or things which are full of curves. This will be clearer by an example. For this reason, too, determinate things are preferred to indeterminate things, in which no reason for a choice can be discerned. Thus, if a scientist were to decide to mark out three points in some space, and there were no reason for one sort of triangle rather than another, he would choose an equilateral triangle, in which the three points are in similar relations. Again, if three equal and similar globes are to be arranged, and no other condition is given, they will be arranged in such a way that they touch each other.

hat is, a being the reason for whose existence is contained in ts own essence, so that there is no need for a reason outside it. Even if one went on to infinity in giving reasons for con- ingent things, yet outside their series (in which there is not a sufficient reason) a reason for the whole series must be found. From this it also follows that the necessary being is one in number, and is all things potentially, since it is the ultimate reason of things, in so far as they contain realities or per- fections. And since the full reason for a thing is the aggregate of all primitive requisites (which do not need other re- quisites) it is evident that the causes of all things can be re- duced to the attributes of God.

If there were no eternal substance, there would be no eternal truths; so this too affords a proof of God, who is the root of possibility, for his mind is the very region of ideas or truths. But it is highly erroneous to suppose that eternal truths[c] and the goodness of things depend on the divine will; for every act of will presupposes a judgement of the intellect about goodness—unless by a change of names one transfers all judgement from the intellect to the will; and even then it cannot be said that the will is a cause of truths, since the judge- ment is not such a cause. The reason for truths lies in the ideas of things, which are involved in the divine essence itself. And who will dare to say that the truth of the divine existence depends on the divine will?

Each substance has something of the infinite in so far as it involves its cause, God; i.e. it has some trace of omniscience and omnipotence. For in the perfect notion of each individual substance there are contained all its predicates, both neces- sary and contingent, past, present and future; indeed, each substance expresses the whole universe according to its position and point of view, in so far as the others are related to it. Hence it is necessary that certain of our perceptions, although clear, are confused, since they involve an infinite number of things—e.g. colour, heat, and the like.[1] And so

---

[1] Note by Leibniz. Further, multiple finite substances are simply differ- ent expressions of the same universe in accordance with different relations and the limitations proper to each. Just as one ground plan has infinite . . . (The manuscript is defective at this point, but Leibniz seems to be re-

what Hippocrates said[d] about the human body is true of the whole universe: namely, that all things conspire and are sympathetic, i.e. that nothing happens in one creature of which some exactly corresponding effect does not reach all others. Nor, again, are there any absolutely extrinsic denominations in things.

By this, the difficulties about predestination and the cause of evil are removed. For it can be understood that God does not decide whether Adam should sin, but whether that series of things in which there is an Adam whose perfect individual notion involves sin should nevertheless be preferred to others. This was also seen by Hugh of St. Victor,[e] who answered the question why God chose Jacob and not Esau by simply saying: because Jacob is not Esau. For in the perfect notion of an individual substance, considered in a pure state of possibility by God before every actual decree of existence, there is already whatever will happen to it if it exists, and indeed the whole series of things of which it forms a part. And so it should not be asked whether Adam will sin, but whether an Adam who will sin is to be admitted to existence. For there is this difference between universal[f] and individual substances: that in the notion of the latter, contingent predicates also are involved. For there is no doubt that God saw what would happen to Adam before he decided to create him, and so there is no obstruction to freedom from this quarter. Again, the notion of a possible Adam also contains the decrees of free will, divine and human, considered as possible. Further, each possible series of the universe rests on certain free primary decrees appropriate to it, considered under the aspect of possibility. For just as no line can be drawn, with however casual a hand, which is not geometrical and has a certain constant nature, common to all its points, so also no possible series of things and no way of creating the world can be conceived which is so disordered that it does not have its own fixed and determinate order and its laws of pro-

---

ferring to the way in which a single ground plan is related to an infinite number of perspectival drawings. Cf. to Arnauld, 9 Oct., 1687, p. 72 above, and *Primary Truths*, p. 90.)

gression—though as in the case of lines, so also some series have more power and simplicity than others, and so they provide more perfection with less equipment.[g] From this it is also clear that the cause of evil is not from God, but is from the essential limitation of creatures, i.e. from their original imperfection before every lapse, just as the impetus impressed on some body produces less velocity if the mass of the body, i.e. its natural inertia, is greater.

From the notion of an individual substance it also follows in metaphysical rigour that all the operations of substances, both actions and passions, are spontaneous, and that with the exception of the dependence of creatures on God, no real influx from one to the other is intelligible. For whatever happens to each one of them would flow from its nature and its notion even if the rest were supposed to be absent, for each one expresses the entire universe. However, that whose expression is the more distinct is judged to act, and that whose expression is the more confused is judged to be passive, since to act is a perfection and to be passive is an imperfection. Again, that thing is thought to be a cause from whose state a reason for changes is most easily given. Thus, one may suppose that a solid which is in motion in a fluid stirs up various waves, yet the same events can be understood if the solid is supposed to be at rest in the middle of the fluid and equivalent motions of the fluid are assumed;[h] indeed, the same phenomena can be explained in an infinite number of ways. But though motion is something relative, the hypothesis which ascribes motion to the solid, and from this deduces the waves of the liquid, is infinitely more simple than the others, and so the solid is thought to be the cause of the motion. Causes are assumed, not from a real influx, but from the need to give a reason.

The truth of this also appears in physics, from an accurate inspection of the fact that no impetus is transferred from one body to another, but each body is moved by its innate force, which is determined only by the occasion or relation of another. For eminent men have already recognised that the cause of the impulse one body receives from another is the body's elasticity itself, by which it recoils from the other. But the cause of elasticity is the internal motion of the parts c the elastic body; for though this may be derived from som general fluid, yet while the parts of the permeating fluid pas through it they are in it. To understand this correctly, th proper motion of each body which gives a blow must be dis tinguished from its common motion, which can always b understood even before the blow and is preserved after th blow; but the proper motion, which alone constitutes a obstacle to the other, does not have an effect in the body c another except through the elasticity of that other.ʲ

Similarly, the very union of soul and body receives a ful explanation from our notion of substance. For some have be lieved that something or other passes from the soul to th body, and conversely; this is the 'hypothesis of real influx'. I seemed to others that God excites thoughts in the soul corres ponding to the motion of the body and, conversely, motion in the body corresponding to the thoughts of the soul; this i the 'hypothesis of the occasional cause'. But there is n need to summon a *deus ex machina* in a matter which clearl follows from our principles. For each individual substance which expresses the same universe in its own measure accord ing to the laws of its own nature, is such that its changes anc states correspond perfectly to the changes and states of othe substances, but the soul and the body correspond to on another most, and their intimate union consists in the mos perfect agreement. Even if this did not have an *a priori* proof it would maintain the position of a most plausible hypo thesis. For why should one not assume that God initiall created the soul and body with so much ingenuity that whilst each follows its own laws and properties and operations all things agree most beautifully among themselves? This i what I call the 'hypothesis of concomitance'. Consequently there is no need of some perpetual and special operation o God to produce agreement, nor is some real influx called in which certainly cannot be explained.[1]

---

[1] Leibniz wrote the following note on a small sheet of paper:
The system of occasional causes must be partly admitted and partl rejected. Each substance is the true and real cause of its *immanent* action and has the power of acting, and though it may be sustained by the divin

It also follows from the notion of an individual substance that a substance cannot be generated or corrupted, nor can it originate or be destroyed except by creation or annihilation; consequently, the immortality of the soul is so necessary that it cannot be taken away except by a miracle. It follows also, either that there are no corporeal substances and bodies are merely phenomena which are true or consistent with each other, such as a rainbow or a perfectly coherent dream, or that in all corporeal substances there is something analogous to the soul, which old authors called a form or species.[k] For that is not one substance or one being which consists merely of an aggregation, such as a heap of stones, nor can beings be understood where there is no one true being. Therefore, either there are atoms (which Cordemoy tried to prove by his very argument) so that we may have some first principle of one being; or rather, since it is to be held as proved that every body is actually subdivided into other parts (as will shortly be stated at greater length) the reality of a corporeal substance consists in a certain individual nature; that is, not in mass, but in a power of acting and being acted on.

It must also be known (though it might seem to be a paradox) that the notion of extension is not as clear as is commonly believed. For from the fact that no body is so small that it is not actually divided into parts which are excited by various motions, it follows that no determinate shape can be assigned to any body, nor is an exact straight line, nor a circle, nor any assignable figure of any body found in the nature of things, though in the derivation of an infinite series certain rules are observed by nature. And so shape involves something imaginary, and no other sword can cut the knots we weave for ourselves by our imperfect understanding of the composition of the continuum.

---

concourse, it cannot happen that it is merely passive; this is true in the case of both corporeal and incorporeal substances. But each substance (with the sole exception of God) is only the occasional cause of those of its actions which are *transient* with regard to another substance. So the true *reason for the union between soul and body*, and the cause of the fact that one body accommodates itself to the state of another body, is simply the fact that the different substances of the same world system were so created initially that they agree among themselves by the laws of their own natures.

The same is to be said of motion; for motion, just as much as place, consists in relation alone—a fact rightly recognised by Descartes—nor is there any way of determining exactly how much absolute motion is to be ascribed to each subject. But motive power, i.e. the power of acting, is something real and can be discerned in bodies.[1] And so the essence of a body is not to be located in extension and its modifications, namely shape and motion, for these involve something imaginary, no less than heat and colour and the other sensible qualities. It is to be located in the power of acting and resisting alone, which we perceive with the intellect and not with the imagination. Even if, in the case of body, action were to be ascribed to the former, yet they do not have resistance. But all substance is contained in the power of acting and being acted on.

Further, there are no atoms, but every part has other parts which are actually separate from it and excited by various motions; or, what follows from this, every body, however small, has parts which are actually infinite, and in every particle there is a world of innumerable creatures. This is established in many ways, one of which is the fact that every portion of matter is agitated by the motions of the entire universe, and is acted upon in some way by all other parts of matter, however distant, in proportion to their distance. Now since every case of being acted on has some effect, it is necessary that the particles of this mass which are exposed in a different way to the actions of others are agitated differently, and that consequently the mass is subdivided.

Neither is a vacuum consistent with the reasons for things; for, to pass over the fact that space is nothing real, it is certain that a vacuum is inconsistent with the perfection of things. Since, therefore, it is not necessary (for what prevents some body being assumed in an empty place, and another in the remainder, and so ad infinitum?) it has no place. Moreover, it interrupts the communication of bodies, and the mutual strife of all with all.

But there remains a doubt about the souls or forms (analogous to the soul) which we have recognised in corporeal substance. For, not to speak of other corporeal substances (as it seems to some that there are grades of perception and appetite), if, in the lower animals at least, souls are found, it will follow from our principles that the lower animals too are immortal. However, just as some have held that every birth of an animal is only a transformation of that same animal which is already alive, and is as it were an accretion, in order that it may be made sensible; so it seems that one can with equal reason defend the position that every death is a transformation of something living into something less animal, and is as it were a diminution, by which it is rendered insensible. This seems to have been the express opinion of the author of the book *On Diet*, which is ascribed to Hippocrates, nor did Albertus Magnus and John Bacon[m] shrink from it; for they admitted neither a natural production nor destruction of forms. If, therefore, living things are free from birth and death alike, so also their souls, if they have any, will be perpetual and immortal, and (as is the case with all substances) will not begin or end except by creation or annihilation. And instead of the transmigration of souls (which has been imperfectly understood, I believe) one must maintain the transformation of animals. But minds must be excepted from the fate of other souls; for it agrees with the divine wisdom both that they are created by God, and that when free from the body they have their own operations, so that they should not be agitated without reason by the innumerable vicissitudes of matter. For God is both the cause of things and the king of minds, and since he himself is a mind, he has a special association with them. Moreover, since each mind is an expression of the divine image (for it can be said that other substances express the universe, but minds express God) it is clear that minds are the most important part of the universe, and that everything was established for their sake; that is, in choosing the order of things, the greatest account was taken of them, all things being arranged in such a way that they appear the more beautiful the more they are understood. So it must be held certain that God has taken the greatest account of justice, and that just as he sought the perfection of things, so he sought the happiness of minds. So we should not wonder that minds are distinguished from the souls of the lower animals both in the origin of the animal which we call a man and in its extinction, and though all are immortal, memory is given only to those in whom there is consciousness and the understanding of rewards and punishments.

I am also inclined to believe that there are souls in the lower animals because it pertains to the perfection of things that when all those things are present which are adapted to a soul, the souls also should be understood to be present. For souls, or at any rate forms, do not impede one another, and so it seems much less likely that there is a vacuum of forms (which was also rejected by older writers) than that there is a vacuum of bodies. But no one should think that it can with equal justice be inferred that there must also be minds in the lower animals; for it must be known that the order of things will not allow all souls to be free from the vicissitudes of matter, nor will justice permit some minds to be abandoned to agitation. So it was sufficient that souls should be given to the lower animals, especially as their bodies are not made for reasoning, but destined to various functions—the silkworm to weave, the bee to make honey, and the others to the other functions by which the universe is distinguished.

To prevent anyone from complaining that the notion of the soul, in so far as it is distinguished from the mind, is insufficiently clear, and that the notion of a form is much less clear, it must be known that these depend on the notion of substance explained above. For it is the nature of an individual substance to have a complete notion, in which all the predicates of the same subject are involved. Thus, though it does not belong to the notion of a circle that a circle should be of wood or iron, yet there belongs to the notion of this present circle not only the fact that it is iron, but also whatever is to happen to it. But since all things have a connexion with others, either mediately or immediately, the consequence is that it is the nature of every substance to express the whole universe by its power of acting and being acted on, that is, by the series of its own immanent operations. It is also truly one being, otherwise it would not be a substance, but several substances.[n] This principle of actions, or primitive active force, from which a series of various states follows, is the form of the substance. Also evident is the nature of the perception which belongs to all forms, namely the expression of many things in one, which differs widely from expression in a mirror or in a corporeal organ, which is not truly one. If the perception is more distinct, it makes a sensation. But in the mind there is found, besides the expression of objects, consciousness or reflexion; this constitutes a certain expression or image of God himself, and it is this which brings it about that minds alone are capable of happiness and misery. But though we may assume forms or souls, without which nature in general cannot rightly be understood, yet in the explanation of the phenomena of particular bodies we no more use the soul or form than we refer to the human mind when we describe the functions of the human body.⁰ For we have shown that such is the harmony of things that everything which happens in the soul can be explained from the laws of perception alone, just as everything which happens in the body can be explained from the laws of motion alone, and yet all things agree with each other as if the soul could move the body or the body the soul.

But it is now time for us gradually to proceed to a statement of the laws of corporeal nature. And first: every body has magnitude and shape. Just as one body is not in several places, neither are several bodies in one place. And so the same mass does not occupy a greater or less volume than it did before, and rarefaction and condensation are simply the absorption or squeezing out of what is more fluid. Every body is mobile and receives some degree of speed or slowness, and also some direction. All motions can be compounded amongst themselves, and their line of motion will be one which geometry will designate; consequently, a body which is carried in a curved line has a direction of progress in a straight line tangential to the curve unless it is hindered, a fact which Kepler first observed. Again, every place is filled with body, and every body is divisible and transfigurable, since no reason can be given for atoms. These have long been regarded as established.

To these I add: in every body there is some force or motion. No body is so small that it is not actually divided into parts which are excited by different motions; and therefore in every body there is actually an infinite number of bodies. Every change of any body propagates its effect to bodies at any distance; i.e. all bodies act on all bodies and are acted on by all. Every body is restrained by those which surround it so that its parts do not disperse, and therefore all bodies strive with each other reciprocally, and each body resists the whole universe of bodies.

Each body has some degree of firmness and fluidity; it has its fluidity or divisibility of itself, but its firmness from the motion of bodies.ᵖ

Primary Truths (*c.* 1686)

Primary truths are those which either state a term of itself, or deny an opposite of its opposite. For example, 'A is A', or 'A is not not-A'; 'If it is true that A is B, it is false that A is not B, or that A is not-B'; again, 'Each thing is what it is', 'Each thing is like itself, or is equal to itself', 'Nothing is greater or less than itself'—and others of this sort which, though they may have their own grades of priority, can all be included under the one name of 'identities'.

All other truths are reduced to primary truths by the aid of definitions—i.e. by the analysis of notions; and this constitutes *a priori proof*, independent of experience. I will give an example.[a] A proposition accepted as an axiom by mathematicians and all others alike is 'The whole is greater than its part', or 'A part is less than the whole'. But this is very easily demonstrated from the definition of 'less' or 'greater', together with the primitive axiom, that of identity. The 'less' is that which is equal to a part of another ('greater') thing. (This definition is very easily understood, and agrees with the practice of the human race when men compare things with one another, and find the excess by taking away something equal to the smaller from the larger.) So we get the following reasoning: a part is equal to a part of the whole (namely to itself: for everything, by the axiom of identity, is equal to itself). But that which is equal to a part of the whole is less than the whole (by the definition of 'less'); therefore a part is less than the whole.

The predicate or consequent, therefore, is always in the subject or antecedent, and this constitutes the nature of truth in general, or, the connexion between the terms of a proposition, as Aristotle also has observed.[b] In identities this connexion and inclusion of the predicate in the subject is express, whereas in all other truths it is implicit and must be shown through the analysis of notions, in which *a priori* demonstration consists.

But this is true in the case of every affirmative truth, universal or particular, necessary or contingent, and in the case of both an intrinsic and an extrinsic denomination. And here there lies hidden a wonderful secret in which is contained the nature of contingency, or, the essential distinction between necessary and contingent truths;[c] and by this also there is removed the difficulty about the fatal necessity of even those things which are free.

From these facts, which have not yet been sufficiently considered because of their excessive easiness, there follow many things of great importance. For from this there at once arises the accepted axiom, 'There is nothing without a reason', or, 'There is no effect without a cause'. For otherwise there would be a truth which could not be proved *a priori*, i.e. which is not analysed into identities; and this is contrary to the nature of truth, which is always, either expressly or implicitly, identical. It also follows that when in the data everything in one part is like everything in another part, then everything will be alike on both sides in the desiderata or consequences also.[d] For no reason can be given for diversity, which must be sought from the data. A corollary, or rather an example of this, is the postulate of Archimedes at the beginning of his book on equilibrium; this states that when the arms of a balance and the weights placed on each side are equal, everything is in a state of equilibrium. Hence *there is a reason even for eternal things*. If it should be supposed that the world has existed from eternity, and that there have been only globules in it, a reason must be given why there should be globules rather than cubes.

From this it follows also that *there cannot be in nature two individual things which differ in number alone*. For it must be possible to give a reason why they are diverse, which must be sought from some difference in them. And so St. Thomas' recognition of the fact that separate intelligences never differ in number alone must be applied to other things as well; two perfectly similar eggs, or two perfectly similar leaves[e] or blades of grass, will never be found. Perfect similarity, therefore, holds only in the case of incomplete and abstract notions, where things are not considered in all respects, but only with respect to a certain mode of consideration—as when we consider shapes only, and neglect the matter which has the shape. Consequently, in geometry two triangles are properly considered to be similar, although two material triangles which are perfectly alike are never found. We may also consider gold and other metals, salts, and many liquids as homogeneous bodies; but that can be admitted only as far as the senses are concerned, and even so is not exactly true.

It also follows that *there are no purely extrinsic denominations*, which have no foundation in the thing denominated. For the notion of the subject denominated must involve the notion of the predicate; consequently, as often as the denomination of the thing is changed, there must be some variation in the thing itself.

The complete or perfect notion of an individual substance involves all its predicates—past, present and future. For that a future predicate is future is true now, and so is contained in the notion of the thing. Therefore, in the perfect individual notion of Peter or Judas, considered under the aspect of possibility by abstracting the mind from the divine decree to create him, there are present and there are seen by God all the things that will happen to them, both necessary and free. From this it is manifest that God chooses, from an infinity of possible individuals, those which he thinks most consistent with the highest hidden ends of his wisdom. Nor is it exact to say that he decrees that Peter shall sin, or that Judas shall be damned; he decrees only that a Peter who will sin—certainly, indeed, though not necessarily but freely—and a Judas who will suffer damnation shall come into existence in preference to other possibles. In other words, God decrees that a possible notion shall become actual. And although the future salvation of Peter is also contained in his eternal possible notion, yet that is not without the concourse of grace; for in that same perfect notion of this possible Peter, the assistance of divine grace which is to be given to him is also contained under the aspect[f] of possibility.

Every individual substance involves in its perfect notion the whole universe, and everything existing in it, past, present and future. For there is no thing on which some true denomination cannot be imposed from another, at all events a denomination of comparison and relation. But there is no purely extrinsic denomination. I show the same thing in many other inter-related ways.

Further, *all created individual substances are diverse expressions of the same universe*, and of the same universal cause, namely God. But these expressions vary in perfection, like different representations or projective drawings of the same town from different points of view.

Every created individual substance exercises physical action on, and is acted on by all others. For if a change is made in one, some corresponding change follows in all the others, since the denomination is changed. This agrees with our experience of nature: for we see that in a vessel full of liquid (and the whole universe is such a vessel) a motion set up in the middle is propagated to the edges, although it becomes more and more imperceptible the farther it recedes from its point of origin.

Strictly, it can be said that *no created substance exercises on another a metaphysical action or influx*. For—to say nothing of the fact that it is impossible to explain how anything passes from one thing into the substance of another—it has already been shown that from the notion of any given thing all its future states already follow. What we call 'causes' are, in meta-physical rigour, merely concomitant requisites. This is illus-trated by our experience of nature: for bodies recede from other bodies by the force of their own elasticity and not by any external force—even if another body is required for the elasticity, which arises from something intrinsic to the body itself, to be able to act.

Further, having posited the diversity of soul and body, we can explain their union from the above without the common hypo-thesis of an influx, which is unintelligible, and without the hypothesis of an occasional cause, which calls in a *Deus ex machina*. For God has from the beginning fashioned soul and body alike with such wisdom and such skill that, from the very first constitution or notion of each of these, all the things that happen in the one correspond perfectly of themselves to all the things that happen in the other, just as if they had passed from the one into the other. I call this the 'hypothesis of concomitance'. This is true of all substances in the whole universe, but it is not to be perceived in all of them, as it is in the soul and the body.

There is no vacuum. For the diverse parts of an empty space would be perfectly similar and congruent and could not be distinguished from one another, and so they would differ in number alone, which is absurd. In the same way in which it is proved that space is not a thing, it is also proved that time is not a thing.

There is no atom; on the contrary, there is no body so small that it is not actually subdivided. Whilst it is being acted on by all other bodies in the entire universe, and receives some effect from all of them (which must cause some variation in the body) it has also preserved all past impressions and contains in advance future impressions. If anyone says that the effect is contained in the motions impressed on the atom, which produce the effect in the whole without its being divided, it can be replied that not only must effects result in the atom from all the impressions of the universe, but it must also be possible in turn to infer from the atom the state of the whole universe, and from the effect the cause. But from the mere shape and motion of an atom we cannot infer back to the impressions by which the motion has reached it, since the same motion can be obtained from various impressions—to say nothing of the fact that no reason can be given why bodies of a certain degree of smallness are not divisible further.

From this it follows that *in every particle of the universe there is contained a world of infinite creatures*. However, the continuum is not divided into points, nor is it divided in all possible ways. Not into points, because points are not parts, but limits; not in all possible ways, because not all creatures are present in the same thing, but only a certain infinite progression of them—just as a man who supposes a straight line and any bisected part of it is establishing other divisions than a man who supposes a trisected part.

There is no actual determinate shape in things, for there is none which can satisfy infinite impressions. So neither a circle, nor an ellipse, nor any other line definable by us exists except in the intellect, nor any lines before they are drawn, or parts before they are cut off.

Extension and motion and bodies themselves, in so far as they consist of these alone, are not substances but true appearances, like rainbows and mock suns. For shapes do not exist objectively, and bodies, if they are considered as extension alone, are not one substance but several.

For the substance of bodies something without extension is required; otherwise there will be no principle of the reality of appearances, nor of true unity. Bodies are always held to be plural, and never one; therefore they are not really even plural.g By means of a similar argument Cordemoy tried to prove that there are atoms; as these are excluded there remains something without extension, analogous to the soul, which was once called a form or species.

A corporeal substance can neither arise nor perish except by creation or annihilation. For since it once endures it will always endure, for there is no reason for a difference, and the dissolution of the parts of a body has nothing in common with the destruction of the body itself. Consequently, *things which have souls do not arise or perish, but are only transformed.*

The Nature of Truth (*c.* 1686)

If one builds a house in a sandy place, one must continue digging until one meets solid rock or firm foundations; if one wants to unravel a tangled thread one must look for the beginning of the thread; if the greatest weights are to be moved, Archimedes demanded only a stable place. In the same way, if one is to establish the elements of human knowledge some fixed point is required, on which we can safely rest and from which we can set out without fear.

I think that this principle is to be sought in the general nature of truths, and that we are to hold to this above all: *every proposition is either true or false*. That is *false* which is the contradictory of the true; those propositions are *contradictory* which differ only in that one of them is affirmative and the other negative. These principles are such that it is vain to demand a proof of them. For since one can only bring forward as proof other propositions, it would be vain to bring them forward if it were at the same time both granted and denied that they are true or false, and all inquiry into truth would cease at the very outset. Further, as often as some proposition is used it is thought to be true, unless warning is given to the contrary.

A true proposition is one whose predicate is contained in its subject, or, more generally, whose consequent is contained in its antecedent, and it is therefore necessary that there should be some connexion between the notions of the terms, i.e. that there should be an objective foundation from which the reason for the proposition can be given, or, an *a priori* proof can be found. This holds in the case of every true affirmative proposition, universal or particular, necessary or contingent—that the notion of the predicate is in the notion of

the subject, either expressly or virtually; expressly in the case
of an identical proposition, virtually in the case of any other.
The predicate can be proved from the subject or the consequent from the antecedent by the analysis either of the
antecedent or subject alone, or of the antecedent and
consequent or subject and predicate simultaneously. The
connexion is necessary in the case of propositions of eternal
truth, which follow from ideas alone or from definitions of
universal ideas. But if a proposition is contingent there is no
necessary connexion, but it varies in time and depends on an
assumed divine decree and on free will. In such a case a reason
can always be given (at any rate by the one who knows all)
from the nature of the thing, or from the notion of the terms,
why that which has been done *has* been done, rather than not
done. But that reason only inclines, and does not impose necessity. From this there follows an axiom of the greatest use, from
which much in physics and in morals is derived: *nothing
happens for which a reason cannot be given why it should happen as it
does rather than otherwise.* For example, it is assumed by Archimedes, as one of the foundations of the whole of statics, that
two equal weights A and B, which are equally distant from
the centre of motion C, are in equilibrium.[a] This is a corollary
of our axiom; for if there should be any diversity, then some
reason can be given for it (by our axiom). But this cannot be
given (by hypothesis), for everything on both sides is assumed
to be in the same state, and so nothing diverse can follow
from this.

Now that we have understood that every proposition is
either true or false, and that every proposition which is not
true of itself, or immediate, can be proved *a priori*, it follows
that we should state the method of proof. This is contained
above all in the axiom: *without loss of truth, the predicate can be
put in place of the subject of a universal affirmative proposition, or the
consequent in place of the antecedent of an affirmative proposition, in
another proposition where the subject of the former proposition is the
predicate, or where the antecedent of the former is the consequent.*[b] But
we must except reduplicative propositions, in which we state
of some term that it is so strictly expressed that we refuse to
substitute another for it;[c] for these propositions are re-

flexive, and in respect of our thoughts are like material propositions in respect of speech.[d] The reason for this axiom is evident from what precedes. Let us suppose that there is a universal affirmative proposition, 'All B is C', and another proposition, 'A is B'. I assert that in the latter, C can be substituted for B. For since A contains B and B contains C (by the preceding axiom), A will also contain C, which (by the same axiom) is sufficient for us to say that A is C. I do not wish to follow up here the variety of propositions and to establish logical rules, for it is sufficient to have indicated the basis of substitution.

If a notion is complete, i.e. is such that from it a reason can be given for all the predicates of the subject to which this notion can be attributed, this will be the notion of an individual substance; and conversely.[e] For an individual substance is a subject which is not in another subject, but others are in it, and so all the predicates of that subject are all the predicates of the individual substance. For these, therefore, a reason can be given from the notion of the individual substance, and from it alone, as is clear from the second axiom. So the notion which affords this is the notion of the individual substance.

Necessary and Contingent Truths
(*c.* 1686)

An affirmative truth is one whose predicate is in the subject; and so in every true affirmative proposition, necessary or contingent, universal or particular, the notion of the predicate is in some way contained in the notion of the subject, in such a way that if anyone were to understand perfectly each of the two notions just as God understands it, he would by that very fact perceive that the predicate is in the subject. From this it follows that all the knowledge of propositions which is in God, whether this is of the simple intelligence, concerning the essence of things, or of vision, concerning the existence of things, or mediate knowledge concerning conditioned existences, results immediately from the perfect understanding of each term which can be the subject or predicate of any proposition. That is, the *a priori* knowledge of complexes arises from the understanding of that which is not complex.[a]

An *absolutely necessary* proposition is one which can be resolved into identical propositions, or, whose opposite implies a contradiction. I will cite a numerical example. I shall call every number which can be exactly divided by two, 'binary', and every one which can be divided by three or four 'ternary' or 'quaternary', and so on. Further, we may understand that every number is resolved into those which divide it exactly. I say, therefore, that the proposition 'A duodenary[b] is a quaternary' is absolutely necessary, for it can be resolved into identical propositions in this way. A duodenary is a binary senary (by definition); a senary is a binary ternary (by definition). Therefore a duodenary is a binary binary ternary. Further, a binary binary is a quaternary (by definition); therefore a duodenary is a quaternary ternary. Therefore a duodenary is a quaternary; q.e.d. But even if other definitions were given, it could always be shown that the matter would come to this in the end. This type of necessity, therefore, I call metaphysical or geometrical. That which lacks such necessity I call contingent, but that which implies a contradiction, or whose opposite is necessary, is called *impossible*. The rest are called *possible*.

In the case of a contingent truth,[c] even though the predicate is really in the subject, yet one never arrives at a demonstration or an identity, even though the resolution of each term is continued indefinitely. In such cases it is only God, who comprehends the infinite at once, who can see how the one is in the other, and can understand *a priori* the perfect reason for contingency; in creatures this is supplied *a posteriori*, by experience. So the relation of contingent to necessary truths is somewhat like the relation of surd ratios (namely, the ratios of incommensurable numbers) to the expressible ratios of commensurable numbers. For just as it can be shown that a lesser number is in a larger, by resolving each of the two into its largest common measure, so also propositions or truths of essence are demonstrated by carrying out a resolution of terms until one arrives at terms which, as is established by the definitions, are common to each term. But just as a larger number contains another which is incommensurable with it, though even if one continues to infinity with a resolution one will never arrive at a common measure, so in the case of a contingent truth you will never arrive at a demonstration, no matter how far you resolve the notions. The sole difference is that in the case of surd relations we can, none the less, establish demonstrations, by showing that the error involved is less than any assignable error, but in the case of contingent truths not even this is conceded to a created mind. And so I think that I have disentangled a secret which had me perplexed for a long time; for I did not understand how a predicate could be in a subject, and yet the proposition would not be a necessary one. But the knowledge of geometry and the analysis of the infinite lit this light in me, so that I might understand that notions too can be resolved to infinity.

From this we learn that there are some propositions which

pertain to the essences, and others to the existences of things. Propositions of essence are those which can be demonstrated by the resolution of terms; these are necessary, or virtually identical, and so their opposite is impossible, or virtually contradictory. The truth of these is eternal; not only will they hold whilst the world remains, but they would have held even if God had created the world in another way. Existential or contingent propositions differ entirely from these. Their truth is understood *a priori* by the infinite mind alone, and cannot be demonstrated by any resolution. These propositions are such as are true at a certain time; they express, not only what pertains to the possibility of things, but also what actually exists, or would exist contingently if certain things were granted—for example, that I am now alive, or that the sun is shining. For even if I say that the sun is shining at this hour in our hemisphere because its previous motion was such that, granted its continuation, this event would certainly follow, yet (to say nothing of the fact that its obligation to continue is not necessary) the fact that its motion was previously such is similarly a contingent truth, for which again a reason must be sought. And this cannot be given in full except as a result of a perfect knowledge of all the parts of the universe—a task which surpasses all created powers. For there is no portion of matter which is not actually subdivided into others; so the parts of any body are actually infinite, and so neither the sun nor any other body can be known perfectly by a creature. Much less can we arrive at the end of our analysis if we seek the mover of each body which is moved, and again the mover of this; for we shall always arrive at smaller bodies without end. But God does not need this transition from one contingent to another contingent which is prior or more simple, a transition which can have no end. (Further, one contingent thing is not really the cause of another, even though it seems so to us.) Rather, in each individual substance, God perceives the truth of all its accidents from its very notion, without calling in anything extrinsic; for each one in its way involves all others, and the whole universe. So all propositions into which existence and time enter have as an ingredient the whole series of things, nor can 'now' or 'here' be understood except in relation to other things. Consequently, such propositions do not admit of demonstrations, i.e. of a terminable resolution by which their truth may appear. The same applies to all the accidents of individual created substances. Indeed, even if some one could know the whole series of the universe, even then he could not give a reason for it, unless he compared it with all other possibles. From this it is evident why no demonstration of a contingent proposition can be found, however far the resolution of notions is continued.

But it must not be thought that only particular propositions are contingent, for there are (and can be inferred by induction) certain propositions which are for the most part true; there are also propositions which are almost always true, in the course of nature at any rate, so that an exception would be ascribed to a miracle. Indeed, I think that in this series of things there are certain propositions which are true with absolute universality,[d] and which cannot be violated even by a miracle. This is not to say that they could not be violated by God, but rather that, when he chose this series of things, by that very act he decreed that he would observe them, as the specific properties of just this chosen series. And through these propositions, once they have been established by the force of the divine decree, a reason can be given for other universal propositions, or even of many of the contingent things which can be observed in this universe. For from the first essential laws of the series—true without exception, and containing the entire purpose of God in choosing the universe, and so including even miracles—there can be derived subordinate laws of nature, which have only physical necessity and which are not repealed except by a miracle, through consideration of some more powerful final cause. Finally, from these there are inferred others whose universality is still less; and God can reveal even to creatures the demonstrations of universal propositions of this kind, which are intermediate to one another, and of which a part constitutes physical science. But never, by any analysis, can one arrive at the absolutely universal laws nor at the perfect reasons for individual things; for that knowledge necessarily belongs to God alone. It should not disturb anyone that I have just said that there are certain essential laws for this series of things, though I said above that these same laws are not necessary and essential, but are contingent and existential. For since the fact that the series itself exists is contingent and depends on the free decrees of God, its laws also will be contingent in the absolute sense; but they will be hypothetically necessary and will only be essential *given the series*.

This will now help us to distinguish free substances from others. The accidents of every individual substance, if predicated of it, make a contingent proposition, which does not have metaphysical necessity. That this stone tends downwards when its support has been removed is not a necessary but a contingent proposition, nor can such an event be demonstrated from the notion of this stone by the help of the universal notions which enter into it, and so God alone perceives this perfectly. For he alone knows whether he will suspend by a miracle that subordinate law of nature by which heavy things are driven downwards; for others neither understand the absolutely universal laws involved, nor can they perform the infinite analysis which is necessary to connect the notion of this stone with the notion of the whole universe, or with absolutely universal laws. But at any rate it can be known in advance from subordinate laws of nature that unless the law of gravity is suspended by a miracle, a descent follows. But free or intelligent substances possess something greater and more marvellous, in a kind of imitation of God. For they are not bound by any certain subordinate laws of the universe, but act as it were by a private miracle, on the sole initiative of their own power, and by looking towards a final cause they interrupt the connexion and the course of the efficient causes that act on their will. So it is true that there is no creature 'which knows the heart'[e] which could predict with certainty how some mind will choose in accordance with the laws of nature; as it could be predicted (at any rate by an angel) how some body will act, provided that the course of nature is not interrupted. For just as the course of the universe is changed by the free will of God, so the course of the mind's thoughts is changed by its free will; so that, in the case of minds, no subordinate universal laws can be established (as is possible in the case of bodies) which are sufficient for predicting a mind's choice. But[f] this does not prevent the fact that the future actions of the mind are evident to God, just as his own future actions are. For he knows perfectly the import of the series of things which he chooses, and so also of his own decree; and at the same time he also understands what is contained in the notion of this mind, which he himself has admitted into the number of things which are to exist, inasmuch as this notion involves the series of things itself and its absolutely universal laws. And although it is most true that the mind never chooses what at present appears the worse, yet it does not always choose what at present appears the better; for it can delay and suspend its judgement until a later deliberation, and turn the mind aside to think of other things. Which of the two it will do is not determined by any adequate sign or prescribed law. This at any rate holds in the case of minds which are not sufficiently confirmed in good or evil; the case of the blessed is different.

From this it can be understood what is that 'indifference' which accompanies freedom. Just as contingence is opposed to metaphysical necessity, so indifference excludes not only metaphysical but also physical necessity. It is in a way a matter of physical necessity that God should do everything in the best way possible, though it is not in the power of any creature to apply this universal law to individual things, and to draw from this any certain conclusions concerning free divine actions. It is also a matter of physical necessity that those who are confirmed in the good—the angels or the blessed—should act in accordance with virtue, so that in certain cases, indeed, it could even be predicted with certainty by a creature what they will do. Again, it is a matter of physical necessity that something heavy tends downwards, and that the angles of incidence and reflection are equal, and other things of this sort. But it is not a matter of physical necessity that men should choose something in this life, however specious and apparent a particular good may be; though there is sometimes a very strong presumption to that effect. It may indeed never be possible for there to be an absolute metaphysical indifference, such that the mind is in exactly the same state with respect to each contradictory, and that anything should be in a state of equilibrium with, so to speak, its whole nature.[g] For we have already noted that a predicate, even if future, is already truly in the notion of the subject, and that the mind is not, therefore, metaphysically speaking indifferent; for God already perceives all its future accidents from the perfect notion he has of it, and the mind is not at present indifferent with respect to its own eternal notion. Yet the mind has this much physical indifference, that it is not even subject to physical necessity, far less metaphysical; that is, no universal reason or law of nature is assignable from which any creature, no matter how perfect and well-informed about the state of this mind, can infer with certainty what the mind will choose—at any rate naturally, without the extraordinary concourse of God.

So far we have expounded, as far as our purpose went, the nature of truth, of contingence, of indifference, and (above all) the freedom of the human mind. Now, however, we must examine in what way contingent things, and especially free substances, depend in their choice and operation on the divine will and predetermination. My opinion is that it must be taken as certain that there is as much dependence of things on God as is possible without infringing divine justice. In the first place, I assert that whatever perfection or reality things have is continually produced by God, but that their limitation or imperfection belongs to them as creatures, just as the force impressed on any body by an agent receives some limitation from the body's matter or mass and from the natural slowness of bodies, and the greater the body the less (other things being equal) is the motion which arises. So also that which is real in some ultimate determination of a free substance is necessarily produced by God, and I think that this fact covers what can reasonably be said about physical predetermination. I understand a 'determination' to be produced when a thing comes into that state in which what it is about to do follows with physical necessity. For there is never any metaphysical necessity in mutable things, since it is not even a matter of metaphysical necessity that a body should continue in motion if no other body impedes it; just as some contingent thing is not determined with meta-physical necessity until it actually exists. That determination is sufficient, therefore, by which some act becomes physically necessary. I understand that determination which is opposed to indifference, namely a determination to some metaphysical or physical necessity, or, a consequence demonstrable from the resolution of terms or from the laws of nature. For a de-termination which does not impose necessity on contingent things, but affords certainty and infallibility, in the sense in which it is said that the truth of future contingents is deter-mined—such a determination never *begins*, but always *was*,[h] since it is contained from eternity in the very notion of the subject, perfectly understood, and is the object of a kind of divine knowledge, whether of vision, or mediate knowledge.[j]

From this it is now apparent that it is possible to reconcile with the divine predetermination the actual conditioned decree of God (or at any rate that decree which depends on certain foreseen factors) by which God decides to bestow his predetermination. For God understands perfectly the notion of this free individual substance, considered as possible, and from this very notion he foresees what its choice will be, and therefore he decides to accommodate to it his predetermina-tion in time, it being granted that he decides to admit it among existing things. But if one examines the innermost reasons a new difficulty arises. For the choice of a creature is an act which essentially involves divine predetermination, without which it is impossible for that choice to be exercised; further, we cannot accept the placing of an impossible con-dition on the divine decree. From this it follows that God, whilst he foresees the future choice of the creature, by that very act foresees his own predetermination also, and so his own future predetermination; therefore he foresees his own decree, in so far as all contingent things essentially involve the divine decrees. Therefore he would decree something because he sees that he has already decreed it, which is absurd.

This difficulty, which indeed is very great in this argument, can, I think, be met in this way. I grant that when God de-cides to predetermine the mind to a certain choice because he has foreseen that it would choose in this way if it were admitted to existence, he foresees also his own predetermination and his own decree of predetermination—but only as possible; he does not decree because he *has* decreed. The reason is that God first considers a mind as possible before he decrees that it should actually exist. For the possibility or notion of a created mind does not involve existence. But while God considers it as possible, and knows perfectly in it all its future events as possible but as connected with it (connected contingently, yet infallibly), at that very moment he understands, that is he knows perfectly, all that which will follow its existence. Further, whilst he understands perfectly the notion of this individual substance, still considered as possible, by that very fact he also understands his own decrees, similarly considered as possible; for just as necessary truths involve only the divine intellect, so contingent truths involve the decrees of the will. God sees that he can create things in infinite ways, and that a different series of things will come into existence if he chooses different laws of the series, i.e. other primitive decrees. And so, whilst he considers this mind, which involves in itself this series of things, by that very act he also considers the decree which this mind and this series involve. But he considers each of them as possible, for he has not yet decided to make a decree; or, he has not yet decreed what special decrees of the series, both general decrees and the special decrees connected with them, he is to choose. But when God chooses one of the series, and this particular mind (to be endowed in future with these events) which is involved in it, by that very fact he also decrees concerning his other decrees or the laws of things which are involved in the notions of the things to be chosen. And because God, whilst he decides to choose this series, by that very fact also makes an infinite number of decrees concerning all that is involved in it, and so concerning his possible decrees or laws which are to be transferred from possibility to actuality—from this it is apparent that there is one decree which God has regard to in deciding, but another by which God decides to render this decree actual; namely, that by which he chooses for existence this series of things, this mind which is in the series, and that decree which is in it. That is to say, the possible decree which is involved in the notion of the series and the things which enter into the series, and which God decides to render actual, is one thing; but the decree by which he decides to render actual that possible decree is another. We should the less wonder at this reflection of one decree by another, since it may also be objected against the divine intellect that the free decrees of the divine will are understood before they are made. For God does not do what he does not know that he does. From this we now understand how the physical necessity of divine predetermination can be consistent with the decree of predetermination from foreseen acts. We understand that God is far from decreeing absolutely that Judas must become a traitor; rather, he sees from the notion of Judas, independently of his actual decree, that he will be a traitor. God, therefore, does not decree that Judas must be a traitor. All that he decrees is that Judas, whom he foresees will be a traitor, must nevertheless exist, since with his infinite wisdom he sees that this evil will be counterbalanced by an immense gain in greater goods, nor can things be better in any way. The act of betrayal itself God does not will, but he allows it in his decree that Judas the sinner shall now exist, and in consequence he also makes a decree that when the time of betrayal arrives the concourse of his actual predetermination is to be accommodated to this. But this decree is limited to what there is of perfection in this evil act; it is the very notion of the creature, in so far as it involves limitation (which is the one thing that it does not have from God) that drags the act towards badness. And so I believe that if we hold to these two points—that all perfection in creatures is from God, and all imperfection from their own limitation—all other opinions can, after being carefully considered, be reconciled in the last analysis.

On Freedom (*c*. 1689)

It is a very old doubt of mankind, how freedom and contingency can be reconciled with the series of causes and with providence. The difficulty of the matter has been increased by the dissertations of Christian authors on God's justice in procuring the salvation of men.

For my part, I used to consider that nothing happens by chance or by accident, except with respect to certain particular substances; that fortune, as distinct from fate, is an empty word; and that nothing exists unless its individual requisites[a] are given, and that from all these taken together it follows that the thing exists. So I was not far from the view of those who think that all things are absolutely necessary; who think that security from compulsion is enough for freedom,[b] even though it is under the rule of necessity, and who do not distinguish the infallible—that is, a truth which is certainly known—from the necessary.

But I was dragged back from this precipice by a consideration of those possibles which neither do exist, nor will exist, nor have existed. For if certain possibles never exist, then existing things are not always necessary; otherwise it would be impossible for other things to exist instead of them, and so all things that never exist would be impossible. For it cannot be denied that many stories, especially those which are called 'romances', are possible, even if they do not find any place in this series of the universe, which God has chosen—unless someone supposes that in the vast magnitude of space and time there exist the regions of the poets, where you could see wandering through the world King Arthur of Britain, Amadis of Gaul, and Dietrich von Bern, famed in the stories of the Germans. A certain distinguished philosopher of our century[c] seems to have been close to this opinion, for he says expressly somewhere that matter takes on successively all the forms of which it is capable (*Principles of Philosophy*, Part III, art. 47). This view is indefensible, for it would remove all the beauty of the universe and all choice, to say nothing here of other arguments by which the contrary can be shown.

Once I had recognised the contingency of things, I then began to consider what a clear notion of truth would be; for I hoped, not unreasonably, to derive from this some light on the problem of distinguishing necessary from contingent truths. However, I saw that it is common to every true affirmative proposition—universal and particular, necessary or contingent—that the predicate is in the subject, or that the notion of the predicate is in some way involved in the notion of the subject, and that this is the principle of infallibility in every kind of truth for him who knows everything *a priori*. But this seemed to increase the difficulty. For if, at a given time, the notion of the predicate is in the notion of the subject, then how, without contradiction and impossibility, can the predicate not be in the subject at that time, without destroying the notion of the subject?

A new and unexpected light finally arose in a quarter where I least hoped for it—namely, out of mathematical considerations of the nature of the infinite. There are two labyrinths of the human mind: one concerns the composition of the continuum, and the other the nature of freedom, and both spring from the same source—the infinite. That distinguished philosopher whom I mentioned above could not unravel these knots, or at any rate was unwilling to make his opinion known, but preferred to cut them with a sword. For he says (*Principles of Philosophy*, Part I, arts. 40 and 41) that we can easily involve ourselves in great difficulties if we try to reconcile God's preordination with the freedom of the will, and that we must abstain from discussing them, since God's nature cannot be comprehended by us. He also says (Part II, art. 35) that we ought not to doubt that matter is divided *ad infinitum*, even though we cannot understand this. But this is not enough: for it is one thing for us not to understand a thing, and another for us to understand its contradictory.

So it is at all events necessary to be able to answer those arguments which seem to imply that freedom or the division of matter imply a contradiction.

It must be known, therefore, that all creatures have impressed on them a certain mark of the divine infinity, and that this is the source of many wonders which amaze the human mind.

For example, there is no portion of matter so small that there does not exist in it a world of creatures, infinite in number. Again, every individual created substance, however imperfect, acts on all others and is acted on by all others, and contains in its complete notion (as this exists in the mind of God) the whole universe, and whatever is, was or will be. Further, every truth of fact or of individual things depends on a series of infinite reasons, and all that is in this series can be seen by God alone. This is also the reason why God alone knows contingent truths *a priori*, and sees their infallibility in another way than by experience.

When I had considered these more attentively, a profound difference between necessary and contingent truths came to light. Every truth is either original or derivative. Original truths are those of which a reason cannot be given; such truths are identical or immediate, and they affirm a term of itself or deny a contradictory of its contradictory.[d] Derivative truths are again of two sorts: some are analysed into original truths, others admit of an infinite process of analysis. The former are necessary, the latter contingent. A necessary proposition is one whose contrary implies a contradiction, such as all identical propositions and all derivative propositions which are analysable into identical propositions. These are the truths which are said to be of metaphysical or geometrical necessity. For demonstration consists simply in this: by the analysis of the terms of a proposition, and by substituting for a defined term a definition or part of a definition, one shows a certain equation or coincidence of predicate with subject in a reciprocal proposition, or in other cases at least the inclusion of the predicate in the subject, in such a way that what was latent in the proposition and as it were contained in it virtually is rendered evident and express by the demonstration.

For example:[e] if we understand by a ternary, senary or duodenary (etc.) number one which can be divided by 3, 6 and 12 respectively, we can demonstrate the proposition 'Every duodenary is a senary'. For every duodenary is a binary-binary ternary (for this is the analysis of a duodenary into its prime factors, $12 = 2 \times 2 \times 3$: i.e. the definition of a duodenary). Now, every binary-binary ternary is a binary ternary (which is an identical proposition), and every binary ternary is a senary (this is the definition of a senary: $6 = 2 \times 3$). Therefore every duodenary is a senary (12 is the same as $2 \times 2 \times 3$; $2 \times 2 \times 3$ is divisible by 2×3; 2×3 is the same as 6; therefore 12 is divisible by 6).

But in the case of contingent truths, even though the predicate is in the subject, this can never be demonstrated of it, nor can the proposition ever be reduced to an equation or identity. Instead, the analysis proceeds to infinity, God alone seeing—not, indeed, the end of the analysis, since it has no end—but the connexion of terms or the inclusion of the predicate in the subject, for he sees whatever is in the series; indeed, this very same truth has arisen in part from his own intellect and in part from his will, and expresses in its own way his infinite perfection and the harmony of the whole series of things.

However, there have been left to us two ways of knowing contingent truths; one is the way of experience and the other the way of reason. The way of experience is when we perceive a thing clearly enough by our senses; the way of reason is derived from the general principle that nothing happens without a reason, or, that the predicate is always in some way in the subject. So we can regard it as certain that everything is done by God in the most perfect way, that he does nothing which is contrary to reason, and that nothing ever happens without the man who understands it understanding its reason—why, that is, the state of things is as it is rather than otherwise. So reasons can be given for the actions of minds no less than for the actions of bodies, although in the case of the choices that minds make there is no necessity. Sins arise from the original limitation of things; but God does not so much decree sins as admit to existence certain possible substances, already involving in their complete notion, under the aspect of possibility, a free sin, and so involving the whole series of things which they will be in. For there can be no doubt that there are hidden reasons, transcending the understanding of every creature, why one series of things (although it includes sin) is preferred by God to another. However, God decrees only perfection, or what is positive; but limitation, and the sin which arises from it, is permitted by him, since given certain positive decrees it cannot absolutely be rejected, and reasons known to wisdom require that it should be redeemed by a greater good which cannot otherwise be obtained. But this cannot be considered here.

But to fix our attention better, so that the mind does not wander through vague difficulties, there occurs to me an analogy that holds between truth and proportions that seems to clarify the whole issue splendidly and put it in a clear light. Just as, in every proposition, the smaller number is contained in the larger, or an equal in an equal, so in every truth the predicate is in the subject. Further, in every proportion between homogeneous quantities one can carry out a kind of analysis of equal or congruent terms and subtract the smaller from the larger, by removing from the larger a part equal to the smaller; and similarly a residue can be subtracted from what has been subtracted, and so on either to a given point, or to infinity. So also, in the analysis of truths, one always substitutes for a term its equivalent, so that the predicate may be analysed into the terms which are contained in the subject. Now, in the case of proportions the analysis is sometimes completed and one arrives at a common measure, which is contained in each term of the proportion an integral number of times. Sometimes, however, the analysis can be continued to infinity, which occurs in the comparison of a rational number and a surd, or of a side and the diagonal in a square. Similarly, truths are sometimes demonstrable or necessary, and sometimes they are free or contingent; the latter cannot be reduced by any analysis to an identity, as to a common measure. This is the essential distinction both between proportionals and between truths.

However, incommensurable proportions have been mastered by the science of geometry, and we even have demonstrations about infinite series. Much more are contingent or infinite truths subject to the knowledge of God; they are known by him, not by a demonstration indeed (for that would imply a contradiction) but by an infallible vision. But this vision that God has must not be conceived as a kind of experiential knowledge, as if he saw something in things which are distinct from himself, but rather as *a priori* knowledge (through the reasons for truths). For he sees things which are possible in themselves by a consideration of his own nature, but he sees existent things by the consideration of his own free will and his own decrees, of which the first is to do everything in the best way and with supreme reason. What is termed 'mediate knowledge' is simply the knowledge of contingent possibles.

When these matters have been properly considered, I do not believe that any difficulty can arise in this topic whose solution cannot be derived from what has been said above. If one admits this concept of necessity—which all do admit—namely, that those propositions are necessary whose contrary implies a contradiction, it is readily apparent that the nature of demonstration and analysis can be explained, and also that there must be truths which are not reduced by any analysis to identical truths or to the principle of contradiction, but which furnish an infinite series of reasons, which God alone can see through. This is the nature of everything which is called free and contingent, and in particular that which involves space and time. It has been shown adequately above that this follows from the infinity of the parts of the universe and the mutual penetration and connexion of things.

A Letter on Freedom (*c.* 1689)

I realised, sir, from the little talk I had the honour to have with you, that you meditate deeply on the nature of human freedom. And this it is which drives me to expound to you more clearly what I referred to in conversation, so that I may profit by your opinion of it. I hold that it is in the interests of piety and faith to reconcile the way in which our will acts not only with the dogmas of faith, but also with the great principles of reason, which hold sway everywhere else, and are the foundations of our knowledge. Otherwise we seem to be yielding the victory to impious men and atheists, or at the least to be confirming and strengthening them in their errors. This is why I never could fancy the opinion of those who maintain that the principle of contradiction is not always applicable *in Divinis*, and that we do in fact find an exception to it in the case of the Trinity of the Divine Persons, as is admitted to some extent by those who introduce certain virtual distinctions. Now it is the same reason which makes me doubt whether it is fitting to say that another principle, which is of hardly less general application than the principle of contradiction, does not apply with regard to freedom—the principle, namely, that nothing ever takes place without its being possible for one who knew everything to give some reason why it should have happened rather than not. All the more so, because it seems to me that this principle is of just the same use to us in contingent matters as is the principle of contradiction in matters of necessity. It is for this reason that the laws of motion depend on it, because they are not of geometrical necessity, since they originate from the will of God, regulated by wisdom. Now since the principle of contradiction is the principle of necessity, and the principle that a reason must be given is the principle of contingency, it seems to me that we must not except freedom from them. Archimedes takes it for granted that a balance will not tip more in one direction than in the other, when everything is equal on both sides, and in the same way all those who reason about morals and politics, with a view to discovering about human actions, tacitly make use of this same foundation, that there is always a reason or cause which inclines the will. We shall, moreover, never find a contrary instance, and no one but a Scholastic, buried in abstractions, thinks otherwise. To show that the will ought to be excepted it would be necessary to have a means of determining the limitation of this principle *a priori*. This we can never find; and any foundation which might be adduced for such a distinction will always go further than we wish. It therefore seems to me that we do not need even to seek this exception, and that free choice is not incompatible with the general principle I have just established. To explain myself more clearly: I say that Adam sinned without necessity, although he who knows everything could give a reason why he rather let himself sin than remain in innocence. Even Holy Writ, in the account it gives of the method adopted by the serpent to betray Eve, also seems to hint that there was some reason or inclination which prevailed over the will of Eve. It looks as though the soul is never in that state of complete indifference, in which everything is equal, both within and without. There is always a reason, that is to say a greater inclination, for what has in fact been chosen, which may come not only from arguments good or bad, but also from passions, habits, dispositions of the organs and of the mind, external impressions, greater or less attention, etc. But this inclination does not master freedom, although it inclines it. There is a great deal of difference between a necessary cause and a certain concomitant. It is my view also that if we established the opposite, and claimed that the perpetual accompaniment of a stronger reason for choice destroys freedom, it would follow that inclination or the strongest reason would destroy freedom on every occasion that it accompanied it. From which it would follow further that we should almost never be free, since the cases when we are completely indifferent, or have a metaphysical freedom of choice, are at the least extremely rare, if they ever occur. Thus when we choose what is best, because it is best, it would be from necessity. Consequently the most perfect actions would be the least free and the least praiseworthy, since it is in freedom that we seek the reason for praise and blame, or rewards and punishments. The more perfect and the more inclined towards good a man was, the less free and praiseworthy he would be. Thus man would have to be reduced to a complete nudity, and despoiled of good qualities and graces, if he were to be allowed any merit. This is a vision favoured by some of our moderns, who seek the notion of freedom in indifference; which is as far removed from good sense as are their doctrines about probability and about knowledge of the badness of the action being necessary for sin. Whence has recently arisen that extraordinary distinction between philosophical and theological sin, which is upheld by certain authors who maintain that an assassination or an adultery is not a mortal sin, when the man who commits it does not actually reflect that he is offending God; because they imagine that otherwise the action is not sufficiently voluntary, that is to say, according to them, sufficiently indifferent, when the man does not give sufficient thought to everything which might dissuade him from it.

New System, and Explanation of the New System (1695–6)

It is now some years since I conceived this system, and entered into communication about it with several learned men, and in particular with one of the greatest theologians and philosophers of our time,[1] who had heard of some of my opinions from a personage of the highest rank, and found them highly paradoxical. But when he had received my explanations, he retracted in the most generous and edifying way imaginable, expressed his approval of a part of my propositions, and withdrew his censure of the others with which he still did not agree. Since that time I have continued my meditations as opportunity offered, so as to give to the public well-considered opinions only: and I have tried also to satisfy the objections raised against my essays on dynamics, which have some connexion with this. Some distinguished people, moreover, have desired to see my opinions more clearly expressed, and so I venture to offer these meditations, although they are in no way popular, nor such as to be to the taste of all kinds of minds. My chief aim is to give myself the benefit of the judgement of those who are enlightened in these matters, since it would be too difficult to seek out and call to my aid individually those who would be prepared to give me instruction—which I shall always be very happy to receive, provided the love of truth appears therein, and not merely a passion for preconceived opinions.

Although I am one of those who have done much work on

---

[1] Arnauld. Cf. pp. 48–74.

mathematics, I have constantly meditated on philosophy from my youth up, for it has always seemed to me that in philosophy there was a way of establishing something solid by means of clear proofs. I had travelled far into the world of the Scholastics when mathematics and modern writers lured me out again, while still a young man. I was charmed with their beautiful way of explaining nature mechanically, and scorned, with justice, the method of those who only make use of forms or faculties, from which we learn nothing. But later, when I tried to get to the bottom of the actual principles of mechanics in order to give an explanation of the laws of nature which are known through experience, I became aware that the consideration of an *extended mass* is not of itself enough, and that use must also be made of the notion of *force*, which is fully intelligible, although it falls within the sphere of metaphysics. It seemed to me also that the opinion of those who transform or degrade the lower animals into mere machines,[a] although it seems possible, is improbable, and even against the order of things.

At first, when I had freed myself from the yoke of Aristotle, I had believed in the void and atoms, for it is this which best satisfies the imagination. But returning to this view after much meditation, I perceived that it is impossible to find *the principles of a true unity* in matter alone, or in what is merely passive, since everything in it is but a collection or accumulation of parts *ad infinitum*. Now a multiplicity can be real only if it is made up of *true unities* which come from elsewhere and are altogether different from mathematical points, which are nothing but extremities of the extended and modifications out of which it is certain that nothing *continuous* could be compounded. Therefore, to find these *real unities*, I was constrained to have recourse to what might be called a *real and animated point* or to an atom of substance which must embrace some element of form or of activity in order to make a complete being. It was thus necessary to recall and in a manner to rehabilitate *substantial forms*, which are so much decried today, but in a way which makes them intelligible and separates the use which must be made of them from their previous abuse. I found then that their nature consists of force and that from this there follows something analogous to feeling and to appetite; and that therefore it was necessary to form a conception of them resembling our ordinary notion of *souls*. But just as the soul must not be used to explain the detail of the economy of the animal's body, so I judged in the same way that these forms ought not to be used to explain the particular problems of nature, although they are necessary to establish true general principles. Aristotle calls them *first entelechies*;[b] I call them, more intelligibly perhaps, *primitive forces*, which contain not only the *act*, or the fulfilment of possibility, but also an original *activity*.

I saw that these forms and these souls must be indivisible like our mind; and indeed I recollected that this had been the opinion held by St. Thomas concerning the souls of the lower animals.[c] But this truth revived the great difficulties about the origin and duration of souls and forms. For since every *simple substance* which possesses a true unity can have its beginning and end by miracle alone, it follows that they could not begin except by creation, nor come to an end except by annihilation. Thus (with the exception of such souls as God still wills to create expressly) I was obliged to recognise that the constitutive forms of substance must have been created with the world and that they go on subsisting always. Moreover, some of the Scholastics, such as Albertus Magnus and John Bacon, had a notion of some part of the truth about their origin. Nor ought our view to appear extraordinary, since we are only attributing to forms duration, which was granted to their atoms by the followers of Gassendi.[d]

Nevertheless I deemed that we ought not to mix without distinction or to confuse with other forms or souls, *minds* or rational souls, which are of a superior order and have incomparably more perfection than those forms embedded in matter which, on my view, are to be found everywhere, since in comparison with these others, minds or rational souls are little gods, made in the image of God, and having in them some glimmering of Divine light. This is why God governs minds as a prince governs his subjects, or as a father cares for his children; whereas he disposes of other substances as an engineer handles his machines. Thus minds have special laws which set them above the revolutions of matter, by the very order God has introduced into them; and it may truly be said that all the rest is made for them alone, the very revolutions being arranged for the felicity of the virtuous and the punishment of the wicked.

But to return to ordinary forms or *brute souls*, the fact that duration must now be attributed to them instead of to atoms as previously, might give rise to the doubt whether they do not pass from one body to another; this would be *metempsychosis*, more or less as some philosophers have thought it to occur in the transmission of movement and of species. But this fancy is very far removed from the nature of things. There is no such passing. It is here that the *transformations* of MM. Swammerdam, Malpighi, and Leeuwenhoek,[e] who are among the best observers of our day, have come to my assistance and have made me admit more readily that the animal and every other organised substance does not begin when we think, but that its apparent generation is only a development, a kind of increase. I have noticed, too, that the author of the *Recherche de la Vérité*,[1] M. Regis, M. Hartsoeker,[f] and other clever men have not been very far removed from this opinion.

But there still remained the more important question of what becomes of these souls or forms at the death of the animal, or at the destruction of the individual unit of organised substance. This question is the more awkward, inasmuch as it seems unreasonable that souls should remain useless in a chaos of confused matter. This ultimately made me decide that there was only one sensible thing to believe; that is to maintain the conservation not only of the soul but also of the animal itself and of its organic machine; even though the destruction of its grosser parts has reduced it to such smallness that it evades our senses, just as it did before birth. Moreover, nobody can mark precisely the true time of death, which may for a long time pass for a mere suspension of observable actions, and fundamentally is never anything else but that in the case of simple animals; witness the *resuscitations* of flies which have been drowned and then buried under powdered chalk, and several similar instances, which make

[1] Malebranche.

us realise that there might be other resuscitations, and in cases which were much further gone, if men were in a position to readjust the machine. And it looks as though it were something of this nature which was discussed by the great Democritus, thoroughgoing atomist though he was, although it was made fun of by Pliny.[g] It is therefore natural that since the animal has always been living and organised (as some people of fine penetration are beginning to recognise), it should also always continue to be so. And since there is thus no first birth or entirely new generation of the animal, it follows that it will suffer no final extinction or complete death, in the strict metaphysical sense; and that consequently instead of a *transmigration* of souls, there occurs only a *transformation* of one and the same animal, according as its organs are differently folded, and more or less developed.

But rational souls obey much more exalted laws, and are immune from anything which could make them lose the status of citizens of the society of minds, since God has so well provided that no changes of matter could make them lose the moral qualities of their personality. And it may be said with truth that everything tends to the perfection not only of the universe in general, but also of these created beings in particular, who are destined for so high a degree of happiness that the universe becomes concerned in it by virtue of the divine goodness which is communicated to each created being, in so far as sovereign wisdom can permit.

As regards the ordinary body of animals and other corporeal substances, which have hitherto been held to suffer complete extinction, and whose changes depend rather on mechanical rules than on moral laws, I was pleased to note that the ancient author of the book *Concerning Diet*, which is attributed to Hippocrates, had some notion of the truth when he expressly says that animals neither are born nor die, and that the things which are thought to come into being and to perish merely appear and disappear. This was also the opinion of Parmenides and of Melissus according to Aristotle[h]. For these ancient thinkers are sounder than is supposed.

I am as willing as any man to give the moderns their due;

but I think they have carried reform too far, among other things in confusing the natural with the artificial, through not having had sufficiently exalted ideas of the majesty of Nature. They conceive that the difference between her machines and ours is but the difference between the great and the small. This recently led a very clever man[1] to remark that when looking at Nature from near at hand she appears less admirable than we thought, being no more than a workman's shop. I believe that this does not give a sufficiently just idea, or one sufficiently worthy of her, and there is no system except mine which properly exhibits the immense distance which really lies between the least productions and mechanisms of Divine wisdom and the greatest achievements of the skill of a limited mind. This difference is one not merely of degree, but of kind also. It must be recognised that Nature's machines possess a truly infinite number of organs, and are so well protected and armed against all accidents that it is not possible to destroy them. A natural machine still remains a machine in its least parts, and, what is more, it always remains the very same machine that it was, being merely transformed by the different foldings it receives, and being sometimes stretched, sometimes contracted and as it were concentrated, when we think that it is destroyed.

Furthermore, by means of the soul or form, there is a true unity which corresponds to what is called the *I* in us; a thing which could not occur in artificial machines, nor in the simple mass of matter, however organised it may be. This can only be regarded as like an army or a flock, or like a pond full of fish, or a watch made up of springs and wheels. Yet if there were no true *substantial unities*, there would be nothing real or substantial in the collection. It was this that compelled M. Cordemoy to abandon Descartes, and to adopt Democritus's theory of atoms, in order to find a true unity. But *atoms of matter* are contrary to reason, besides the fact that they also are composed of parts, since the invincible attachment of one part to another (granted that this could be reasonably conceived or supposed) would not destroy their

---

[1] Fontenelle (1657–1757): author of *Entretiens sur la pluralité des mondes* (1686).

diversity. It is only *atoms of substance*, that is to say unities which are real and absolutely without parts, which can be the sources of actions, and the absolute first principles of the composition of things, and as it were the ultimate elements into which substantial things can be analysed. They might be called *metaphysical points*; there is about them *something vital* and a kind of *perception*, and *mathematical points* are their *points of view* for expressing the universe. But when corporeal substances are contracted all their organs constitute for us but a *physical point*. Thus physical points are indivisible in appearance only: mathematical points are exact, but they are nothing but modalities. It is only metaphysical points, or points of substance (constituted by forms or souls), which are both exact and real; and without them there would be nothing real, since without true unities there would be no plurality.

Once I had established these things, I thought I had reached port; but when I set myself to reflect on the union of the soul with the body, I seemed to be cast back again into the open sea. For I could find no way of explaining how the body causes something to happen in the soul, or vice versa, nor how one created substance can communicate with another. M. Descartes left the field at this stage, as far as we can gather from his writings; but his disciples, realising that the common opinion is inconceivable, maintained that we are aware of the qualities of bodies because God produces thoughts in the soul on the occasion of the movements of matter; and when our soul wishes to move the body in its turn, they deemed that it is God that moves it for the soul. And as the communication of motion seemed to them likewise inconceivable, they maintained that God gives motion to a body on the occasion of the motion of another body. This is what they call *the System of occasional causes*, which has become very fashionable owing to the fine reflections of the author of the *Recherche de la Vérité*.[1]

It must be admitted that they have gone a great way in regard to this problem by showing what cannot possibly take place; but their explanation of what does in fact occur does not remove the difficulty. It is quite true that in the

[1] Malebranche.

strict metaphysical sense there is no real influence exerted by one created substance on another, and that all things, with all their realities, are continually produced by the power of God: but to solve these problems it is not enough to make use of the general cause, and to drag in what is called the *deus ex machina*. For when this is done without giving any further explanation in terms of the order of secondary causes, this is properly speaking to fall back on miracle. In philosophy, we must attempt to give an explanation showing in what way things are brought about by the Divine wisdom, in conformity with the notion of the subject in question.

Being thus constrained to grant that it is impossible for the soul or for any other true substance to receive anything from without, except by Divine omnipotence, I was insensibly led to adopt a view which surprised me, but which seems inevitable, and which does in fact possess very great advantages and considerable beauties. This view is that we must say that God first created the soul, and every other real unity, in such a way that everything in it must spring from within itself, by a perfect *spontaneity* with regard to itself, and yet in a perfect *conformity* with things outside. And thus, since our internal sensations (those, that is to say, which are in the soul itself and not in the brain or in the subtle parts of the body) are but phenomena dependent upon external entities, or rather are really appearances, and, as it were, well ordered dreams, these internal perceptions within the soul itself must arise in it from its own original constitution, that is to say through the natural representative ability (capable of expressing entities outside itself in relation to its organs) with which it has been endowed since its creation, and which constitutes its individual character. It follows from this that, since each of these substances exactly represents the whole universe in its own way and from a certain point of view, and since the perceptions or expressions of external things reach the soul at the proper time by virtue of its own laws and, as it were, in a world apart, as if nothing else existed but only God and itself (if I may make use of a way of speaking employed by a certain writer with a most exalted mind and famous for her holiness[j]), there will be a perfect agreement between all these substances, producing the same effect as would occur if these communicated with one another by means of a transmission of species or qualities, as the common run of philosophers[k] maintain. Furthermore, the organised mass, within which is the point of view of the soul, is itself more nearly expressed by it, and finds itself in its turn ready to act of itself according to the laws of the corporeal machine whenever the soul desires, without either disturbing the laws of the other, the animal spirits and the blood having precisely at the given moment the motions necessary to make them respond to the passions and perceptions of the soul; and it is this mutual relation, regulated in advance in every substance in the universe, which produces what we call their *communication*, and which alone constitutes *the union of the soul and the body*. And this makes it possible to understand how the soul has its seat in the body by an immediate presence, which could not be closer than it is, since it is present in the way in which the unity is present in that resultant of unities which is a plurality.

This hypothesis is very possible. For why should not God be able in the first instance to give to substance a nature or internal force capable of producing for it in an orderly way (as if it were an *automaton,*[1] *spiritual and formal, but free* in the case of a substance which has a share of reason) everything that is going to happen to it, that is to say all the appearances and expressions it is going to have, and that without the assistance of any created thing? This is rendered all the more probable by the fact that the nature of substance necessarily requires and essentially involves a progress or change, without which it would have no force to act. And since it is the very nature of the soul to be representative of the universe in a very exact way (although with varying distinctness), the sequence of representations which the soul produces for itself will naturally correspond to the sequence of changes in the universe itself: while on the other hand the body has also been adjusted to the soul, in regard to the experiences in which the latter is conceived as acting outside itself. This is all the more reasonable in that bodies are only made for those minds which are capable of entering into society with God, and of celebrating His glory. Thus once we recognise the possibility of this *hypothesis of agreements*, we recognise also that it is the most reasonable one, and that it gives a wonderful idea of the harmony of the universe and of the perfection of the works of God.

There is in it this great advantage also, that instead of saying that we are free only in appearance and in a manner adequate for practice, as several ingenious men have held, we must rather say that we are determined in appearance only; and that in strict metaphysical language we are perfectly independent as regards the influence of all other created things. This again shows up in a marvellously clear light the immortality of our soul, and the ever uniform conservation of our individual self, which is perfectly well regulated of its own nature, and is beyond the reach of all accidents from outside, whatever the appearances to the contrary. No system has ever so clearly exhibited our exalted position. Since each mind is as it were a world apart, sufficient unto itself, independent of all other created things, including the infinite, expressing the universe, it is as lasting, as subsistent, and as absolute as the very universe of created things itself. We must therefore conclude that it must always play its part in the way most suited to contribute to the perfection of that society of all minds which constitutes their moral union in the City of God. Here, too, is a new and wonderfully clear proof of the existence of God. For this perfect agreement of all these substances, which have absolutely no communication with one another, could only come from the one common cause.

Besides the fact that this hypothesis is recommended by all these advantages, it may be added that it is something more than a hypothesis, since it seems hardly possible to explain things in any other intelligible way, and since several serious difficulties which have hitherto exercised men's minds seem to disappear of themselves when once it is properly understood. Ordinary ways of speaking can still be easily retained. For it may fairly be said that when the particular disposition of a given substance is the explanation of a change taking place in an intelligible manner, so that we can infer that it is to this substance that the others have been adjusted in this regard from the beginning, in accordance with the order of the decrees of God, then that substance ought to be conceived as in that respect *acting* upon the others. Further, the action of one substance on another is not a giving forth, or transplanting of an entity, as is commonly supposed; and it can reasonably be understood only in the way I have just described. It is true that we can easily conceive of matter both as giving out and as taking in parts; and it is in this way that we rightly explain in terms of mechanics all the phenomena of physics; but as the material mass is not a substance, it can be seen that action in regard to substance itself can only be such as I have just described.

These considerations, metaphysical though they may appear, are yet wonderfully useful in physics, for establishing the laws of motion, as my *Dynamics* will be able to establish. For the truth is that in the shock of impact each body suffers only from its own elasticity, caused by the motion which is already in it. And as for absolute motion, nothing can determine it mathematically, since everything terminates in relations. This means that there is always a perfect equivalence of hypotheses, as in astronomy; so that whatever number of bodies we take, we may at our own discretion assign rest, or a certain degree of velocity, to any particular one of them we wish, without its being possible for us to be refuted by the phenomena of motion, whether in a straight line, circular, or composite. It is, however, reasonable to attribute to bodies true motions, in accordance with the supposition which explains phenomena in the most intelligible way; and this way of speaking is in conformity with the notion of activity which we have just established.[m]

EXPLANATION OF THE NEW SYSTEM OF THE COMMUNICATION OF SUBSTANCES, IN REPLY TO WHAT IS SAID ABOUT IT IN THE 'JOURNAL' OF 12 SEPT. 1695[1]

I recollect, sir, that I thought I was complying with your desire in imparting to you my philosophical hypothesis

---

[1] A letter from Foucher to Leibniz was published in this copy of the *Journal des Savants*, giving a number of objections to the New System.

some years ago, though at the same time I pointed out that I had not yet decided to acknowledge it. In return I asked your opinion of it; but I do not remember receiving any objections from you, otherwise with my usual docility I should certainly not have given you occasion to raise the same ones a second time. Yet they are still not too late, although they reach me after publication, for I am not one of those for whom the being committed to a view takes the place of sound reasoning, as you will find when you are able to say you have adduced some precise and pressing reason against my opinions—which, it appears, is not your aim. You wish rather to speak as an able Academic, and thereby to provide an opportunity of going more deeply into the matter.

1. It was my aim here to expound, not the principles of extension, but the principles of that which is in fact extended, or of bodily mass. These principles, according to me, are the real units, that is to say substances that possess a true unity.

2. The unity of a clock, to which you refer, is on my view quite other than the unity of an animal; the latter may be a substance possessing a true unity, like that in us which is called the *I*; whereas a clock is nothing but an assemblage.

3. It is not in the disposition of the organs that I find the principle of sensation in animals; I agree that this disposition concerns nothing but the bodily mass.

4. I mention these things to prevent misunderstandings and to show that what you say about them is not contrary to what I have propounded. It seems that you do not make me out to be wrong when I demand true unities, and when that makes me rehabilitate substantial forms. But when you appear to say that the souls of brutes must have some share of reason if they are allowed to have sensation, that is a conclusion the proof of which I do not see.

5. You recognise with commendable sincerity that my hypothesis of harmony or concomitance is a possible one. But none the less you are still somewhat averse to it, no doubt because you believed that it was purely arbitrary, and did not realise that it follows from my view of unities, and that my whole contention stands or falls together.

6. You therefore ask me, sir, what can be the purpose of

all this artifice which I attribute to the Author of nature—as if it were possible for too much artifice to be attributed to him, and as if this exact correspondence of unities with one another through their own laws, which each received at the beginning, were not a thing admirably beautiful in itself and worthy of its Author. You further ask what advantage I find in this theory.

7. I might refer to what I have already said about this. Still, I answer in the first place that when a thing cannot not be so, it is not necessary to ask what can be the purpose of it before admitting it. What is the purpose of the incommensurability of the side with the diagonal?

8. In the second place I answer that this correspondence serves the purpose of explaining the communication of substances and the union of the soul with the body by means of the laws of nature established in advance, without having recourse either to a transmission of species, which is inconceivable, or to a fresh intervention of God, which seems hardly conceivable. For we must realise that as there are natural laws in matter, so there are also natural laws in souls or forms, and these laws mean what I have just stated.

9. I am further asked how it happens that God is not content to produce all the thoughts and *modifications* of the soul, without these *useless* bodies which the soul (it is said) can neither *move* nor *know*. The answer is easy. It is that it was God's will that there should be a greater rather than a lesser number of substances, and he found it good that these *modifications* should correspond to something outside.

10. There is no *useless* substance; they all have their contribution to make to God's design.

11. Also I do not admit that the soul *does not know* bodies, though this knowledge arises without their influencing one another.

12. I should have no objection even to saying that the soul *moves* the body; in the same way as a Copernican rightly speaks of the rising of the sun, a Platonist of the reality of matter, a Cartesian of the reality of sensible qualities, provided these statements are sanely understood, so I believe that it is very true to say that substances act upon one

another, provided it is understood that the one is the cause of changes in the other in consequence of the laws of harmony.

13. The objection touching the *lethargy* of bodies (namely that the bodies might be inactive even when the soul believed them to be in motion) cannot stand because of this same unfailing correspondence, established by Divine wisdom.

14. I have no knowledge of these *vain, useless, and inactive masses*, to which reference is made. There is activity everywhere; indeed, I maintain this more than the received philosophy, because I hold that there is no body without motion, nor substance without effort.

15. I do not understand the precise nature of the objection contained in the words: *In truth, sir, can we not see that these views are formed with a set purpose, and that these systems, coming after the event, have only been manufactured to save certain principles?* All hypotheses are formed *with a set purpose*, and all systems come *after the event* to save phenomena[n] or appearances. But I do not see which are the principles in favour of which I am supposed to be prejudiced, and which I want to save.

16. If this means that I am led to my hypothesis by *a priori* reasons also, or by fixed principles, as is in fact the case, this is rather a commendation of the hypothesis than an objection to it. It commonly suffices for a hypothesis to be proved *a posteriori*, because it satisfies the phenomena; but when we have other reasons as well, and those *a priori*, it is so much the better.

17. But perhaps what is meant is that when I had invented a new view for myself, I was very glad to make use of it, more to assume airs on account of its novelty than because I recognised it to be useful. I do not know, sir, whether you have so poor an opinion of me as to attribute such thoughts to me. For you know that I love truth; and that if I had such a feeling for novelties, I should be in a greater hurry to produce them, especially those whose solidity is recognised. But in order that those who know me less well should not endow your words with a meaning which we should not like, suffice it to say that in my view it is impossible to explain *transeunt activity*[o] in conformity with the laws of nature in any other way, and that I believed that the value of my hypo-

thesis would be recognised in view of the difficulty which the ablest philosophers of our time have found in the communication of minds and bodies, and even of bodily substances one with another. I do not know whether you yourself have encountered any of these difficulties.

18. It is true that there are, on my view, efforts in all substances; but these efforts are, strictly speaking, only in the substance itself; and what follows from them in the other substances is only by virtue of a *pre-established harmony*, if I may use the word, and not by any real influence, or by the transmission of some species or quality. As I have explained the nature of activity and passivity, the nature of effort and of resistance can readily be inferred.

19. You say, sir, *that you know that there are still many more questions to be put before we can decide those which we have been discussing*. But perhaps you will find that I have already put them: I am not sure that your Academics have put into practice the valuable parts of their method more rigorously and effectively than I myself have done. I strongly approve of the attempt to prove truths from first principles; this is more useful than is commonly supposed, and I have often put this precept into practice. Thus I welcome what you say on this subject, and I hope your example will lead our philosophers to think about it as they should.

20. I will add a further reflection which seems to me to be of considerable assistance towards the better understanding of the reality and value of my system. You know that M. Descartes believed that the same quantity of motion is conserved in bodies.[p] It has been demonstrated that he was mistaken in this; but I have shown that it is always true that the same motive force—instead of, as he thought, the same quantity of motion—is conserved. Even so, the changes which take place in the body as a consequence of the modifications of the soul caused him embarrassment, because they seemed to violate this law. He thought therefore that he had found a way out of the difficulty, which is certainly ingenious, by saying that we must distinguish between motion and direction of motion; and that the soul cannot increase or diminish the motive force, but that it changes the direction

or determination of the course of the animal spirits, and it is in this way that voluntary motions take place. It is true that he made no attempt to explain how the soul sets about changing the course of bodies—and in fact this seems as inconceivable as saying that it gives them motion, unless you have recourse, as I do, to pre-established harmony. But the truth is that there is *another law of nature*, which I have discovered and proved, and which M. Descartes did not know: namely, that *there is conserved* not only the same quantity of motive force, but also *the same quantity of direction from whatever side in the world it be taken*. That is to say: take any straight line you like, and take also any number of bodies, chosen as you please; you will find that, considering all these bodies together without leaving out any of those which act on any of those which you have taken, there will always be the same quantity of progression from the same side in all the lines parallel to the straight line you have chosen: provided care is taken that the sum total of progression is estimated by deducting that of the bodies which go in the opposite direction from that of those which go in the direction chosen. This law is as beautiful and as general as the other, and deserves as little to be violated: and this is so in my system, which conserves both force and direction, and, in a word, all the natural laws of bodies, notwithstanding the changes which occur in them as a result of those in the soul.

PS.   Hanover, 3/13 January 1696.

I see clearly from your reflexions that I need to throw some light on that idea of mine which a friend caused to be inserted in the *Journal des Savants*. You say, sir, that you do not see how I could prove what I propounded concerning the communication or harmony of two substances as different as the soul and the body. It is true that I thought I had supplied the means of doing so. And I hope that what follows will satisfy you.

Imagine two clocks or watches which are in perfect agreement. Now this agreement may come about *in three ways. The first* consists of a natural influence. This is what M. Huygens tried with a result that surprised him. He suspended two pendulums from the same piece of wood; the continual strokes of the pendulums communicated similar vibrations to the particles of the wood; but since these different vibrations could not well persist independently and without interfering with one another, unless the pendulums were in agreement, it happened by some sort of miracle that even when their strokes had been purposely disturbed, they soon went back to swinging together, rather like two strings[1] which are in unison. *The second method* of achieving the constant agreement of two clocks, albeit imperfect ones, would be to have them continually supervised by a skilful craftsman who should be constantly setting them right. *The third method* is to construct the two clocks so skilfully and accurately at the outset that one could be certain of their subsequent agreement.

Now substitute the soul and the body for these two watches. Their agreement or sympathy will also arise in one of these three ways. *The way of influence* is that of ordinary philosophy; but as it is impossible to conceive of either material particles, or immaterial species or qualities, as capable of passing from one of these substances to the other, we are obliged to abandon this view. *The way of assistance* is that of the system of occasional causes. But I hold that this is bringing in the *deus ex machina* for a natural and ordinary thing, where reason requires him to intervene only in the way he concurs with all other things in nature. Thus there remains only my hypothesis, that is to say *the way of pre-established harmony*— pre-established, that is, by a Divine anticipatory artifice, which so formed each of these substances from the beginning, that in merely following its own laws, which it received with its being, it is yet in accord with the other, just as if they mutually influenced one another, or as if, over and above his general concourse, God were for ever putting in his hand to set them right. After this I do not think there is anything for me to prove, unless I am desired to prove that God possesses the cleverness necessary for making use of this anticipatory artifice, of which we see samples even among men, in proportion as they are clever people. And supposing that he can, it is clear that this is the finest way and the

[1] i.e. strings of a musical instrument.

worthiest of him. You had some suspicion that my explanation would be opposed to the rather different idea we have of mind and body. But now you see clearly, sir, that no one has better established their independence. For so long as it was necessary to explain their communication by a kind of miracle, it was always left open to some people to fear that the distinction between them might not be what it was supposed to be, because it was necessary to go to such lengths to uphold it. Now all these scruples disappear. My essays on dynamics are connected with this; in them I had to inquire more deeply into the notion of bodily substance, which on my view lies rather in the force of acting and resisting than in extension, which is but a repetition or diffusion of something anterior, that is to say, of this force. And as these thoughts of mine, which to some have appeared paradoxical, have caused me to exchange letters with various well-known men, I could produce a *Commercium Epistolicum* on the subject, into which would come my correspondence with M. Arnauld, of which I spoke in my previous letter. It will contain a curious mixture of thoughts about philosophy and mathematics, which will perhaps sometimes have the charm of novelty. I leave you to judge, sir, whether the explanations I have just given are suitable for sounding the opinions of enlightened people through the intermediary of your journal.q But do not give my name, as it was not given in the *Journal des Savants* either.

On the Principle of Indiscernibles
(*c.* 1696)

A consideration which is of the greatest importance in all philosophy, and in theology itself, is this: that there are no purely extrinsic denominations, because of the interconnexion of things, and that it is not possible for two things to differ from one another in respect of place and time alone, but that it is always necessary that there shall be some other internal difference. So there cannot be two atoms which are at the same time similar in shape and equal in magnitude to each other; for example, two equal cubes. Such notions are mathematical, that is, they are abstract and not real. For all things which are different must be distinguished in some way, and in the case of real things position alone is not a sufficient means of distinction. This overthrows the whole of purely corpuscularian philosophy. First, there cannot be any atoms, otherwise there could be two things which differ only extrinsically. Then, if place by itself does not make a change, it follows that there can be no change which is merely local. In general, place, position and quantity, such as number and proportion, are merely relations, and result from other things which by themselves either constitute or terminate a change. To be in a place seems, abstractly at any rate, to imply nothing but position. But in actuality, that which has a place must express place in itself; so that distance and the degree of distance involves also a degree of expressing in the thing itself a remote thing, either of affecting it or of receiving an affection from it. So, in fact, situation really involves a degree of expressions. When thinking about the categories I used to distinguish, in the accepted manner, the category of quantity from that of relation, since quantity and position (both of which are included in this category) seem to be produced by motion *per se*, and are usually conceived by people in this way. But when I considered the matter more accurately I saw that they are mere results, which do not constitute any intrinsic denomination *per se*, and so they are merely relations which demand a foundation derived from the category of quality, that is, from an intrinsic accidental denomination.

We may compare our conception of position with that of existence. Existence is conceived by us as having nothing in common with essence; but this cannot be so, since there must be more in the concept of a thing which exists than in that of one which does not exist, that is, existence must be a perfection, since all that is explicable in existence is being an ingredient of the most perfect series of things.[a] In the same way we conceive position as something extrinsic, which adds nothing to the thing posited, though it does add the way in which it is affected by other things.

Further, transition or variation itself—which is called an action when joined with perfection, and being acted on when joined with imperfection—is simply a complex of two states which are immediate and opposite to each other, together with a force or reason for the transition, which reason is itself a quality. So action or being acted on itself is a result of simple states. From this it appears that two intrinsic denominations are required, a power of transition and that to which the transition is made. In what this consists, no one has yet explained. It must be something other than active force; for this says merely 'that which the transition follows', but does not explain what it consists in, and what it is to which the transition is made. At one time I called this 'light', from which our phenomena result, and which differs in different monads, according to the manner of each. It could be called a possible quality. Just as shape is to extension, and derived force is to an entelechy, so are phenomena to light; light is in a way the matter of images. This cannot be located in the mere power of acting, since action is again something relative to a state which varies. What is sought, therefore, is something ultimate; that is, the matter of images, which at the same time has a transition from image to image; or, there are ideas which are active, and so to speak 'alive', just as the monads themselves are living mirrors.

All that we have said here arises from that great principle, that the predicate is in the subject. When I once advanced this, Arnauld wrote that he was struck and moved by this; 'J'en ay esté frappé', he said.[b]

On the Ultimate Origination of Things (23 Nov. 1697)

Besides the world or aggregate of finite things we find a certain Unity which is dominant, not only in the sense in which the soul is dominant in me, or rather in which the self or *I* is dominant in my body, but also in a much more exalted manner. For the dominant Unity of the universe not only rules the world, but also constructs or makes it; and it is higher than the world and, if I may so put it, extramundane; it is thus the ultimate reason of things. For neither in any one single thing, nor in the whole aggregate and series of things, can there be found the sufficient reason of existence. Let us suppose[a] the book of the elements of geometry to have been eternal, one copy always having been written down from an earlier one; it is evident that, even though a reason can be given for the present book out of a past one, nevertheless out of any number of books taken in order going backwards we shall never come upon a full reason; since we might always wonder why there should have been such books from all time—why there were books at all, and why they were written in this manner. What is true of the books is true also of the different states of the world; for what follows is in some way copied from what precedes (although according to certain laws of change), And so, however far you go back to earlier states, you will never find in those states a full reason why there should be any world rather than none, and why it should be such as it is.

Therefore, even if you suppose the world eternal, as you will still be supposing nothing but a succession of states and will not in any of them find a sufficient reason, nor however many states you assume will you advance one step towards giving a reason, it is evident that the reason must be sought elsewhere. For in things which are eternal, though there may be no cause, nevertheless a reason must be discerned; which reason in things that are permanent is necessity itself or essence, but in the series of changeable things (if this is supposed *a priori* to be eternal[b]) it will be, as will be presently understood, the prevailing of inclinations, in a sphere where reasons do not necessitate (by an absolute or metaphysical necessity, in which the contrary implies a contradiction), but incline. From this it is evident that even by supposing the world to be eternal we cannot escape the ultimate, extramundane reason of things, or God.

The reasons of the world then lie in something extramundane, different from the chain of states, or series of things, whose aggregate constitutes the world. And so we must pass from physical or hypothetical necessity, which determines the subsequent things of the world by the earlier, to something which is of absolute or metaphysical necessity, for which no reason can be given. For the present world is necessary physically or hypothetically, but not absolutely or metaphysically. In other words, granted that it is once such and such, it follows that such and such things will come into being. Since then the ultimate root must be in something which is of metaphysical necessity, and since there is no reason of any existent thing except in an existent thing, it follows that there must exist some one Being of metaphysical necessity, that is, to whose essence existence belongs; and so there must exist something different from the plurality of beings, that is the world, which, as we have allowed and have shown, is not of metaphysical necessity.

Let me explain a little more distinctly how out of truths that are eternal or essential or metaphysical there arise truths that are temporal, contingent, or physical. First we must notice, from the very fact that something exists rather than nothing, that there is in things that are possible, or in possibility or essence itself, a certain need for existence, or (if I may so put it) a claim to exist; and, to put it in a word, that essence in itself tends towards existence. From this it further follows that all things which are possible, or express essence or possible reality, tend by equal right towards existence[c] in proportion to the quantity of essence or reality which they include, or in proportion to the degree of perfection which belongs to them; for perfection is nothing else than quantity of essence.

Hence it is seen to be most evident that out of the infinite combinations of possibles, and the infinite possible series, that one exists by whose means the greatest possible amount of essence or possibility is brought into existence. There is always to be found in things a principle of determination which turns on considerations of greatest and least; namely, that the greatest effect should be produced with (if I may so put it) the least expenditure. And the time, the place, or (in a word) the receptivity or capacity of the world, may here be taken to be the expenditure, or the ground on which a building is to be raised as fittingly as possible, while the variety of forms is in accordance with the fitness of the building and with the number and elegance of its rooms. It is very much like what happens in certain games, in which all the spaces on the board have to be filled in according to certain rules: unless you show some ingenuity you will find yourself at the end kept out of certain refractory spaces, and thereby compelled to leave empty more spaces than you need have done, and more than you wished. There is, however, a definite formula by which the greatest possible success in filling the spaces is most easily obtained. For instance, if we suppose ourselves told to construct a triangle, there being no other principle of determination, the result is that we draw an equilateral triangle;[d] and if we are required to go from one point to another, and nothing further is added to determine the way, we shall choose the path that is easiest or shortest. Similarly, once it has been granted that being prevails over not-being, that is, that there is a reason why something should exist rather than nothing, or that transition from possibility to actuality is to take place, then, even if nothing further is determined, the consequence is that there exists as much as is possible in accordance with the capacity of time and place (or of the possible order of existing)—in very much the same way as tiles are fitted together so as to put in as many as possible within the given area.

From this it is now wonderfully clear how in the very origination of things a certain Divine mathematics or metaphysical mechanics is employed, and how a determination of the maximum holds good. It is on this principle that of all the angles the right angle is the determinate angle in geometry, and that liquids when placed in heterogeneous media form themselves into the most capacious shape, that is, the spherical; but the best instance of all is that in common mechanics itself, when several heavy bodies are operating against one another, the result is that movement which secures the greatest descent on the whole. For just as all things that are possible with equal right tend towards existence in proportion to their reality, so in the same way all weights with equal right tend towards descent in proportion to their gravity; and just as in the latter case there results a motion involving the greatest possible descent of the heavy bodies, so in the former case there results a world involving the greatest production of things that are possible.

Thus we now have physical necessity based on metaphysical necessity. For although the world is not metaphysically necessary, such that its contrary would imply a contradiction or logical absurdity, nevertheless it is necessary physically, that is, determined in such a way that its contrary would imply imperfection or moral absurdity. And as possibility is the principle of essence, so perfection or degree of essence (through which there exists the largest number of compossibles) is the principle of existence. This makes it evident at the same time how there can be freedom in the Author of the world, although he does everything determinately, because he acts from the principle of wisdom or perfection. Indifference arises from ignorance, and the wiser a man is, the more is he determined to that action which is most perfect.

But (you will say) this comparison of a certain metaphysical determining mechanism with the physical mechanism of heavy bodies, elegant though it may appear, has nevertheless this fault: there really exist heavy bodies acting against one another, but possibilities or essences prior to or beyond existence are imaginary or fictitious, and therefore one cannot seek in them the reason of existence. I answer, that neither the essences nor the truths about them which are known as eternal truths, are fictitious; they exist (if I may so put it) in a certain region of ideas, that is, in God himself, the fount of all essence and of the existence of other things. That this is no merely arbitrary assertion is shown by the very existence of the actual series of things. For since in the series a reason cannot be found, as I have shown above, but must be sought in metaphysical necessities or eternal truths; since, too, existent things cannot come into being except from existent things, as I have explained previously; it follows that eternal truths must have their existence in some subject which is absolutely or metaphysically necessary, that is in God, through whom these truths, which would otherwise be imaginary, are (to use a barbarous but expressive word) *realised*.[1]

And indeed in actual fact we find that everything in the world takes place in accordance with the laws of the eternal truths, not only geometrical but also metaphysical laws; that is, not only according to material necessities, but also according to formal necessities. This is not only true in general, in regard to the reason (which I have just explained) why the world should exist rather than not, and why it should exist just as it is rather than otherwise (this reason is to be found in the tendency of possibles towards existence); but more than this, if we come down to details, we see the marvellous way in which metaphysical laws hold sway in the whole of nature—the laws of cause, of power, of activity,— and how they prevail even over the purely geometrical laws of matter themselves, as I found to my great wonder when I was giving an account of the laws of motion; so much so, in- deed, that though from my early youth, when I was more of a materialist, I had defended the law of the geometric com- position of endeavours, I was finally forced to abandon it, as I have explained at greater length elsewhere.[e]

Here then we have the ultimate reason of the reality both of essences and of existences in a Unity, which must certainly be greater, higher, and prior to the world itself, since through it not only the existent things, which the world contains, but also the things that are possible have their reality. It

[1] The word *realisentur* is a barbarism in Latin.

cannot be found except in one single source, because of the interconnexion of all these things with one another. It is evident that from this source existent things are continually issuing and being produced, and have been produced, since it is not clear why one state of the world rather than another, yesterday's state rather than today's, should flow from the world itself. It is also evident how God acts not only physically but also freely; and how there lies in him not only the efficient but also the final cause; and how from him proceeds the reason not only of the greatness or potency that there is in the mechanism of the universe as now established, but also of the goodness or wisdom involved in the establishing of it.

In case someone may think that moral perfection or goodness is here being confused with metaphysical perfection or greatness, and may admit the latter while denying the former, it should be pointed out that it follows from what has been said not only that the world is the most perfect physically, or, if you prefer it, metaphysically, or in other words that that series of things will be forthcoming which in actual fact affords the greatest quantity of reality, but also that the world should be the most perfect morally, because true moral perfection is physical perfection in minds themselves. Hence the world is not only the most wonderful machine, but also in regard to minds it is the best commonwealth,[f] by whose means there is bestowed on minds the greatest possible amount of felicity or joyfulness; and it is in this that their physical perfection consists.

But, you will say, we find in the world the very opposite of this. Often the worst of sufferings fall upon the best men; the innocent (I speak not only of the brutes, but of men also) are afflicted, and are slain even with tortures; indeed the world, especially if we look at the government of the human race, seems rather a confused chaos than an affair ordained by some supreme wisdom. So it appears at first sight, I allow: but on deeper examination it must be agreed that the opposite is the case. It is evident *a priori* from those very principles which I have adduced that without doubt there is secured in the world the highest perfection that there could possibly be of all things, and therefore of minds.

And indeed it is unreasonable, as the jurisconsults say, to give a judgement without inspecting the whole law. We have knowledge of a tiny part of that eternity which stretches out immeasurably. For how small a thing is the memory of the few thousand years which history hands down to us! And yet out of so little experience we rashly make judgements about the immeasurable and the eternal; just as men who had been born and bred in prison or in the subterranean salt-mines of Sarmatia might think that there was no other light in the world than the treacherous flicker of torches, which was hardly sufficient to guide their footsteps. Look at the most lovely picture, and then cover it up, leaving uncovered only a tiny scrap of it. What else will you see there, even if you look as closely as possible, and the more so as you look from nearer and nearer at hand, but a kind of confused medley of colours, without selection, without art! And yet when you remove the covering, and look upon the whole picture from the proper place, you will see that what previously seemed to you to have been aimlessly smeared on the canvas was in fact accomplished with the highest art by the author of the work. What happens to the eyes in painting is equally experienced by the ears in music. The great composers frequently mingle discords with harmonious chords so that the listener may be stimulated and pricked as it were, and become, in a way, anxious about the outcome; presently when all is restored to order he feels so much the more content. In the same way we may take pleasure in small dangers, or in the experience of ills, from the very sense or proof they give us of our own power or felicity. Or again at the spectacle of rope-walking or sword-dancing we are delighted by the very element of fear that is involved, and we ourselves in play with children hold them as if we were going to fling them away, and half let them go—in very much the same way as the ape carried Christian, King of Denmark, when he was still an infant wrapped in long clothes, to the edge of the roof, and then, when everybody was in terror, put him back into his cradle safe and sound, as if in play. On the same principle it has an insipid effect if we always eat sweet things; sharp, acid, and even bitter things should be mixed in to stimulate the taste.

He who has not tasted what is bitter has not earned what is sweet, nor will he appreciate it. This is the very law of enjoyment, that pleasure does not come from an even course; such things produce weariness, and make men dull, not joyful.

What I have said, however, about the possibility of a part being disturbed without upsetting the harmony of the whole must not be interpreted to mean that no account is taken of the parts; or that it is sufficient for the world to be perfect as a whole, even though it should turn out that the human race was wretched, and that there was in the universe no care for justice and no account was taken of us—as is maintained by some people whose judgement about the sum of things is ill-grounded. For the truth is that, just as in a well regulated commonwealth care is taken that as far as possible things shall be to the interest of the individual, in the same way the universe would not be sufficiently perfect unless, as far as can be done without upsetting the universal harmony, the good of individual people is considered. Of this there could be established no better measure than the very law of justice itself, which dictates that each should have a part in the perfection of the universe and in his own happiness in proportion to his own virtue and to the extent to which his will is directed towards the common good; by which is fulfilled what we call the charity and love of God, in which alone, according to the judgement of wise theologians also, stands the whole force and power of the Christian religion. Nor ought it to seem remarkable that all this deference should be paid to minds in the universe, since they bear the closest resemblance to the image of the supreme Author, and their relation to him is not that of machines to their artificer (like the rest of the world) but rather that of citizens to their prince; moreover they will endure as long as the universe itself, and they, in some manner, express and concentrate the whole in themselves; so that it might be said that minds are whole parts.

As for the afflictions of men, and especially of good men, we must hold ourselves assured that they lead to the greater good of those who suffer them; and this is true not only theologically, but physically also, just as a grain of wheat cast into the earth must suffer before it bears fruit.[g] And in general it is true to say that afflictions are for the time being evil, but in effect good, since they are short cuts to a greater perfection. Similarly in physics the liquids which ferment slowly are also more slowly purified, whereas those in which there is a more violent disturbance throw off the foreign parts with greater force and so more quickly become pure. You might fairly say that this is a case of taking a step back in order to make a stronger leap forward (*reculer pour mieux sauter*). These things must be allowed to be not only pleasant and consoling, but also most true. Indeed in general I hold that there is nothing truer than happiness, and nothing happier and sweeter than truth.

Further, we realise that there is a perpetual and a most free progress of the whole universe towards a consummation of the universal beauty and perfection of the works of God, so that it is always advancing towards a greater development.[h] Thus, even now a great part of our earth has received cultivation, and will receive it more and more. And though it is true that there are times when some parts of it go back again to virgin forest, or are destroyed again and oppressed, this must be understood in the same sense as I just now interpreted the meaning of affliction, namely, that this very destruction and oppression contributes to achieve something greater, so that in some way we receive profit from our very loss.

To the objection that may perhaps be offered that if this were so the world would long ago have become a paradise, the answer is at hand: although many substances have already come to great perfection, yet owing to the infinite divisibility of what is continuous, there always remain in the abyss of things parts that are asleep, and these need to be awakened and to be driven forward into something greater and better— in a word, to a better state of development. Hence this progress does not ever come to an end.

A Résumé of Metaphysics (c. 1697)

1. There is a reason in Nature why something should exist rather than nothing. This is a consequence of the great principle that nothing happens without a reason, and also that there must be a reason why this thing exists rather than another.

2. This reason must be in some real entity, or cause. For a *cause* is simply a real reason, and truths about possibilities and *necessities* (that is, where the possibility of the opposite has been denied) would not produce anything unless those possibilities were founded on a thing which actually exists.

3. This entity must be necessary; otherwise a cause must again be sought outside it for the fact that it exists rather than does not exist, which is contrary to the hypothesis. This entity is the ultimate reason for things, and is usually called by the one word 'God'.

4. There is, therefore, a cause for the prevalence of existence over non-existence; or, *the necessary being is existence-creating.*[a]

5. But the cause which brings it about that something exists, or that possibility demands existence, also brings it about that everything possible has an urge to existence; for a reason for restricting this to certain possible things in the universe cannot be found.

6. So it can be said that *everything possible demands existence,*[b] inasmuch as it is founded on a necessary being which actually exists, and without which there is no way by which something possible may arrive at actuality.

7. But it does not follow from this that all possibles exist; though this would follow if all possibles were compossible.

8. But since some things are incompatible with others, it follows that certain possibles do not arrive at existence;

again, some things are incompatible with others, not only with respect to the same time, but also universally, since future events are involved in present ones.

9. Meanwhile, from the conflict of all possibles demanding existence this at any rate follows, that there exists that series of things through which the greatest amount exists, or, the greatest of all possible series.

10. This series alone is determinate, as among lines the straight line is determinate, among angles the right angle, and among figures the most capacious, namely the circle or sphere. And just as we see liquids spontaneously collect in spherical drops, so in the nature of the universe the most capacious series exists.

11. There exists, therefore, that which is the most perfect, since *perfection* is simply quantity of reality.

12. Further, perfection is not to be located in matter alone, that is, in something filling time and space, whose quantity would in any way have been the same; rather, it is to be located in form or variety.

13. So it follows that matter is not everywhere alike, but is rendered dissimilar by its forms; otherwise it would not obtain as much variety as it can. I pass over what I have shown elsewhere, that otherwise no diverse phenomena will arise.

14. It follows also that that series has prevailed through which there arises the greatest amount of what is distinctly thinkable.

15. Distinct cogitability gives order to a thing and beauty to a thinker. For order is simply a distinctive relation of several things; confusion is when several things are present, but there is no way of distinguishing one from another.

16. This removes atoms, and in general those bodies in which there is no reason for distinguishing one part from another.

17. It also follows in general that the world is a cosmos, full of ornament; that is, that it is made in such a way that it gives the greatest satisfaction to an intelligent being.

18. An intelligent being's *pleasure* is simply the perception of beauty, order and perfection. All pain contains something disordered, though only relative to the percipient; for in the absolute sense all things are ordered.

19. So when something in the series of things displeases us, that arises from a defect of our understanding. For it is not possible that every mind should understand everything distinctly; and to those who observe only some parts rather than others, the harmony in the whole cannot appear.

20. The consequence of this is that in the universe, justice also is observed; for *justice* is simply order or perfection with respect to minds.

21. And the greatest account is taken of minds, since through them there arises the greatest variety in the smallest space.

22. It can also be said that minds are the primary unities of the world and are the closest likenesses of the first Being, for they distinctly perceive necessary truths, that is, the reasons which moved the first Being, and must have formed the universe.

23. Further, the first cause is of the highest *goodness*, for whilst it produces as much perfection as possible in things, at the same time it bestows on minds as much pleasure as possible, since *pleasure* consists in the perception of perfection.

24. So much so, that evils themselves serve a greater good, and the fact that pains are found in minds is necessary if they are to reach greater pleasures.

New Essays on the Human Understanding (c. 1704)

PREFACE

Since the *Essay on the Human Understanding*, by a famous Englishman,[1] is one of the finest and most highly esteemed works of our time, I have resolved to make some remarks on it, because, having long meditated on the same subject and on the greater part of the matters therein considered, I thought this would be a good opportunity for publishing something under the title of *New Essays on the Human Understanding*, and for securing a favourable reception for my reflections by putting them in such good company. I further thought that I might profit by someone else's labour, not only to diminish my own (since in fact it is less trouble to follow the thread of a good author than to work at everything afresh), but also to add something to what he has given us, which is always an easier task than making a start; for I think I have removed certain difficulties which he had left entirely on one side. Thus his reputation is of advantage to me; and since I am moreover inclined to do justice to him, and am very far from wishing to lessen the high opinion commonly entertained of his work, I shall increase his reputation if my approval has any weight. It is true that I am

[1] John Locke (1632–1704). When his *Essay* was published in 1690 Leibniz sent him some short papers in criticism. Locke seems to have paid little attention to these. In 1700, Coste's translation of the *Essay* into French was published, and Leibniz set himself to write the *New Essays*, an elaborate work in which he examines and criticises Locke's doctrines in a running commentary. He delayed publication, however, both because of Locke's death in 1704, and because a new and improved edition of the French translation was promised. The *New Essays* were not published until 1765.

often of another opinion from him, but, far from denying the merit of famous writers, we bear witness to it by showing wherein and wherefore we differ from them, when we deem it necessary to prevent their authority from prevailing against reason in certain important points; besides the fact that, in convincing such excellent men, we make the truth more acceptable, and it is to be supposed that it is chiefly for truth's sake that they are labouring.

In fact, although the author of the *Essay* says a thousand fine things of which I approve, our systems are very different. His bears more relation to Aristotle, mine to Plato; although we both of us depart in many things from the doctrine of these two ancient philosophers. He is more popular, while I am sometimes compelled to be a little more *acroamatic* and abstract, which is not an advantage to me, especially when writing in a living language. But I think that by making two characters speak, of whom one expounds the views derived from our author's *Essay*,[1] while the other gives my observations, I shall show the relation between us in a way that will be more to the reader's taste than dry remarks, the reading of which would have to be constantly interrupted by the necessity of referring to his book in order to understand mine. Nevertheless it will be well sometimes to compare our writings and to judge of his opinions by his own work only, although I have as a rule retained his expressions. It is true that the necessity of having to follow the thread of another person's argument in making my remarks has meant that I have been unable to think of achieving the graces of which the dialogue form is capable: but I hope the matter will make up for this defect in the manner.

---

[1] Philalethes gives Locke's views, and Theophilus those of Leibniz. The words of Philalethes are sometimes obviously a translation of Locke's own words, sometimes a paraphrase or summary of a particular passage in Locke, and sometimes a free re-statement of Locke's doctrine. Where his words are obviously meant to be a translation, instead of retranslating them I have printed Locke's own words in italics, as it may be of advantage to the reader to see at a glance what is the original Locke, and what is Leibniz's summary or re-statement. In some places of course it is difficult to tell whether to treat the French as translation or as paraphrase; but as a general rule it is clear enough.

Our differences are on subjects of some importance. The question at issue is whether the soul itself is entirely void, like a tablet whereon nothing has yet been written (*tabula rasa*), as is the view of Aristotle and the author of the essay,[a] and everything marked on it comes solely from the senses and from experience, or whether the soul contains originally the principles of various notions and doctrines, which external objects simply recall from time to time, as is my view and that of Plato, and even of the Schoolmen, and of all those who attribute this meaning to the passage from St. Paul (Rom. ii. 15), where he says that the law of God is writ in men's hearts. The Stoics call these principles *prolepses*,[b] that is to say assumptions which are fundamental or taken as agreed in advance. The mathematicians call them *common notions*[c] (κοιναὶ ἔννοιαι). Modern philosophers give them other fine names, and Julius Scaliger[d] in particular called them *semina aeternitatis*[1] and again *zopyra*, meaning to say living fires, flashes of light, hidden within us, but caused to appear by the contact of the senses, like the sparks which the shock of the flint strikes from the steel. And it is not an unreasonable belief that these flashes are a sign of something divine and eternal, which makes its appearance above all in necessary truths. From this arises another question, whether all truths depend on experience, that is to say on induction and on instances, or whether there are some which have another basis also. For if certain events can be foreseen before we have made any trial of them, it is clear that we contribute in those cases something of our own. The senses, although they are necessary for all our actual knowledge, are not sufficient to give us the whole of it, since the senses never give anything but instances, that is to say particular or individual truths. Now all the instances which confirm a general truth, however numerous they may be, are not sufficient to establish the universal necessity of this same truth, for it does not follow that what happened before will happen in the same way again. For example, the Greeks and the Romans, and all the other peoples of the earth known to the ancients, always observed that before the passage of twenty-four hours day

[1] 'seeds of eternity'.

changes to night and night to day. But they would have been wrong if they had believed that the same rule holds good everywhere, for since that time the contrary has been experienced during a visit to Nova Zembla. And any one who believed that in our zone at least this is a necessary and eternal truth which will last for ever, would likewise be wrong, since we must hold that the earth and even the sun do not exist of necessity, and that there may perhaps come a time when that beautiful star and its whole system will exist no longer, at least in its present form. From which it appears that necessary truths, such as we find in pure mathematics, and particularly in arithmetic and geometry, must have principles whose proof does not depend on instances, nor consequently on the testimony of the senses, although without the senses it would never have occurred to us to think of them. This is a distinction that should be carefully noted; and it is one which Euclid understood so well that he often proves by reason what is evident enough through experience and sensible images. Logic also, together with metaphysics and morals, the one of which forms natural theology and the other natural jurisprudence, are full of such truths; and consequently proof of them can only arise from inner principles, which are called innate. It is true that we must not imagine that we can read in the soul these eternal laws of reason as in an open book, as the edict of the praetor can be read in his *album* without trouble or deep scrutiny.[e] But it is enough that we can find them in ourselves by dint of attention, opportunities for which are afforded by the senses. The success of experiments serves also as a confirmation of reason, more or less as verifications serve in arithmetic to help us to avoid erroneous calculation when the reasoning is long. It is in this also that the knowledge of men differs from that of the brutes: the latter are purely empirical, and guide themselves solely by particular instances; for, as far as we can judge, they never go so far as to form necessary propositions; whereas men are capable of the demonstrative sciences. This also is why the faculty the brutes have of making *sequences* of ideas is something inferior to the reason which is in man. The sequences of the brutes are just like those of the pure empiricists who claim that what has happened sometimes will happen again in a case where what strikes them is similar, without being capable of determining whether the same reasons hold good. It is because of this that it is so easy for men to catch animals, and so easy for pure empiricists to make mistakes. And people whom age and experience has rendered skilful are not exempt from this when they rely too much on their past experience, as some have done in civil and military affairs; they do not pay sufficient attention to the fact that the world changes, and that men become more skilful by discovering countless new contrivances, whereas the stags and hares of today are no more cunning than those of yesterday. The sequences of the brutes are but a shadow of reasoning, that is to say, they are but connexions of imagination, transitions from one image to another; for in a fresh experience, which appears like the preceding one, there is the expectation that what was hitherto joined thereto will occur again, as though the things were connected in fact, because their images are connected in the memory. It is true that reason also teaches us to expect in the ordinary course of events to see occur in the future what conforms to a long experience of the past, but it is not therefore a necessary and infallible truth, and we may cease to be successful when we least expect it, when the reasons which have maintained it change. This is why the wisest people do not rely on it to the extent of not trying to discover, if it is possible, something of the reason of what happens, so as to judge when exceptions must be made. For reason alone is capable of setting up rules which are certain, and of supplying what is lacking to those which are not certain, by inserting the exceptions, and in short of finding connexions which are certain in the force of necessary consequences. This often provides the means of foreseeing the event, without its being necessary to experience the sensible connexions between images which is all that the brutes can do; so that to vindicate the existence within us of the principles of necessary truths is also to distinguish man from the brutes.

Perhaps our gifted author will not entirely dissociate himself from my opinion. For after having devoted the

whole of his first book to the rejection of innate ideas, understood in a certain sense, he yet admits in the beginning of the
second and in what follows that ideas whose origin is not in
sensation arise from reflexion. Now reflexion is nothing but
an attention to what is in us, and the senses do not give us
what we already bring with us. This being so, can we deny
that there is a great deal that is innate in our mind, since we
are innate, so to speak, to ourselves, and since there is in
ourselves being, unity, substance, duration, change, activity, perception, pleasure, and a thousand other objects
of our intellectual ideas? And since these objects are immediate to our understanding and are always present (although they cannot always be apperceived on account of our
distractions and our needs), why be surprised that we say that
these ideas, and everything which depends on them, are
innate in us? This is why I have taken as an illustration a
block of veined marble, rather than a wholly uniform block
or blank tablets, that is to say what is called *tabula rasa* in
the language of the philosophers. For if the soul were like
these blank tablets, truths would be in us in the same way as
the figure of Hercules is in a block of marble, when the marble
is completely indifferent whether it receives this or some other
figure. But if there were veins in the stone which marked
out the figure of Hercules rather than other figures, this
stone would be more determined thereto, and Hercules
would be as it were in some manner innate in it, although
labour would be needed to uncover those veins, and to clear
them by polishing, and by cutting away what prevents them
from appearing. It is in this way that ideas and truths are
innate in us, like natural inclinations and dispositions, natural
habits or potentialities, and not like activities, although these
potentialities are always accompanied by some activities which
correspond to them, though they are often imperceptible.

It seems that our gifted author claims that there is in us
nothing *potential*, nor even anything which we do not always
actually apperceive; but he cannot take this quite strictly,
otherwise his opinion would be too paradoxical, since acquired
habits also and the contents of our memory are not always
apperceived, and do not even always come to our aid when

needed, although we often easily recall them to mind on some trivial occasion which reminds us of them, in the same way as we only need the beginning of a song to make us remember the rest. Moreover he limits his doctrine in other places by saying that there is nothing in us which we have not at least previously apperceived. But besides the fact that nobody can guarantee by reason alone how far our past apperceptions which may have been forgotten may have gone, especially in view of the Platonic doctrine of reminiscence, which, mythical though it is, is not incompatible, in part at least, with bare reason: besides this, I say, why should it be necessary that everything should be acquired by us by apperceptions of external things, and nothing be able to be unearthed in ourselves? Is our soul of itself alone so empty that apart from images borrowed from without it is nothing? This is not, I am convinced, an opinion that our judicious author could approve. And where are there to be found tablets which have not in themselves a certain amount of variety? We shall never see a perfectly level and uniform surface. Why, therefore, should we not also be able to provide some sort of thought from deep within ourselves, when we are willing to delve there? Thus I am led to believe that fundamentally his opinion on this point does not differ from mine, or rather from the common opinion, inasmuch as he recognises two sources of our knowledge, the senses and reflexion.

I am not sure that it will be so easy to reconcile him with us and with the Cartesians when he maintains that the mind does not always think, and in particular that it is without perception during dreamless sleep; and when he protests that since bodies can exist without motion, souls also might well exist without thought. But here I answer somewhat differently from what is usual; for I maintain that, naturally, a substance cannot exist without activity, and that there never even exists a body without motion. Experience is already in my favour on this point, and to be persuaded of it it is only necessary to consult the illustrious Mr. Boyle's book[1] against absolute rest. But I believe that reason also supports it,

[1] *Of Absolute Rest in Bodies.* Robert Boyle (1627–91) was a famous chemist and physicist.

and this is one of the proofs which I use for refuting the theory of atoms.

Besides, there are a thousand signs which make us think that there are at all times an infinite number of *perceptions* in us, though without apperception and without reflexion; that is to say changes in the soul itself which we do not apperceive because their impressions are either too small and too numerous, or too unified, so that they have nothing sufficiently distinctive in themselves, though in combination with others they do not fail to have their effect and to make themselves felt, at least confusedly, in the mass. It is thus that habituation causes us not to notice the motion of a mill or waterfall, after we have lived near by for some time. It is not that the motion does not continue to affect our organs, and that something does not still take place in the soul to correspond to it, on account of the harmony of the soul and the body; it is that these impressions which are in the soul and in the body, when they are devoid of the attractions of novelty, are not strong enough to attract our attention and memory, when these are attached to more absorbing objects. For all attention demands some memory, and often when we are not admonished, so to speak, and warned to pay attention to certain of our present perceptions, we let them pass without reflexion and even without noticing them; but if someone draws attention to them immediately afterwards, and makes us notice, for example, some sound that has just been heard, we remember it, and we apperceive that we did have some sensation of it at the time. Thus there were perceptions which we did not immediately apperceive, apperception in this case only arising through our attention having been aroused after an interval, however small. In order the better to form an opinion of these minute perceptions which we cannot distinguish in the crowd, I generally make use of¹ the example of the roar or noise which strikes us when we are on the shore. To hear this noise as we do, we must surely hear the parts of which the whole is made up, that is to say the noises of each wave, although each of these little noises only makes itself heard in the confused combination of all the others together, that is to say in the actual roar, and would not be noticed if the wave which makes it were the only one. For it is necessary that we should be slightly affected by the motion of this wave, and that we should have some perception of each of these noises, however small they may be; otherwise we should not have the perception of a hundred thousand waves, since a hundred thousand nothings cannot make a something. We never sleep so soundly but that we have some feeble and confused sensation, and we should never be awakened by the loudest noise in the world, if we had not some perception of its beginning, small as it is; just as we should never break a rope by the greatest exertion in the world, if it were not to some small extent strained and stretched by lesser efforts, although the slight extension they produce is not apparent.

These minute perceptions are therefore more efficacious in their consequences than we think. They it is that constitute that indefinable something, those tastes, those images of the qualities of the senses, clear in the mass but confused in the parts, those impressions which surrounding bodies make on us, which include the infinite, that link which connects every being with all the rest of the universe. It may even be said that as a result of these minute perceptions the present is big with the future and laden with the past, that everything is in league together (σύμπνοια πάντα, as Hippocrates said), and that in the smallest substance eyes as piercing as those of God could read the whole sequence of things in the universe:

Quae sint, quae fuerint, quae mox futura trahantur.[1]

These insensible perceptions are also the signs and constituents of personal identity: the individual is characterised by the traces or expressions of his previous states which these perceptions preserve by connecting them with his present state, and which can be known by a superior spirit, even though the individual himself may not be conscious of them, that is to say though he may no longer expressly recollect them. But they (these perceptions, I mean) also provide the

[1] 'The things that are, the things that have been, and those that are presently to come.' (Cf. Virgil, *Georgics*, IV, 393.)

means of rediscovering this recollection at need through periodic developments which may one day occur. This is why, because of them, death can only be a sleep, and cannot even go on being that, since, in animals, the perceptions only cease to be sufficiently distinguished and become reduced to a state of confusion which suspends apperception, but which cannot last for ever—not to speak here of man, who must in this have great privileges in order to retain his personality.

It is, moreover, these insensible perceptions which afford the explanation of that wonderful pre-established harmony of soul and body, and indeed of all monads or simple substances, which takes the place of the untenable theory of the influence of the one on the other, and which in the opinion of the author of the greatest of dictionaries[1] exalts the grandeur of the Divine perfections beyond what has ever been conceived. After this I should be adding but little if I said that it is these minute perceptions which *determine* us in many experiences without our giving them a thought, and which deceive the common herd by giving the appearance of an *indifference of equilibrium*, as if we were entirely indifferent whether, for example, we turned to the right or to the left. Nor is it necessary that I should point out here, as I have done in the book itself,[g] that they cause that *uneasiness* which, on my showing, consists in something which differs from pain only as the small from the great, and which yet often creates our desire and even our pleasure, giving it a kind of savour. It is moreover, these insensible parts of our sensible perceptions which bring it about that there is a relation between those perceptions of colour, heat, and other sensible qualities and the motions in the bodies which correspond to them; whereas the Cartesians and our author, penetrating though he is, conceive of the perceptions which we have of these qualities as being arbitrary, that is to say, as if God had given them to the soul at his good pleasure without any regard to any essential relation between perceptions and their

---

[1] i.e. Bayle. The reference is to the article 'Rorarius' in Bayle's *Dictionary* (cf. *Monadology*, par. 16). It should perhaps be added that in making this remark, Bayle was not being complimentary. (Cf. to Clarke, 5.87.)

objects: an opinion which surprises me, and which seems to me hardly worthy of the wisdom of the Author of things, who does nothing without harmony and without reason.

In a word, the *insensible perception* is of as much use in pneumatics[1] as is the insensible corpuscle in physics; and it is equally unreasonable to reject the one or the other on the pretext that it is beyond the reach of our senses. Nothing takes place all at once, and it is one of my most important and best verified maxims that *nature makes no leaps*. This I called the *law of continuity* when I spoke of it in the first *News of the Republic of Letters*;[h] and the use of this law in physics is very considerable: it means that the passage from the small to the great and back again always takes place through that which is intermediate, both in degrees and in parts, and that a motion never arises immediately from rest, nor is reduced to it except through a smaller motion, just as we never manage to traverse any given line or length without first traversing a shorter line—although till now those who have exhibited the laws of motion have not observed this law, believing as they did that a body can receive in a moment a motion contrary to its preceding one.[j] All this brings us to the conclusion that *noticeable perceptions* come by degrees from those which are too small to be noticed. To think otherwise is to have but little knowledge of the immensely subtle composition of things, which always and everywhere include an actual infinity.

I have also noted that, by virtue of insensible variations, two individual things can never be perfectly alike, and that they must always differ more than *numero*. This at once puts out of court the blank tablets of the soul, a soul without thought, a substance without action, the void in space, atoms and even particles not actually divided in matter, absolute rest, complete uniformity in one part of time, place, or matter, the perfect globes of the second element which are the offspring of the original perfect cubes,[2] and a thousand other fictions of the philosophers—fictions arising from their incomplete notions, and not admitted by the nature of things,

[1] An early name for the philosophy of mind or spirit.
[2] The reference is to the vortex theory of Descartes.

but merely allowed to pass because of our ignorance and of the slight attention we pay to the insensible; they can only be made tolerable by being limited to abstractions made by the mind, which protests that it is not denying any of the things which it considers irrelevant to the present inquiry but only setting them on one side. Otherwise, if we thought in good earnest that the things we do not apperceive are not there in the soul or in the body, we should fail in philosophy as in politics, by neglecting τὸ μικρόν,[1] insensible progressions; whereas an abstraction is not an error, provided we know that what we are ignoring is really there. This is the use made of abstractions by mathematicians when they speak of the perfect lines they ask us to consider, and of uniform motions and other regular effects, although *matter* (that is to say the mixture of the effects of the surrounding infinite) is always providing some exception. We proceed in this way so as to distinguish the various considerations from one another, and to reduce the effects to their reasons as far as is possible to us, and to foresee some consequences; for the more careful we are to neglect no consideration which we can regulate, the more does practice correspond to theory. But it belongs to the Supreme Reason, which misses nothing, distinctly to understand the whole infinite, and to see all the reasons and all the consequences. All that we can do in regard to infinities is to know them confusedly, and at least to have distinct knowledge that they exist. Otherwise we should have a very poor recognition of the beauty and grandeur of the universe; we should also be unable to have a sound physics to explain the nature of bodies in general, and still less a sound pneumatics to include the knowledge of God, of souls, and of simple substances in general.

This knowledge of insensible perceptions serves also to explain why and how two souls, whether human or of some other identical species, never come perfectly alike from the Creator's hands, but each has always from the beginning its own relation to the point of view it will have in the universe. But this follows from what I pointed out previously about two individuals, namely that their *difference* is always more

[1] *lit.* 'the small'; i.e. by neglecting very small items.

than a *numerical* one. There is also another important point
on which I am obliged to differ not only from the opinions
of our author, but also from those of the greater part of the
moderns; that is, that like most of the ancients I hold that all
superhuman beings, all souls, all simple created substances,
are always joined to a body, and that there never are entirely
separate souls[k]. I have *a priori* reasons for this, but there will be
found to be this advantage also in my doctrine that it solves all
the philosophical difficulties about the state of souls, their
perpetual conservation, their immortality, and their operation: the difference between one state of the soul and another
is never and has never been anything other than that between the more and the less sensible, the more and the less
perfect, or the other way round, and so the past or future
state of the soul is as explicable as its present state. The
smallest reflexion suffices to show that this is reasonable, and
that a leap from one state to another infinitely different
state could not be natural. I am surprised that the schools
should have causelessly given up natural explanations, and
should have been ready deliberately to plunge into very great
difficulties and thus to provide occasion for the apparent
triumphs of free-thinkers; all of whose reasons collapse at
once on this explanation of things, in which there is no more
difficulty in conceiving the conservation of souls (or rather
on my view of the animal) than there is in the change from
the caterpillar into the butterfly, and in the conservation of
thought during sleep—sleep to which Jesus Christ with divine
propriety likened death. I have already said that no sleep can
last for ever, and it will have least duration, or almost none
at all, in the case of rational souls, which are always destined
to retain the personality which has been given to them in the
City of God, and which consequently have memory, so that
they may be more susceptible of punishments and rewards.
I add further that in general no derangement of its visible
organs is capable of carrying things to the point of complete
confusion in the animal or of destroying all its organs, and of
depriving the soul of the whole of its organic body and of the
ineffaceable remains of all its preceding traces. But the ease
with which the ancient doctrine that angels have subtle

bodies[1] has been abandoned (a doctrine that has been confounded with the corporeality of the angels themselves), the introduction of supposed intelligences without bodies among created things (a view that has been much strengthened by Aristotle's doctrine[1] that such intelligences make the heavens revolve), and finally the mistaken opinion that has existed that the conservation of the souls of the brutes cannot be maintained without falling into metempsychosis and transferring them from body to body, and the perplexity some have felt through not knowing what to do with them—all these things have, in my opinion, led to the neglect of the natural way of explaining the conservation of the soul. This has done much injury to natural religion, and has caused some people to believe that our immortality was but a miraculous grace of God. Our illustrious author also speaks of it with some doubt, as I shall subsequently point out. But it would be well if all those who are of this opinion had spoken of it as wisely and sincerely as he; for it is to be feared that some who speak of immortality through grace[m] merely do so to preserve appearances, and at bottom are not very far from those Averroists and certain pernicious Quietists, who picture an absorption and reunion of the soul with the ocean of Divinity, a notion whose impossibility is perhaps shown up by my system alone.

It appears, moreover, that we differ also in regard to matter, in that the author thinks that the existence of a void is necessary to motion, because he believes that the small parts of matter are rigid.[2] I admit that if matter were composed of such parts, motion in a plenum would be impossible, just as if a room were filled with quantities of small pebbles without there being in it the least empty space. But

---

[1] i.e. made of some more rarefied stuff than ordinary matter. Locke uses the word in this connexion (to represent the Latin *subtilis*) in the correspondence with the Bishop of Worcester.

[2] Locke's own term is *solid*, and *solidity*. He says: *That which hinders the approach of two bodies, when they are moved one towards another, I call solidity . . . but if any one think it better to call it impenetrability, he has my consent* [*Essay*, Bk. II, ch. iv, § 1]. But I do not think that Leibniz's word here (*roide*) can properly be translated by *solid*. The word *hard* is rejected by Locke on the ground that a hard body is no more solid than a soft one.

I do not admit this supposition, for which, moreover, there does not appear to be any reason, although our gifted author goes so far as to hold that rigidity or cohesion of parts is the essence of body. Space should rather be conceived of as full of a matter originally fluid, susceptible of any division, and submitted indeed actually to divisions and subdivisions *ad infinitum*; with this difference, however, that it is divisible and divided unequally in different places on account of motions in it which are more or less harmonious. This means that it has throughout a degree of rigidity as well as of fluidity, and that there does not exist any body which is absolutely hard or absolutely fluid; that is to say that it is impossible to find in any body any atom whose hardness is unsurpassable, or any mass which is entirely indifferent to division. Besides, the order of nature, and particularly the law of continuity, make both equally impossible.

I have also shown that *cohesion*, which was not of itself the result of impulse or of motion,[n] would cause a *traction*, strictly speaking. For if there were a body originally rigid, an Epicurean atom, for example, which contained a part projecting from it in the form of a hook (since we may imagine atoms of all kinds of shapes), this hook when impelled would draw with it the rest of the atom, that is to say the part which was not being impelled, and which did not fall in the line of impulse. Our gifted author, however, is himself opposed to these philosophic tractions, such as were formerly attributed to nature's abhorrence of a vacuum, and reduces them to *impulses*, maintaining in agreement with the moderns that one part of matter can only operate immediately on another by impelling it by contact; wherein I think they are right, because otherwise the operation is in no way intelligible.

I must not, however, conceal the fact that I have observed a kind of recantation on this point on the part of our excellent author, whose modesty and sincerity in this I cannot refrain from praising, just as on other occasions I have admired his penetrating insight. It is in the reply to the second letter of the late Bishop of Worcester, printed in 1699, page 408, where, in order to justify the view he had upheld against this learned prelate, namely that matter was capable of thought, he says among other things: '*It is true, I say "that bodies operate by impulse, and nothing else"* (Essay, *Bk.* II, *ch.* viii, § 11). *And so I thought when I writ it, and can yet conceive no other way of their operation. But I am since convinced by the judicious Mr. Newton's incomparable book, that it is too bold a presumption to limit God's power, in this point, by my narrow conceptions. The gravitation of matter towards matter, by ways inconceivable to me, is not only a demonstration that God can, if he pleases, put into bodies powers and ways of operation, above what can be derived from our idea of body or can be explained by what we know of matter, but also an unquestionable and everywhere visible instance, that he has done so. And therefore in the next edition of my book I shall take care to have that passage rectified.*'[1] I find that in the French translation of this book, which was no doubt taken from the latest editions, this § 11 reads thus: 'It is evident, *at least as far as we can conceive it,*[2] that bodies act upon one another by impulse and not otherwise; for it is impossible for us to understand that a body can act upon that which it does not touch, which is as much as to imagine that it can act where it is not.'[3]

I cannot but praise this modest piety on the part of our famous author, who recognises that God can do things beyond what we can understand, and thus that there may be inconceivable mysteries in the articles of faith: but I should not wish us to be obliged to have recourse to miracles in the ordinary course of nature, and to allow the existence of powers and operations which are absolutely inexplicable. Otherwise we should be granting too much licence to bad philosophers on the strength of what God can do. If we admit these *centripetal powers* or *immediate attractions* from a distance without its being possible to make them intelligible,[o] I see nothing to prevent our Scholastics from saying that everything is done simply through their 'faculties' and from upholding their 'intentional species', which go from objects up to us, and find a way of entering our souls. If this is true:

---

[1] Italics indicate Locke's own exact words.

[2] These italics are Leibniz's.

[3] In the English edition § 11 runs as follows: *The next thing to be considered is, how bodies produce ideas in us; and that is manifestly by impulse, the only way which we can conceive bodies to operate in.*

Omnia jam fient, fieri quae posse negabam.[1]

So that it seems to me that our author, judicious though he is, is in this going rather too much from one extreme to the other. He makes difficulties about the operations of *souls*, when it is only a question of admitting what is not *sensible*, and here we have him granting to bodies what is not even *intelligible*, in allowing them powers and activities beyond everything which, in my opinion, a created mind can do and understand, since he grants them attraction, even at great distance and without limiting himself to any stated sphere of activity, and that in order to uphold a view which seems no less inexplicable, to wit, the possibility of thinking in matter in the natural order.

The question he is discussing with the celebrated prelate, who had attacked him, is *whether matter can think*, and as this is an important point, even for the present work, I cannot avoid going into the subject a little and taking some account of their dispute. I will set forth the substance of it as regards this subject, and will take the liberty of saying what I think about it. The late Bishop of Worcester, being apprehensive, though in my opinion without great cause, that our author's doctrine of ideas was liable to some abuses prejudicial to the Christian faith, undertook to examine certain parts of it in his vindication of the doctrine of the Trinity. He first gives this excellent author his due by recognising that he holds the existence of the mind as certain as that of the body, although one of these substances is as little known as the other; he then asks (page 241 seq.) how reflexion could possibly assure us of the existence of mind, if God can give matter the faculty of thinking (as our author believes, Bk. IV, ch. iii), since in this case the way of ideas, which is required to discriminate between the properties of soul and of body, would become useless; whereas it was said in Book II of the *Essay on the Human Understanding* (ch. xxiii, §§ 15, 27, 28), that the operations of the soul provide us with the idea of mind, and the understanding together with the

[1] 'Everything will now happen which I declared to be impossible.' (Ovid, *Tristia*, Book I, Elegy 8, v. 7.)

will makes this idea as intelligible to us as the nature of body is made intelligible to us by solidity and impulse. This is how our author replies in his first letter (page 65 seq.): '*I think it may be proved from my principles, and I think I have done it, that there is a spiritual substance in us. . . . We experiment in ourselves thinking. The idea of this action, or mode of thinking, is inconsistent with the idea of self-subsistence, and therefore has a necessary connexion with a support or subject of inhesion: the idea of that support is what we call substance . . . for the general idea of substance being the same everywhere, the modification of thinking, or the power of thinking, joined to it, makes it a spirit, without considering what other modifications it has, as whether it has the modification of solidity or not. As, on the other side, substance that has the modification of solidity, is matter, whether it has the modification of thinking or not. And therefore if your lordship means by a spiritual an immaterial substance, I grant I have not proved, nor upon my principles can it be proved, (your lordship meaning, as I think you do, demonstratively proved) that there is an immaterial substance in us that thinks. Though I presume, what I have said about the supposition of a system of matter thinking* (Bk. IV, ch. x, § 16) *(which there demonstrates that God is immaterial) will prove it in the highest degree probable, that the thinking substance in us is immaterial. . . .* Yet, *I have shown* [adds the author, page 68] *that all the great ends of religion and morality are secured barely by the immortality of the soul, without a necessary supposition that the soul is immaterial.*

In his reply to this letter the learned bishop, to show that our author was of another opinion when he wrote the second book of his *Essay*, cites from it on page 51 this passage (taken from the same book, chapter xxiii, § 15), where it is said that *by the simple ideas we have taken from our own minds we are able to frame the complex idea of an immaterial spirit. And thus by putting together the ideas of thinking, perceiving, liberty, and power of moving themselves, and other things, we have as clear a perception and notion of immaterial substances as we have of material.* He further cites other passages to show that the author opposed mind to body. He says (page 54) that the ends of religion and morality are best secured by proving that the soul is immortal by its very nature, that is to say immaterial. He further adduces (page 70) this passage, that *all our ideas of the several sorts of substances are nothing but collections of simple ideas*; and that thus our author believed that the idea of thinking and willing gave a different substance from that given by the idea of solidity and impulse; and (§ 17) regards these ideas as constituting body as opposed to mind.

The Bishop of Worcester might have added that from the fact that the *general idea* of substance is in body and in mind, it does not follow that their *differences* are *modifications* of one and the same thing, as our author has just said in the passage I quoted from his first letter. It is necessary to distinguish properly between modifications and attributes. The faculties of having perception and of acting, extension, and solidity, are attributes, or perpetual and principal predicates; but thinking, impetus, shapes, and motions are modifications of these attributes. Further, we ought to distinguish between *physical* (or rather real) *genus*, and *logical* or ideal *genus*. Things which are of the same *physical* kind or which are *homogeneous*, are of the same matter so to speak, and can often be changed one into another by changing their modifications, like circles and squares. But two *heterogeneous* things may have a common logical genus, and then their *differences* are not simple accidental modifications of one self-same subject or of one self-same metaphysical or physical matter. Thus time and space are quite heterogeneous things, and we should be wrong to imagine some kind of common real subject which had only continuous quantity in general and whose modifications resulted in time or space. However, their common logical genus is continuous quantity.ᴾ People may laugh at these philosophical distinctions between two genera, the one only logical, the other real, and between two matters, one physical —that of bodies—the other only metaphysical or general, as if someone said that two parts of space are of the same matter or that two hours are also of the same matter as one another. Yet these distinctions are not a mere matter of terms, but are in the things themselves; and they seem to be particularly relevant here, where their confusion has given rise to a false conclusion. These two genera have a common notion, and the notion of real genus is common to both matters, so that their genealogy would be as follows:

Genus	*Logical* merely, the variations consisting of simple *differences*.		
	Real, whose differences are modifications, that is to say *matter*.	*Metaphysical* merely, in which there is homogeneity.	
		Physical, in which there is a solid homogeneous mass.	

I have not seen our author's second letter to the bishop, and the answer the latter makes to it hardly touches the point about the thinking of matter. But *our author's reply* to this second answer comes back to it. 'God [he says, nearly in these words, page 397], superadds to the essence of matter what qualities and perfections he pleases; to some parts simple motion, to plants vegetation, and to animals sense. Those who agree with me so far exclaim against me when I go a step further and say, *God may give to matter thought, reason, and volition*, as if that would destroy the essence of matter. To make good this assertion they say that thought and reason are not included in the essence of matter: which proves nothing, for motion and life are just as little included in it. They also urge that we cannot conceive how matter can think: but our conception is not the measure of God's omnipotency.' After this he quotes the example of the attraction of matter, page 399 and particularly page 408, where he speaks of the gravitation of matter towards matter, attributed to Mr. Newton (in the words I have quoted above), admitting that we cannot conceive how the attraction takes place. This, in effect, is going back to qualities which are occult,q or, what is more, inexplicable. He adds (page 401) that nothing is more likely to assist the sceptics than to deny what we do not understand, and (page 402) that we cannot conceive even how the soul thinks. He wants to maintain (page 403) that, since both substances, material and immaterial, can be conceived in their bare essence without any activity, it rests with God to give to the one or to the other the power of thinking. And he wants to take advantage of the admission of his opponent, who had granted sense in brutes, but would not grant them any immaterial substance. He claims that liberty and self-consciousness (page 408) and the power of making abstractions (page 409) can be given to matter, not as matter, but as enriched by a divine power. Finally he reports (page 434) the observation of a traveller as important and judicious as M. de La Loubère[r] that the pagans of the East know of the immortality of the soul without being able to understand its immateriality.

With regard to all this I may say, before coming to the explanation of my opinion, that it is certain that matter is as little capable of mechanically producing sensation as of producing reason, as our author agrees; that I fully recognise that it is not allowable to deny what we do not understand, but I add that we have the right to deny (in the order of nature at least) what is absolutely unintelligible and inexplicable. I maintain also that substances, whether material or immaterial, cannot be conceived in their bare essence without any activity, activity being of the essence of substance in general; and finally that the conception of created beings is not the measure of God's power, but that their conceptivity, or power of conceiving, is the measure of the power of nature; for everything which conforms with the order of nature can be conceived or understood by some created being.

Those who understand my system will see that I cannot agree altogether with either of these excellent authors; their dispute, however, is very instructive. Let me explain myself distinctly: it must above all things be considered that the modifications which can attach to a subject naturally or without miracle, must come to it from the limitations or variations of a real genus, or of an original nature which is constant and absolute. This is how we distinguish in philosophy the modes of an absolute being from that being itself; for instance we know that size, shape, and motion are manifestly limitations and variations of corporeal nature. For it is clear how a limitation of extension gives figures, and that the change which therein takes place is nothing but motion. And every time we find some quality in a subject, we ought to think that, if we understood the nature of this subject and of this quality, we should conceive how this quality could result from it. Thus, in the order of nature (miracles apart) God does not arbitrarily give to substances such and such qualities indifferently, and he never gives them any but those which are natural to them, that is to say qualities which can be derived from their nature as explicable modifications. Thus we see that matter does not naturally have the attraction mentioned above, and does not of itself go in a curve, because it is not possible to conceive how this takes place, that is to say, to explain it mechanically, whereas what is natural ought to be able to be rendered distinctly conceivable, if we were admitted into the secrets of things. This distinction between what is natural and explicable and what is inexplicable and miraculous removes all the difficulties: in rejecting it we should be upholding something worse than occult qualities, and in so doing we should be renouncing philosophy and reason, and throwing open sanctuaries for ignorance[s] and idleness, by a stupid system which admits not only that there are qualities which we do not understand (of which there are only too many), but also that there are some which the greatest mind, even if God provided him with every possible advantage, could not understand—that is to say they would be either miraculous or without rhyme or reason. It would indeed be without rhyme or reason that God should perform miracles in the ordinary course; so that this do-nothing hypothesis would destroy equally our philosophy which searches for reasons, and the Divine wisdom which provides them.

We can now turn to the question of thinking. It is certain that our author recognises in more than one place that thinking cannot be an intelligible modification of matter, or one which could be understood and explained; that is to say, a sentient or thinking being is not a mechanical thing like a watch or a windmill, so that we could conceive of sizes, shapes, and motions in such a mechanical conjunction that they could produce in a mass, in which there was nothing of the kind, something capable of thought and even of sensation, which thinking and sensing would likewise stop if the mechanism got out of order. Thus it is not natural to matter to have sensation and to think, and there are only two ways in which it could do so; one of which is for God to join to it a substance to which thought is natural, and the other for

God to endow it with thought miraculously. In this, then, I am entirely of the opinion of the Cartesians, except that I extend it to brutes also, and hold that they have sensation, and souls which are, properly speaking, immaterial, and as incapable of perishing as the atoms of Democritus or Gassendi; whereas the Cartesians, being needlessly embarrassed about the souls of brutes, and not knowing what to do with them if they were preserved (since it did not occur to them that the animal might be preserved in a minute form), were compelled to deny them even sensation, contrary to all appearances, and to the judgement of mankind. But if it is argued that God, at least, could add the faculty of thinking to such a mechanism, I would answer that if this occurred, and if God added this faculty to matter without at the same time endowing it with a substance of such a kind that this same faculty (as I conceive it) could be inherent in it, that is to say without adding an immaterial soul, then matter would have to be exalted miraculously so as to be able to receive a power of which it is not capable naturally: just as some Scholastics[t] claim that God exalts fire to the point of giving it the power directly to burn spirits separated from matter—which would be a miracle pure and simple. It is enough that we cannot maintain that matter thinks unless we attribute to it an imperishable soul, or rather a miracle, and that thus the immortality of our souls follows from what is natural: since we could not maintain that they are extinguished except by a miracle, whether by exalting matter, or by annihilating the soul. For we know, of course, that the power of God could render our souls mortal, even though they may be immaterial (or immortal by nature alone), since he can annihilate them.

Now this truth of the immateriality of the soul is undoubtedly of consequence. For it is of infinitely more use in religion and morals, especially in our days (when many people have scant respect for revelation by itself or for miracles), to show that souls are naturally immortal, and that it would be a miracle if they were not, than to maintain that our souls must naturally die, and that it is by virtue of a miraculous grace, based solely on the promise of God, that they do not die. We have, moreover, known for a long time that those who wished to destroy natural religion, and reduce everything to revealed religion, as if reason taught us nothing about it, have been held suspect, and not always without reason. But our author is not of their number. He upholds the proof of the existence of God and attributes to the immateriality of the soul *a probability of the highest degree*, which may consequently pass for a *moral certainty*, so that I imagine that, having as much sincerity as penetration, he might quite well come to agree with the doctrine I have just expounded. This doctrine is fundamental in every reasonable philosophy, for otherwise I do not see how we can prevent ourselves from falling back into *fanatical philosophy*, such as the Mosaic philosophy of Fludd,[u] which preserves all phenomena by attributing them immediately and miraculously to God, or into a *barbarous philosophy* like that of certain philosophers and physicians of bygone days, who still savoured of the barbarism of their age, and who today are justly despised; these preserved appearances by expressly fabricating suitable occult qualities or faculties, which were supposed to be like little demons or spirits able to do what was required of them out of hand—just as if there were watches able to tell the time by some 'time-indicative faculty'[v] without the need of wheels, or mills able to crush grain by a 'fractive faculty' without the need of anything in the nature of millstones. As to the difficulty many people have had in conceiving an immaterial substance, that soon ceases to be felt (in part at least) when there is no longer any question of substances separated from matter; such substances do not, I hold, ever naturally exist among created things.

Metaphysical Consequences of the Principle of Reason (c. 1712)

1. The fundamental principle of reasoning is *that there is nothing without a reason*; or, to explain the matter more distinctly, that there is no truth for which a reason does not subsist. The reason for a truth consists in the connexion of the predicate with the subject, that is, that the predicate is in the subject. This is either manifest, as in the case of identical propositions—for example, 'A man is a man', or 'A white man is white'—or it is concealed, but concealed in such a way that the connexion can be shown by the analysis of notions—for example, 'Nine is a square'. For nine is three times three, which is three multiplied by three, which is a number multiplied by itself, which is a square.

2. This principle disposes of all inexplicable occult qualities, and other similar figments. For as often as writers introduce some primitive occult quality they impinge on this principle. For example, suppose that someone thinks that there is in matter some attractive force which is primitive, and therefore not derivable from the intelligible notions of body (namely, magnitude, shape and motion). And suppose he wants it to happen that by this attractive force bodies tend towards some other body without being pushed, as some conceive gravity—namely, as if heavy things were attracted by the body of the earth, or as if they were attracted to it by some sympathy, in such a way that the ulterior reason of this cannot be given from the nature of bodies, and the method of attraction cannot be explained. Such a person admits that there is no reason for the truth that a stone tends towards the earth. For if he thinks that this occurs, not by an occult quality of the body, but by the will of God or by a divinely established law, by that very fact he gives some reason, but a

supernatural or miraculous one. The same is to be said of all those who, where bodily phenomena are to be explained, have recourse to bare faculties, sympathies, antipathies, archaei,[a] operational ideas, plastic force, souls and other incorporeal entities, which (as they have to admit) have no connexion with the phenomenon.

3. The consequence of this is that in the case of bodies everything occurs mechanically, that is, through the intelligible qualities of bodies, namely magnitude, shape and motion; in the case of souls, everything is to be explained in vital terms, that is, through the intelligible qualities of the soul, namely perceptions and appetites. However, we detect in animated bodies a beautiful harmony between vitality and mechanism, such that what occurs mechanically in the body is represented vitally in the soul; and what are perceived exactly in the soul are handed over completely for execution in the body.

4. From this it follows that we can often heal the soul from the known qualities of the body, and can often heal the body from the known affections of the soul. For it is often easier to know what happens in the soul than what happens in the body; often, again, the contrary is the case. As often as we use what the soul indicates to help the body, this may be called vital medicine; this extends more widely than is commonly thought. For the body corresponds to the soul not only in the so-called voluntary motions, but in all others as well; though, on account of habit, we do not notice that the soul is affected by or agrees with the motions of the body, or that the latter correspond to the perceptions and appetites of the soul. For the perceptions of these are confused, so that their agreement does not appear so easily. The soul gives orders to the body in so far as it has distinct perceptions, and serves it in so far as it has confused ones; however, anyone who has some perception in his soul can be certain that he has received some effect of that in his body, and vice versa. Whatever is good, then, in the archaeists or similar writers is reduced to this; for even if there do not exist in the body the disturbances of the archaeus (which they say are anger) and its settlings, and these cannot be conceived except as in

the soul, yet there is something in the body which corresponds to these.

5. Further, it is a fact that we can sometimes arrive at the truth about natural things through final causes, when we cannot arrive at it easily through efficient causes. This is shown, not only by the anatomical doctrine of the use of the members, where we reason correctly from the end to the means, but also (as I myself have shown) by a notable example in optics.[b] For just as in animated bodies what is organic corresponds to what is vital, motions to appetites, so also in the whole of nature efficient causes correspond to final causes, because everything proceeds from a cause which is not only powerful, but also wise; and with the rule of power through efficient causes, there is involved the rule of wisdom through final causes. This harmony of corporeal and spiritual is one of the finest and most evident arguments for a Divinity; for, since the influx of one kind on another is inexplicable, a harmony of things which are entirely different can arise only from the one common cause, that is, God.

6. But we shall arrive at the same point in a more general way by returning to our fundamental principle. We must reflect that space, time and matter—bare matter, in which nothing is considered besides extension and impenetrability[c]— are clearly indifferent with respect to any magnitudes, shapes and motions. Consequently no reason can be found, in these indifferent and indeterminate things, for what is determinate; that is, why the world should exist in such and such a way, and should not have been produced in any other no less possible form. The consequence of this is that the reason for the existence of contingent things must eventually be sought outside matter and in a necessary cause; namely, in that whose reason for existing is not outside itself. This, therefore, is spiritual—in a word, a mind—and is also the most perfect mind, since on account of the connexion of things it extends to all.

7. Further, all creatures are either substantial or accidental. Those which are substantial are either substances or sub-stantiated. I give the name 'substantiated'[d] to aggregates of substances, such as an army of men, or a flock of sheep; and

all bodies are such aggregates. A substance is either simple, such as a soul, which has no parts, or it is composite, such as an animal, which consists of a soul and an organic body. But an organic body, like every other body, is merely an aggregate of animals or other things which are living and therefore organic, or finally of small objects or masses; but these also are finally resolved into living things, from which it is evident that all bodies are finally resolved into living things, and that what, in the analysis of substances, exist ultimately are simple substances—namely, souls, or, if you prefer a more general term, *monads*, which are without parts. For even though every simple substance has an organic body which corresponds to it—otherwise it would not have any kind of orderly relation to other things in the universe, nor would it act or be acted upon in an orderly way—yet by itself it is without parts. And because an organic body, or any other body whatsoever, can again be resolved into substances endowed with organic bodies, it is evident that in the end there are simple substances alone, and that in them are the sources of all things and of the modifications that come to things.

8. But because modifications vary, and whatever is the source of variations is truly active, it must therefore be said that simple substances are active or the sources of actions, and that they produce in themselves a certain series of internal variations. And because there is no means by which one simple substance could influence another, it follows that every simple substance is spontaneous, or the one and only source of its own modifications. Further, since the nature of a simple substance consists of perception and appetite, it is clear that there is in each soul a series of appetites and perceptions, through which it is led from the end to the means, from the perception of one object to the perception of another. So the soul does not depend on anything except a universal cause, or God, through whom (like all things) it continually exists and is conserved; but the rest it has from its own nature.

9. But there would be no order among these simple substances, which lack the interchange of mutual influx, unless they at least corresponded to each other mutually. Hence it is necessary that there is between them a certain relation of

perceptions or phenomena, through which it can be discerned how much their modifications differ from each other in space or time; for in these two—time and place—there consists the order of things which exist either successively or simultaneously. From this it also follows that every simple substance represents an aggregate of external things, and that in those external things, represented in diverse ways, there consists both the diversity and the harmony of souls. Each soul will represent proximately the phenomena of its own organic body, but remotely those of others which act on its own body.

10. It must also be known that, because of the nature of things, in the whole of the universe 'all things conspire', as Hippocrates says of the body of an animal, and everything conspires with everything else in a certain fixed way. For since all places are filled with bodies, and all bodies are endowed with a certain degree of fluidity, so that they give way somewhat to pressure, however small, it follows from this that no body can be moved without its neighbour being moved somewhat, and, for the same reason, the neighbour of its neighbour, and so on over any distance, however great. From this it follows that each corpuscle is acted on by all the bodies in the universe, and is variously affected by them, in such a way that the omniscient being knows, in each particle of the universe, everything which happens in the entire universe. This could not happen unless matter were everywhere divisible, and indeed actually divided *ad infinitum*. Therefore, since every organic body is affected by the entire universe by relations which are determinate with respect to each part of the universe, it is not surprising that the soul, which represents to itself the rest in accordance with the relations of its body, is a kind of mirror of the universe, which represents the rest in accordance with (so to speak) its point of view—just as the same city presents, to a person who looks at it from various sides, projections which are quite different.

11. But it must not be thought that, when I speak of a mirror, I mean that external things are always depicted in the organs and in the soul itself. For it is sufficient for the expression of one thing in another that there should be a

certain constant relational law, by which particulars in the one can be referred to corresponding particulars in the other.[e] Thus, a circle can be represented by an ellipse (that is, an oval curve) in a perspective projection, and indeed by a hyperbola, which is most unlike it, and does not even return upon itself; for to any point of the hyperbola a corresponding point of the circle which projects the hyperbola can be assigned by the same constant law. From this it comes about that a created soul necessarily has many confused perceptions, representing an aggregation of innumerable external things, but it perceives distinctly what is closer or more prominent, and accommodated to its organs. But since it also understands reasons, the mind is not only a mirror of the created universe, but is also an image of God. But this belongs to rational substances alone.

12. From this it follows that a simple substance does not come into existence naturally (unless with the origin of things), nor can it cease to exist, but it always remains the same. For since it does not have parts, it cannot suffer dissolution; since it is the source of variations, it proceeds in a continuous series of change; and since by its own nature it is a mirror of the universe, it no more ceases to exist than the universe itself. But if it should arrive at that state in which it has perceptions which are almost all confused, we call this 'death'; for then a stupor arises, as in a profound sleep or in apoplexy. But since nature gradually unravels confusions, then that which we suppose to be death cannot be perpetual. But is is only rational substances which preserve, not only their individuality, but also their personality, by retaining or recovering consciousness of themselves, so that they can be citizens in the city of God, capable of reward and punishment. In them, therefore, the kingdom of nature serves the kingdom of grace.[f]

13. Indeed I go further, and I assert that not only the soul but also the animal itself lasts perpetually, from the very beginning of things. For a soul is always endowed with an organic body, so that it has that through which it may represent the other external things in an orderly way; and so its body can indeed be reduced to a great fineness, but cannot be

utterly destroyed. And though it may be that the body consists of a perpetual flux, and it cannot be said that any particle of matter is constantly assigned to the same soul, yet an entire organic body can never be given to or taken away from the soul. However much the animal grows at conception, yet it had a seminal organism before it could be brought forth through conception and could grow; and however much it may diminish at death, yet once its skin has been cast, it retains a subtle organism superior to all the forces of nature, since it extends to infinity through repeated subdivisions. For since nature has been made by a most wise artificer, it is everywhere organic within, and the organism of living things is nothing other than a divine mechanism, increasing in subtlety to infinity. No one fittingly understands the works of God unless he sufficiently recognises in them this fact: that the effect is the trace of its cause.

Monadology (1714)

1. The *monad*, of which we shall speak here, is nothing but a simple substance which enters into compounds; *simple,* that is to say, without parts.

2. And there must be simple substances, because there are compounds; for the compound is nothing but a collection or *aggregatum* of simples. — *How can simple substances make compound ones*

3. Now where there are no parts, there neither extension,[a] nor shape, nor divisibility is possible. And these monads are the true atoms of nature and, in a word, the elements of things.

4. Moreover, there is no fear of dissolution, and there is no conceivable way in which a simple substance could perish in the course of nature.

5. For the same reason there is no way in which a simple substance could begin in the course of nature, since it cannot be formed by means of compounding.

6. Thus it may be said that monads can only begin and end all at once, that is to say they can only begin by creation and end by annihilation, whereas what is compound begins or ends by parts.

7. There is also no means of explaining how a monad can be altered or changed within itself by any other created thing, since it is impossible to displace anything in it or to conceive of the possibility of any internal motion being started, directed, increased, or diminished within it, as can occur in compounds, where change among the parts takes place. Monads have no windows, by which anything could come in or go out. Accidents cannot become detached, or wander about outside substances, as the 'sensible species' of the Scholastics used to do.[b] Thus neither substance nor accident can enter a monad from without.

8. Monads, however, must have some qualities, otherwise they would not be beings at all. And if simple substances did not differ by their qualities, there would be no way of perceiving any change in things, since what is in the compound can only come from its simple ingredients; and if monads were without qualities, they would be indistinguishable from one another, since they do not differ in quantity either. And consequently, supposing space to be a plenum, each place would always only receive, when motion occurred, the equivalent of what it had before; and one state of things would be indistinguishable from another.

9. Indeed, every monad must be different from every other. For there are never in nature two beings which are precisely alike, and in which it is not possible to find some difference which is internal, or based on some intrinsic denomination.

10. I also take it as granted that every created thing, and consequently the created monad also, is subject to change, and indeed that this change is continual in each one.

11. It follows from what we have just said, that the natural changes of monads come from an *internal principle*, since an external cause would be unable to influence their inner being.

12. But besides the principle of change, there must be *differentiation within that which changes*,[c] to constitute as it were the specification and variety of simple substances.

13. This differentiation must involve a plurality within the unity or the simple. For since every natural change takes place by degrees, something changes, and something remains; and consequently the simple must contain a large number of affections and relations, although it has no parts.

14. The passing state, which involves and represents a plurality within the unity or simple substance, is nothing other than what is called *perception*, which must be carefully distinguished from apperception or consciousness, as will appear presently. And herein lies the great mistake of the Cartesians, that they took no account of perceptions which are not apperceived. It is this also which made them believe that minds alone are monads, and that neither brutes nor other entelechies[d] have souls. For the same reason also they fell into the common error of confusing death, properly so

called, with a prolonged unconsciousness; and this made
them favour the Scholastic conviction that souls are entirely
separate from bodies, and even confirmed some ill-balanced
minds in the opinion that souls are mortal.

15. The action of the internal principle which produces the
change or passage from one perception to another may be
called *appetition*; it is true that the appetite cannot always
attain completely the whole of the perception towards which
it tends, but it always attains something of it, and arrives at
new perceptions.

16. We ourselves experience plurality within a simple
substance, when we find that the least thought which we
apperceive involves a variety in its object. So everyone who
acknowledges that the soul is a simple substance must acknowledge this plurality within the monad; and M. Bayle
should not have found any difficulty in this, as he does in his
Dictionary, in the article 'Rorarius'.[e]

17. We are moreover obliged to confess that *perception* and
that which depends on it *cannot be explained mechanically*, that
is to say by figures and motions. Suppose that there were a
machine so constructed as to produce thought, feeling, and
perception, we could imagine it increased in size while retaining the same proportions, so that one could enter as one
might a mill. On going inside we should only see the parts
impinging upon one another; we should not see anything
which would explain a perception. The explanation of perception must therefore be sought in a simple substance, and
not in a compound or in a machine. Moreover, there is nothing
else whatever to be found in the simple substance except just
this, viz. perceptions and their changes. It is in this alone that
all the *internal actions* of simple substances must consist.

18. We may give the name *entelechies* to all created simple
substances or monads. For they have in themselves a certain
perfection (ἔχουσι τὸ ἐντελές), there is a self-sufficiency (αὐτάρκεια)
in them which makes them the sources of their internal
actions—incorporeal automata,[f] if I may so put it.

19. If we wish to give the name 'soul' to everything which
has *perceptions* and *appetites* in the general sense I have just
explained, all created simple substances or monads might be

called souls; but as feeling is something more than a simple perception, I agree that the general name—monad or entelechy—should be enough for simple substances which have no more than that, and that those only should be called souls, whose perception is more distinct and is accompanied by memory.

20. For we experience within ourselves a state, in which we remember nothing and have no distinguishable perception; as when we fall into a swoon, or when we are overcome by a deep dreamless sleep. In this state the soul does not sensibly differ from a simple monad; but as this state is not permanent, and as the soul emerges from it, the soul is something more.

21. And it does not follow that when in that state the simple substance has no perception at all. Indeed, that is not possible for the above reasons; for it cannot perish, nor can it subsist without some affection in some way, and this affection is nothing but its perception. But when there are a very great number of small perceptions with nothing to distinguish them, we are stupefied, just as it happens that if we go on turning round in the same direction several times running, we become giddy and go into a swoon, so that we can no longer distinguish anything at all. And death can throw animals[1] into this state for a time.

22. And as every state of a simple substance is a natural consequence of its preceding state, so that the present state of it is big with the future,

23. and since, on awakening from our stupor, we apperceive our perceptions, it must be the case that we received the perceptions the moment before, though we did not apperceive them; for a perception cannot arise in the course of nature except from another perception, as one motion can only arise in the course of nature from another motion.

24. From this we see that if we had nothing in our perceptions to distinguish them, nothing so to speak heightened and of a keener savour, we should always be in this stupor. And this is the state of bare monads.

[1] By 'animals' Leibniz means all living creatures up to and including man. The lower animals, as distinguished from man, he refers to as 'brutes'.

25. We see also that Nature has given heightened perceptions to animals from the care she has taken to provide them with organs which collect several rays of light, or several undulations of the air, so as to make these more effective by being united. There is something of the kind in smell, taste, and touch, and perhaps in many other senses which are unknown to us. I will explain later how what occurs in the soul represents what takes place in the organs.

26. Memory provides souls with a kind of *consecutiveness*, which copies reason but must be distinguished from it. What I mean is this: we often see that animals, when they have a perception of something which strikes them, and of which they had a similar perception previously, are led, by the representation of their memory, to expect what was united with this perception before, and are moved to feelings similar to those they had before. For example, when dogs are shown a stick, they remember the pain which it has caused them in the past, and howl or run away.

27. The powerful imagination, which strikes and moves them, arises either from the magnitude or from the number of the preceding perceptions. For often a vivid impression has in a moment the effect of long *habit*, or of many moderate perceptions oft repeated.

28. Men act like brutes in so far as the sequences of their perceptions arise through the principle of memory only, like those empirical physicians who have mere practice without theory. We are all merely empiricists as regards three-fourths of our actions. For example, when we expect it to be day tomorrow, we are behaving as empiricists, because until now it has always happened thus. The astronomer alone knows this by reason.

29. But it is the knowledge of necessary and eternal truths which distinguishes us from mere animals, and gives us *reason* and the sciences, raising us to knowledge of ourselves and God. It is this in us which we call the rational soul or *mind*.

30. Further it is by the knowledge of necessary truths and by their abstractions that we are raised to *acts of reflection*, which make us think of what is called the *self*, and consider

that this or that is within *us*. And it is thus that in thinking of ourselves, we think of being, of substance, of the simple and the compound, of the immaterial and of God himself, conceiving that what is limited in us, in him is limitless. And these acts of reflection provide the chief objects of our reasonings.

31. Our reasonings are based on two great principles: the *principle of contradiction*, by virtue of which we judge to be false that which involves a contradiction, and true that which is opposed or contradictory to the false;

32. and the *principle of sufficient reason*, by virtue of which we consider that no fact can be real or existing and no proposition can be true unless there is a sufficient reason, why it should be thus and not otherwise, even though in most cases these reasons cannot be known to us.

33. There are also two kinds of *truths*: truths of *reasoning* and truths of *fact*. Truths of reasoning are necessary and their opposite is impossible; those of fact are contingent and their opposite is possible. When a truth is necessary, the reason for it can be found by analysis, that is, by resolving it into simpler ideas and truths until the primary ones are reached.

34. It is in this way that in mathematics speculative *theorems* and practical *canons* are reduced by analysis to *definitions*, *axioms*, and *postulates*.

35. Finally there are simple ideas of which no definition can be given; there are also axioms and postulates, or in a word *primary principles*, which cannot be proved and have no need of proof. These are *identical propositions*, whose opposite contains an express contradiction.

36. But a *sufficient reason* also must be found in the case of *contingent truths* or *truths of fact*; that is to say, in the case of the series of things spread over the universe of created things; here resolution into particular reasons might go on into endless detail on account of the immense variety of things in nature and the division of bodies *ad infinitum*. There are an infinite number of shapes and motions, both present and past, which enter into the efficient cause of my present writing; and there are an infinite number of minute inclinations and dispositions of my soul, both present and past, which enter into its final cause.

37. And as all this differentiation involves only other prior or more differentiated contingent things, all of which need a similar analysis to explain them, we are no further advanced: and the sufficient or ultimate reason must be outside the succession or *series* of this differentiation of contingent things, however infinite it may be.

38. This is why the ultimate reason of things must lie in a necessary substance, in which the differentiation of the changes only exists eminently as in their source; and this is what we call *God*.

39. Now since this substance is a sufficient reason of all this differentiation, which is itself likewise all connected, *there is only one God, and this God is enough*.

40. We may also judge that since this Supreme Substance, who is unique, universal, and necessary, has nothing outside himself independent of himself, and is a simple consequence of possible being, he must be incapable of being limited, and must contain just as much reality as is possible.

41. Whence it follows that God is absolutely perfect, since *perfection* is nothing but magnitude of positive reality, in the strict sense, setting aside the limits or bounds in things which are limited. And there, where there are no bounds, that is to say in God, perfection is absolutely infinite.

42. It follows also that created things owe their perfections to the influence of God, but that they owe their imperfections to their own nature, which is incapable of being without limits. For it is in this that they are distinguished from God.

43. It is true likewise, that in God is the source not only of existences but also of essences, in so far as they are real, that is of all the reality there is in possibility. This is because the Understanding of God is the region of eternal truths or of the ideas on which they depend, and because without him there would be nothing real in the possibilities—not only nothing existent, but also nothing possible.

44. For if there is a reality in essences or possibilities, or indeed in eternal truths, this reality must be founded on something existent and actual; and consequently on the existence of the Necessary Being in whom essence involves existence, or in whom it is enough to be possible in order to be actual.

45. Thus God alone (or the Necessary Being) has the privilege that he must exist if he is possible. And as nothing can prevent the possibility of that which has no limits, no negation, and consequently no contradiction, this alone is sufficient for us to know the existence of God *a priori*. We have proved it also by the reality of eternal truths. And we have now just proved it *a posteriori* also, since there exist contingent beings, which can only have their ultimate or sufficient reason in the Necessary Being, who has the reason for his existence in himself.

46. We must not, however, imagine, as some do, that because the eternal truths are dependent on God, they are therefore arbitrary and depend on his will, as Descartes, and after him M. Poiret,[g] seem to have thought. This is true only of contingent truths, whose principle is *fitness* or the choice of *the best*; whereas necessary truths depend solely on his understanding, of which they are the internal object.

47. Thus God alone is the primary Unity, or original simple substance, from which all monads, created and derived, are produced, and are born, so to speak, by continual fulgurations of the Divinity from moment to moment, limited by the receptivity of the created being, which is of its essence limited.

48. There is in God *power*, which is the source of everything, *knowledge*, which contains the differentiation of the ideas, and finally *will*, which causes changes and productions according to the principle of what is best. And these correspond to what provides the ground or basis in created monads, the perceptive faculty and the appetitive faculty. But in God these attributes are absolutely infinite or perfect, while in created monads or in *entelechies* (or *perfectihabiae*, as Hermolaus Barbarus[h] translated this word) there are only limitations of them, in proportion to the perfection there is in the monad.

49. The created thing is said to *act* outwardly in so far as it has perfection, and to be *passively affected* by another in so far as it is imperfect. Thus *activity* is attributed to the monad in so far as it has distinct perceptions, and *passivity* in so far as it has confused perceptions.

50. And one created thing is more perfect than another

when there is found in it that which explains *a priori* what happens in the other; and it is because of this that we say that it acts upon the other.

51. But in simple substances the influence of one monad over another is *ideal* only; it can have its effect only through the intervention of God, inasmuch as in the ideas of God a monad rightly demands that God, in regulating the rest from the beginning of things, should have regard to itself. For since it is impossible for a created monad to have a physical influence on the inner nature of another, this is the only way in which one can be dependent on another.

52. And this is why actions and passions are mutual between created things. For when God compares two simple substances he finds in each reasons which oblige him to adapt the other to it, and consequently what is active in certain aspects is passive from another point of view: *active* in so far as what is distinctly known in it explains what occurs in another, and *passive* in so far as the reason for what occurs in it is found in what is distinctly known in another.

53. Now as there is an infinite number of possible universes in the ideas of God, and as only one can exist, there must be a sufficient reason for God's choice, determining him to one rather than to another.

54. And this reason can only be found in the *fitness*, or in the degrees of perfection, which these worlds contain, each possible world having the right to claim existence in proportion to the perfection which it involves.

55. And it is this which causes the existence of the best, which God knows through his wisdom, chooses through his goodness, and produces through his power.

56. Now this *connexion* or adaptation of all created things with each, and of each with all the rest, means that each simple substance has relations which express all the others, and that consequently it is a perpetual living mirror of the universe.

57. And just as the same town, when looked at from different sides, appears quite different and is, as it were, multiplied *in perspective*, so also it happens that because of the infinite number of simple substances, it is as if there were

as many different universes, which are however but different
perspectives of a single universe in accordance with the different
points of view of each monad.

58. And this is the means of obtaining as much variety as
possible, but with the greatest order possible; that is to say,
it is the means of obtaining as much perfection as possible.

59. Further it is this hypothesis alone (which I venture to
regard as proved) which properly exalts the greatness of God.
This M. Bayle recognised, when in his *Dictionary* (in the
article 'Rorarius') he made objections, in which he was even
inclined to believe that I attributed too much to God, and
more than is possible. But he could not advance any reason
why this universal harmony, which causes each substance
exactly to express all the others through the relations which
it has with them, should be impossible.

60. Moreover, there are evident from what I have just said
the *a priori* reasons why things could not be otherwise than
they are: namely, because God in regulating the whole
had regard to each part, and particularly to each monad.
The nature of the monad is representative, and consequently
nothing can limit it to representing a part of things only,
although it is true that its representation is confused as
regards the detail of the whole universe and can only be
distinct as regards a small part of things; that is to say as
regards those which are either the nearest or the largest in
relation to each of the monads; otherwise each monad would
be a divinity. It is not in the object, but in the modification
of the knowledge of the object, that monads are limited. In
a confused way they all go towards the infinite, towards the
whole; but they are limited and distinguished from one
another by the degrees of their distinct perceptions.

61. And in this the compounds agree with the simples.¹
For as the whole is a plenum, which means that the whole
of matter is connected, and as in a plenum every movement
has some effect on distant bodies in proportion to their distance, so that each body not only is affected by those which
touch it, and is in some way sensitive to whatever happens
to them, but also by means of them is sensitive to those which
touch the first bodies by which it is itself directly touched; it

follows that this communication stretches out indefinitely. Consequently every body is sensitive to everything which is happening in the universe, so much so that one who saw everything could read in each body what is happening everywhere, and even what has happened or what will happen, by observing in the present the things that are distant in time as well as in space; σύμπνοια πάντα, as Hippocrates said.[k] But a soul can read in itself only what is distinctly represented there; it is unable to develop all at once all the things that are folded within it, for they stretch to infinity.

62. Thus although each created monad represents the whole universe, it represents more distinctly the body which is particularly affected by it, and whose entelechy it is: and as this body expresses the whole universe by the connexion of all matter in the plenum, the soul represents the whole universe also in representing the body which belongs to it in a particular way.

63. The body belonging to a monad, which is that body's entelechy or soul, constitutes together with the entelechy what may be called a *living thing*, and with the soul what is called an *animal*. Now this body of a living thing or animal is always organic; for since every monad is in its way a mirror of the universe, and since the universe is regulated in a perfect order, there must also be an order in that which represents it, that is to say in the perceptions of the soul, and consequently in the body, according to which order the universe is represented therein.

64. Thus each organic body of a living thing is a kind of divine machine, or natural automaton, which infinitely surpasses all artificial automata. Because a machine which is made by the art of man is not a machine in each of its parts; for example, the tooth of a metal wheel has parts or fragments which as far as we are concerned are not artificial and which have about them nothing of the character of a machine, in relation to the use for which the wheel was intended. But the machines of nature, that is to say living bodies, are still machines in the least of their parts *ad infinitum*. This it is which makes the difference between nature and art, that is to say between Divine art and ours.

65. And the Author of nature was enabled to practise this divine and infinitely marvellous artifice, because each portion of matter is not only infinitely divisible, as the ancients recognised, but is also actually subdivided without limit, each part into further parts, of which each one has some motion of its own: otherwise it would be impossible for each portion of matter to express the whole universe.

66. Whence it is evident that there is a world of created beings—living things, animals, entelechies, and souls—in the least part of matter.

67. Each portion of matter may be conceived as a garden full of plants, and as a pond full of fish. But every branch of each plant, every member of each animal, and every drop of their liquid parts is itself likewise a similar garden or pond.

68. And although the earth and the air interspersed between the plants in the garden, or the water interspersed between the fish in the pond, are neither plant nor fish, yet they still contain them, though most usually of a subtlety which renders them imperceptible to us.

69. Thus there is nothing waste, nothing sterile, nothing dead in the universe; no chaos, no confusions, save in appearance. We might compare this to the appearance of a pond in the distance, where we can see the confused movement and swarming of the fish, without distinguishing the fish themselves.

70. Thus we see that each living body has a dominant entelechy, which in the case of an animal is the soul, but the members of this living body are full of other living things, plants and animals, of which each has in turn its dominant entelechy or soul.

71. But we must not imagine, as some have done who have misunderstood my view, that each soul has a mass or portion of matter appropriate or attached to itself for ever, and that it consequently possesses other inferior living things, for ever destined to its service. For all bodies are in a perpetual flux like rivers, and parts are passing in and out of them continually.

72. Thus the soul only changes its body bit by bit and by degrees, so that it is never despoiled of all its organs all

together; in animals there is often metamorphosis, but never metempsychosis, nor transmigration of souls: neither are there any entirely *separate souls*, nor *superhuman spirits* without bodies. God alone is entirely detached from body.

73. It is because of this also that there is never, strictly speaking, absolute generation nor perfect death, consisting in the separation of the soul. And what we call *generation* is a development and a growth, while what we call *death* is an envelopment and a diminution.

74. Philosophers have been much embarrassed over the origin of forms, entelechies or souls. But today when exact researches on plants, insects, and animals have revealed the fact that the organic bodies of nature are never produced from a chaos or from putrefaction, but always from seeds, wherein there was certainly some *preformation*, we conclude not only that the organic body was already present before conception, but also that there was a soul in this body; that, in a word, the animal itself was present, and that by means of conception it was merely prepared for a great transformation, so as to become an animal of another kind. We even see something of this kind apart from birth, as when worms become flies, and caterpillars become butterflies.

75. The *animals*, of which some are raised by means of conception to the rank of the larger animals, may be called *spermatic*; but those among them which remain in their own kind (and they are the greater number) are born, multiply, and are destroyed like the large animals; and there is only a small number of elect ones who pass into a greater theatre.

76. But this is only half the truth. And so I have judged that if the animal never begins naturally, neither does it end naturally; and that not only will there be no birth, but also no complete destruction, no death, strictly speaking. And these reasonings, which are *a posteriori* and derived from experience, agree perfectly with the principles which I have deduced *a priori* above.

77. Thus one may say that not only is the soul (the mirror of an indestructible universe) itself indestructible, but so also is the animal itself, although its machine may often perish in part, and cast off or put on particular organic integuments.

78. These principles provide me with a way of explaining naturally the union, or rather the conformity, of the soul and the organic body. The soul follows its own laws, and the body its own likewise, and they accord by virtue of the *harmony pre-established* among all substances, since they are all representations of one and the same universe.

79. Souls act according to the laws of final causes by appetitions, ends, and means. Bodies act according to the laws of efficient causes by motions. And the two kingdoms, of efficient and of final causes, are in harmony with one another.

80. Descartes recognised that souls cannot give force to bodies because there is always the same quantity of force in matter. He believed, however, that the soul could change the direction of bodies. But this is because in his day the law of nature was not known which affirms the conservation of the same total direction in matter.[1] Had he noticed this, he would have stumbled upon my system of Pre-established Harmony.

81. Under this system, bodies act as though, *per impossibile,* there were no souls: and souls act as if there were no bodies, and both act as if each influenced the other.

82. As for minds or rational souls, although I find that what I have just been saying is at bottom true of all living beings and animals (that is to say that the animal and the soul only begin with the world and do not come to an end any more than the world comes to an end), yet rational animals are peculiar in this, that their little spermatic animals, so long as they are that merely, have only ordinary or sensitive souls; but as soon as those which are, so to speak, elect arrive by an actual conception at human nature, then their sensitive souls are raised to the rank of reason and to the prerogative of minds.

83. Among other differences which exist between ordinary souls and minds, some of which I have already pointed out, there is also this, that souls in general are the living mirrors or images of the universe of created things, whereas minds are also images of the Divinity himself, or the Author of nature, capable of knowing the system of the universe, and

of imitating something of it by architectonic patterns, each mind being as it were a little divinity in its own department.

84. This it is which renders minds capable of entering into a kind of society with God, and makes his relation to them not only that of an inventor to his machine (which is God's relation to the rest of created things) but also that of a prince to his subjects, and even of a father to his children.

85. From this it is easy to conclude that the assemblage of all minds must make up the City of God, that is to say the most perfect possible state under the most perfect of monarchs.

86. This City of God, this truly universal monarchy, is a moral world in the natural world, and is the most exalted and the most divine of God's works, and in it truly consists his glory, since he could not be glorified if his greatness and goodness were not known and wondered at by minds: it is also in relation to this divine City that he may properly be said to have goodness, whereas his wisdom and power are manifested everywhere.

87. As we have established above a perfect harmony between two natural kingdoms, the one of efficient and the other of final causes, we ought here also to point out another harmony between the physical kingdom of nature and the moral kingdom of grace; that is to say between God as Architect of the machine of the universe, and God as Monarch of the divine City of Minds.

88. This harmony means that things conduce to grace by the very ways of nature, and that this globe, for example, must be destroyed and repaired by natural ways at the times demanded by the government of minds for the chastisement of some and the reward of others.

89. It can further be said that God as Architect satisfies God as Lawgiver in everything, and that thus sins carry their punishment with them by the order of nature, and by virtue of the mechanical structure of things itself; and that in the same way noble actions will attract their rewards by ways which are mechanical as far as bodies are concerned, although this cannot and should not always happen immediately.

90. Finally, under this perfect government there will be no good action without reward, no evil action without punishment, and everything must turn out for the good of the righteous, of those, that is, who are not dissatisfied in this great State, who trust in Providence when they have done their duty, and who love and imitate fittingly the Author of all good, delighting in the consideration of his perfections after the manner of true *pure love*, which makes us take pleasure in the happiness of the beloved. This it is which makes the wise and virtuous work for whatever seems to conform with the presumptive or antecedent will of God, and yet leaves them satisfied with what God in fact causes to happen by his secret will, which is consequent and decisive,[m] recognising as they do that if we could sufficiently understand the order of the universe, we should find that it surpasses all the desires of the most wise, and that it is impossible to make it better than it is, not only for the whole in general, but also for ourselves in particular, if we are attached as we should be to the Author of the whole, not merely as to the Architect and efficient Cause of our being, but also as to our Master and the final Cause which must constitute the whole end of our will, and which alone can constitute our happiness.

Principles of Nature and of Grace, Founded on Reason (1714)

1. *Substance* is a being capable of action. It is simple or compound. *Simple substance* is that which has no parts. *Compound substance* is the combination of simple substances or *monads*. *Monas* is a Greek word which signifies unity or that which is one. Compounds or bodies are pluralities, and simple substances—that is lives, souls, minds—are unities. There must necessarily be simple substances everywhere, because without simple substances there could be no compounds; consequently the whole of nature is full of life.

2. Monads, having no parts, cannot be made or unmade. They can neither begin nor end naturally, and consequently they last as long as the universe, which will be changed but not destroyed. They cannot have shapes, otherwise they would have parts. Therefore one monad, in itself and at a particular moment, can only be distinguished from another by internal qualities and activities, which can be nothing else but its *perceptions* (that is to say, the representations in the simple of the compound or of that which is outside) and its *appetitions* (that is to say, its tendencies to pass from one perception to another), which are the principles of change. For the simplicity of substance does not preclude the possibility of a multiplicity of modifications, which indeed necessarily exist together in the same simple substance, and these modifications must consist in the variety of the relations of the simple substance to things which are outside. Just as in a *centre* or point, in itself perfectly simple, are found an infinity of angles formed by the lines which meet there.

3. All nature is a plenum. Everywhere there are simple substances, effectively separated from one another by actions of their own which are continually altering their relations;

and each simple substance or distinct monad, which forms the centre of a compound substance (e.g. of an animal) and the principle of its oneness, is surrounded by a *mass* composed of an infinity of other monads which constitute the body belonging to this central monad; corresponding to the affections of its body it represents, as in a kind of *centre*, the things which are outside of it. And this *body* is *organic*, when it forms a kind of automaton or natural machine,[a] which is a machine not only as a whole but also in its smallest observable parts. And since because the world is a plenum everything is connected together, and each body acts on every other body more or less according to the distance, and is affected by it by reaction, it follows that every monad is a mirror that is alive or endowed with inner activity, is representative of the universe from its own point of view, and is as much regulated as the universe itself. The perceptions in the monad spring from one another according to the laws of the appetites or the *final causes of good and evil*, which consist in the observable perceptions, regulated or unregulated—in the same way as the changes of bodies and of external phenomena spring from one another according to the laws of *efficient causes*, that is to say of motions. Thus there is a perfect *harmony* between the perceptions of the monad and the motions of the bodies, pre-established at the outset between the system of efficient causes and the system of final causes. Herein consists the concord and the physical union of the soul and the body, which exists without the one being able to change the laws of the other.

4. Each monad, together with a particular body, makes a living substance. Thus there is not only life everywhere, joined to members or organs, but there are also infinite degrees of it in the monads, some of them more or less dominating over others. But when the monad has its organs adjusted in such a way that by means of them the impressions they receive, and consequently the perceptions which represent them, are distinguished and heightened (as, for example, when by means of the shape of the humours of the eye rays of light are concentrated and act with more force), this may amount to *sensation*, that is to say, to a perception

accompanied by *memory*—a perception, to wit, of which a certain echo long remains to make itself heard on occasion. Such a living being is called an *animal*, as its monad is called a *soul*. And when this soul is raised to the level of *reason*, it is something more sublime, and is reckoned as a mind, as will be explained later. It is true that animals are sometimes in the condition of simple living beings and their souls in the condition of simple monads, to wit, when their perceptions are not sufficiently distinguished to be remembered, as occurs in a deep dreamless sleep or in a swoon. But perceptions which have become entirely confused must necessarily be developed again in animals, for reasons I shall give below (12). Thus it is well to distinguish between *perception*, which is the inner state of the monad representing external things, and *apperception*, which is *consciousness*, or the reflective knowledge of this inner state, and which is not given to all souls, nor at all times to the same soul. It is for want of this distinction that the Cartesians made the mistake of taking no account of perceptions which are not apperceived, as common people take no account of insensible bodies. It is this also which made these same Cartesians believe that minds alone are monads, and that there are no souls in animals, and still less other *principles of life*. And while, in thus denying sensations to animals, they have gone against the common opinion of men too much, so they have, on the other hand, taken too much account of the prejudices of the vulgar, in confusing a *long stupor*, which arises from a great confusion of perceptions, with *actual death*, in which all perception would cease. This teaching of theirs has confirmed the ill-founded belief in the destruction of some souls, and the pernicious view of certain people, self-styled free-thinkers, who have denied the immortality of ours.

5. There is a connexion between the perceptions of animals, which bears some resemblance to reason: but it is based only on the memory of *facts* or effects, and not at all on the knowledge of *causes*. Thus a dog runs away from the stick with which he has been beaten, because memory represents to him the pain which was caused by that stick. And men, in so far as they are empiricists, that is to say in three-fourths of

their actions, only act like brutes. For example, we expect that
day will dawn tomorrow, because we have always experienced
it to be so; it is only the astonomer who foresees it by reason,
and even this prediction will ultimately fail when the cause
of daylight, which is not eternal, ceases. But true reasoning
depends on necessary or eternal truths (like the truths of
logic, numbers, and geometry) which produce the indubitable
connexion of ideas, and infallible inferences. Animals in which
such inferences cannot be observed are called *brutes*; but those
which know these necessary truths are called *rational animals*,
and their souls are called *minds*. These souls are capable of
performing acts of reflexion, and of considering what is
called self, substance, soul, mind—those things and truths, in
short, which are immaterial. It is this which makes us capable
of understanding science or demonstrative knowledge.

6. The researches of the moderns[b] have taught us, and it is
approved by reason, that the living things whose organs we
know, that is to say plants and animals, do not come from
putrefaction or chaos as the ancients believed, but from
pre-formed seeds, and consequently from the transformation
of pre-existing living things. There are little animals in the
seeds of the large ones, which by means of conception assume
a new vesture, which they appropriate, and which enables
them to be nourished and to grow, so as to pass on to a wider
stage, and propagate the large animal. It is true that the
souls of human spermatic animals are not rational and only
become so when through conception these animals are destined for human nature. And as animals are usually not born
completely in conception or *generation*, so neither do they perish
completely in what we call *death*; for it is reasonable that what
does not begin naturally should not come to an end in the
order of nature either. Thus, casting off their masks or their
rags, they merely return to a more subtle scene, on which,
however, they can be as sensible and as well ordered as on
the greater one. And what has just been said of large animals
occurs also in the generation and death of these spermatic
animals themselves; that is to say, they have grown from
other smaller spermatic animals, in comparison with which
they can be reckoned large; for everything in nature proceeds

ad infinitum. Thus not only souls but animals also are in-generable and imperishable: they are only developed, en-veloped, re-clad, stripped, transformed; souls never leave the whole of their body, and do not pass from one body to another which is entirely new to them. Thus there is no *metempsychosis,* but there is *metamorphosis.* Animals change, take on and put off parts only: in nutrition this takes place bit by bit, and by small insensible parts, but continually, while in conception and death when much is acquired or lost all at one time the change takes place rarely, but all at once and in a way that can be noticed.

7. Up till now we have spoken as *physicists* merely; now we must rise to *metaphysics,* making use of the *great principle,* commonly but little employed, which holds that *nothing takes place without sufficient reason,* that is to say that nothing hap-pens without its being possible for one who has enough knowledge of things to give a reason sufficient to determine why it is thus and not otherwise. This principle having been laid down, the first question we are entitled to ask will be: *Why is there something rather than nothing?* For 'nothing' is simpler and easier than 'something'. Further, supposing that things must exist, it must be possible to give a reason *why they must exist just as they do* and not otherwise.

8. Now this sufficient reason of the existence of the universe cannot be found in the series of contingent things, that is to say, of bodies and of their representations in souls. For since matter is in itself indifferent to motion or to rest, and to one motion rather than another, it cannot itself contain the reason of motion, still less of a particular motion. And although the present motion which is in matter arises from the one before it, and this in its turn from the one before that, we are no further on however far we go; for the same question always remains. Thus the sufficient reason, which needs no further reason, must be outside this series of contingent things, and must lie in a substance which is the cause of this series, or which is a necessary being, bearing the reason of its existence within itself; otherwise we should still not have a sufficient reason, with which we could stop. And this final reason of things is called *God.*

9. This simple primary substance must include eminently[c] the perfections which are contained in the derivative substances which are its effects. Thus it will have perfect power, knowledge, and will; that is to say, it will have omnipotence, omniscience, and supreme goodness. And as *justice*, taken in a very general sense, is nothing other than goodness in conformity with wisdom, there must clearly also be supreme justice in God. Reason, which has made things exist through Him, makes them also depend on Him in their existence and operation; and they are continually receiving from Him that which endows them with some perfection; but any imperfection which they retain comes from the essential and original limitation of the created thing.

10. It follows from the supreme perfection of God that in producing the universe He chose the best possible plan, containing the greatest variety together with the greatest order; the best arranged situation, place, and time; the greatest effect produced by the simplest means; the most power, the most knowledge, the most happiness and goodness in created things of which the universe admitted. For as all possible things have a claim to existence in the understanding of God in proportion to their perfections, the result of all these claims must be the most perfect actual world which is possible. Otherwise it would not be possible to explain why things have happened as they have rather than otherwise.

11. The supreme wisdom of God has made Him choose especially the *laws of motion* which are the best adjusted and the most fitted to abstract and metaphysical reasons. According to them[d] there is always conserved the same quantity of total and absolute force or activity; the same quantity of relative force or reaction; the same quantity, finally, of force of direction. Moreover the activity is always equal to the reaction, and the whole effect is always equivalent to its full cause. It is surprising that those laws of motion discovered in our day, some of which I have myself discovered, cannot be explained merely by the consideration of *efficient causes* or of matter. For I have found that it is necessary to have recourse to *final causes*, and that these laws do not depend on the *principle of necessity* as do the truths of logic, arithmetic, and

geometry, but on the *principle of fitness*, that is to say on the choice of wisdom. And this is one of the most effective and sensible proofs of the existence of God for those who are able to go deeply into these matters.

12. It follows, further, from the perfection of the Supreme Author, that not only is the order of the whole universe the most perfect possible, but also that each living mirror which represents the universe from its own point of view, that is to say each *monad*, each substantial centre, must have its perceptions and appetites regulated in the best way which is compatible with all the rest. From which it follows that *souls*, that is to say the most dominant monads, or rather animals themselves, cannot fail to wake up from the state of stupor in which they may be placed by death or by some other accident.

13. For everything is regulated in things once for all with as much order and agreement as possible, since supreme wisdom and goodness cannot act without perfect harmony: the present is big with the future, what is to come could be read in the past, what is distant is expressed in what is near. The beauty of the universe could be learnt in each soul, could one unravel all its folds which develop perceptibly only with time. But as each distinct perception of the soul includes an infinity of confused perceptions which embrace all the universe, the soul itself does not know the things which it perceives, except in so far as it has perceptions of them which are distinct and heightened: and it has perfection in proportion to its distinct perceptions. Each soul knows the in-finite, knows everything, but confusedly. Just as when I am walking along the shore of the sea and hear the great noise it makes, though I hear the separate sounds of each wave of which the total sound is made up, I do not discriminate them one from another; so our confused perceptions are the result of the impressions which the whole universe makes on us. It is the same with each monad. God alone has a distinct knowledge of everything, for he is the source of everything. It has been very well said that he is like a centre which is everywhere; but his circumference is nowhere, since everything is present to him immediately, without being removed from this centre.[e]

14. As regards the rational soul or *mind*, there is in it something more than in monads, or even in simple souls. It is not only a mirror of the universe of created things, but also an image of the Deity. The mind not only has a perception of the works of God, but is even capable of producing something like them, though on a small scale. For, not to mention the wonders of dreams, in which we invent without effort (but also without will) things we could only discover after much thinking when awake, our soul is architectonic in its voluntary activities also, and, discovering the sciences in accordance with which God had regulated things (*pondere, mensura, numero,*[1] etc.), it imitates in its own sphere, and in the little world in which it is allowed to act, what God performs in the great world.

15. For this reason all minds, whether of men or superhuman spirits, entering as they do by virtue of reason and the eternal verities into a kind of society with God, are members of the City of God, that is to say of the most perfect state, formed and governed by the greatest and best of monarchs: where there is no crime without punishment, no good action without proportionate reward, and finally as much virtue and happiness as is possible; and this, not by any derangement of nature, as if what God has in store for the soul might disturb the laws of the body, but by the actual order of natural things, by virtue of the harmony preestablished from all time between the realms of nature and of grace, between God as Architect and God as Monarch, in such a way that nature itself leads to grace, and grace perfects nature in making use of it.

16. Thus although reason cannot teach us the details of the great future, which are reserved for revelation, we can rest assured by this same reason that things are accomplished in a manner which exceeds our desires. Since, too, God is the most perfect and the most happy and consequently the most lovable of substances, and since *pure true love* consists in the state which causes pleasure to be felt in the perfections and happiness of the beloved, this love ought to give us the greatest pleasure of which a man is capable, when God is the object of it.

[1] 'by weight, measure, number', etc.

17. It is easy to love him as we ought if we know him as I have described. For although God is not sensible to our external senses, he is none the less very lovable and gives great pleasure. We see how much pleasure men derive from honours, although they do not consist of qualities that appear to the external senses. Martyrs and fanatics (although the affection of the latter is ill regulated) show of what the pleasure of the mind is capable: and what is more, even the pleasures of the senses are in the last resort intellectual pleasures, confusedly known. Music charms us although its beauty only consists in the harmony of numbers, and in the account which we do not notice, but which the soul none the less takes, of the beating or vibration of sounding bodies, which meet one another at certain intervals. The pleasures which the eye finds in proportions are of the same kind, and those caused by the other senses amount to much the same thing, although we may not be able to explain it so distinctly.

18. It may even be affirmed that love of God gives us here and now a foretaste of future felicity. And although it is disinterested, it constitutes of itself our greatest good and interest, even though we may not seek them in it, and consider only the pleasure which it gives without regard to the utility it produces; for it gives us a perfect confidence in the goodness of our Author and Master, which produces a true tranquillity of mind, not as in the Stoics, who resolutely force themselves to patience, but by a present contentment, which further assures us a future happiness. And apart from the present pleasure, nothing could be more useful for the future, for the love of God also fulfils our hopes, and leads us in the way of supreme happiness, because in virtue of the perfect order established in the universe, everything is done in the best possible way, as much for the general good as also for the greatest particular good of those who believe in it, and who are satisfied by the Divine government: which cannot fail to be the case with those who know how to love the Source of all good. It is true that supreme happiness (with whatever *beatific vision*, or knowledge of God, it may be accompanied) can never be complete because God, being infinite, cannot be entirely known. Thus our happiness will

never consist, and ought not to consist, in a complete enjoyment, in which there would be nothing left to desire, and which would make our mind stupid, but in a perpetual progress to new pleasures and new perfections.

Correspondence with Clarke[1]
(Selections) (1715–16)

LEIBNIZ'S FIRST PAPER[2]

(Extract from a letter written in November 1715)

It appears that even natural religion is growing very much weaker. Many hold that souls are corporeal; others hold that God himself is corporeal. Mr. Locke and his followers are at any rate doubtful whether souls are not material and naturally perishable. Mr. Newton says that space is the organ which God makes use of to perceive things by. But if he stands in need of any medium whereby to perceive them, they do not then depend entirely on him, and were not produced by him. Mr. Newton and his followers have also an extremely odd opinion of the work of God. According to them God has to wind up his watch from time to time.[3] Otherwise it would cease to go. He lacked sufficient foresight to make it a perpetual motion. This machine of God's is even, on their view, so imperfect that he is obliged to clean it from time to time by an extraordinary concourse, and even

---

[1] Samuel Clarke (1675–1729), English philosopher and divine; the most celebrated disciple of Newton.

[2] This paper by Leibniz begins the correspondence. It is given here complete.

[3] Clarke thinks that the passage to which Leibniz is referring is the following, from Newton's *Optics*: 'Whilst the comets move in orbs very eccentrical, with all variety of directions towards every part of the heavens; 'tis not possible it should have been caused by blind fate, that the planets all move with one similar direction in concentrick orbs; excepting only some very small irregularities, which may have arisen from the mutual actions of the planets and comets upon one another; and which 'tis probable will in length of time increase more and more, till the present system of nature shall want to be anew put in order by its Author.' *Optics*, Query 31.

to mend it, as a clockmaker might his handiwork; who will be the less skilful a workman, the more often is he obliged to mend and set right his work. According to my view, the same force and vigour goes on existing in the world always, and simply passes from one matter to another, according to the laws of nature and to the beautiful pre-established order. And I hold that, when God performs miracles, it is not to satisfy the needs of nature, but those of grace. To think otherwise would be to have a very low opinion of the wisdom and power of God.

LEIBNIZ'S SECOND PAPER[1]

It is rightly said in the Paper which was sent to the Princess of Wales, and which Her Royal Highness did me the honour of sending me, that next to vicious passions *the principles of the Materialists* do a great deal to support impiety. But I do not think the author was justified in adding that *the Mathematical Principles of philosophy are opposed to those of the Materialists.* On the contrary, they are the same except that Materialists follow the example of Democritus, Epicurus, and Hobbes, and restrict themselves to mathematical principles alone and admit nothing but bodies; while the Christian Mathematicians admit immaterial substances also. Thus it is not Mathematical Principles (in the ordinary sense of the term) but *Metaphysical Principles* which must be opposed to those of the Materialists. Pythagoras, Plato, and to some extent Aristotle had some knowledge of these, but it is my claim to have established them demonstratively in my *Theodicy*, although I have expounded them in a popular way. The great foundation of mathematics is the *principle of contradiction or of identity*, that is to say, that a statement cannot be true and false at the same time and that thus *A is A, and cannot be not A.* And this single principle is enough to prove the whole of arithmetic and the whole of geometry, that is to say all mathematical principles. But in order to proceed from

---

[1] This *Second Paper* was written in answer to Clarke's reply to Leibniz's *First Paper*. It is given here complete.

mathematics to physics another principle is necessary, as I have observed in my *Theodicy*, that is, the *principle of a sufficient reason*, that nothing happens without there being a reason why it should be thus rather than otherwise. This is why Archimedes, wishing to proceed from mathematics to physics in his book *On Equilibrium*, was compelled to make use of a particular case of the great principle of sufficient reason; he takes it for granted that if there is a balance in which everything is the same on both sides, and if, further, two equal weights be hung on the two ends of the balance, the whole will remain at rest. This is because there is no reason why one side should go down rather than the other. Now by this principle alone, to wit, that there must be a sufficient reason why things are thus rather than otherwise, I prove the existence of the Divinity, and all the rest of metaphysics or natural theology, and even in some manner those physical principles which are independent of mathematics, that is to say, the principles of dynamics or of force.

Our author goes on to say that according to the mathematical principles, that is to say according to the philosophy of Mr. Newton (for mathematical principles here prove nothing one way or the other), *matter is the least considerable part of the universe*. This is because he holds that besides matter there is empty space, and because according to him matter only occupies a very small part of space. But Democritus and Epicurus maintained the same thing, except that in this they differed from Mr. Newton on the point of quantity; according to them there was perhaps more matter in the world than according to Mr. Newton. Wherein I think their view is preferable; for the more matter there is, the more opportunity is there for God to exercise his wisdom and his power; and it is for this, among other reasons, that I hold that there is no void at all.

It is said expressly in the Appendix to Mr. Newton's *Optics* that *space is God's sensorium*.[1] Now the word *sensorium* has always meant the organ of sensation. Let him and his friends

---

[1] Clarke had objected to Leibniz's statement in his *First Paper* that 'Mr. Newton says that space is the organ which God makes use of to perceive things by'. Cf. p. 205.

now give a quite different explanation of their meaning: I
shall not object.

Our author supposes that the presence of the soul is enough
to enable it to perceive what is going on in the brain. But this
is exactly what Malebranche and the whole Cartesian School
deny, and rightly deny. Something quite other than mere
presence is needed for one thing to represent what takes
place in another. For this some explicable communication
is necessary, some kind of influence either of the things upon
one another or of a common cause.[a] Space, according to Mr.
Newton, is intimately present to the body which it contains
and which is commensurate with it. Does it therefore follow
that space perceives what takes place in the body, and re-
members it after the body has left it? Besides, since the soul
is indivisible and its immediate presence in the body could
therefore be conceived to be at a point only, how could it then
perceive what took place outside this point? I claim to be the
first to have shown how the soul perceives what takes place in
the body.

The reason why God perceives everything is not his
simple presence, but his operation also; it is because he
preserves things by an activity which continually produces
all that there is in them of goodness and perfection. But since
souls have no immediate influence on bodies, nor bodies on
souls, their mutual correspondence cannot be explained by
presence.

The real reason which chiefly causes us to praise a machine,
is derived rather from the effect of the machine than from
its cause. We seek information less regarding the power of the
machine-maker than regarding his skill. Thus the reason
alleged for praising God's machine—that he made it entirely
without borrowing any matter from outside—is not enough. It
is a shift to which the author has been compelled to resort. The
reason why God is to be preferred above another machine-
maker is not only because he makes the whole, whereas the
artisan has to seek for his material. This superiority would
arise from power only. But there is another reason for the
excellence of God, which arises from wisdom. This reason is
that his machine also lasts longer and goes more correctly

than that of any other machine-maker whatever. The buyer of the watch does not trouble himself whether the workman made the whole of it, or whether he had the pieces of it made by other workmen and merely adjusted them himself, provided that it goes properly. And if the workman had received from God the gift of creating as well the material for the wheels, the buyer would not be satisfied if the workman had not also received the gift of adjusting them properly. And in the same way the man who wants to be satisfied with God's handiwork will not become so merely for the reason alleged here.

Thus it is needful that God's skill should not be inferior to that of a workman; it must even go infinitely beyond it. The mere production of everything would indeed exemplify the power of God, but it would not sufficiently show his wisdom. Those who maintain the opposite fall exactly into the error of the Materialists and of Spinoza, from whom they protest they differ. They recognise power, but not sufficient wisdom in the principle of things.

I do not say that the corporeal world is a machine or watch which goes without God's *interposition*,[1] and I am insistent enough that created things stand in need of his continual influence. But I do maintain that it is a watch which goes without needing his *correction*: otherwise we should have to admit that God keeps improving upon his own work. God has foreseen everything, he has provided a remedy for everything in advance. There is in his works an already preestablished harmony and beauty.

This view does not exclude the providence or the government of God: on the contrary it makes it perfect. A true providence in God requires a perfect *foresight*, but moreover it further requires not only that he should have *foreseen* everything but also that he should have *provided for* everything by means of suitable preordained remedies: otherwise

---

[1] Clarke had made the (usual) objection to Leibniz: 'The notion of the world's being a great *machine*, going on *without the interposition of God*, as a clock continues to go without the assistance of a clockmaker, is the notion of *Materialism* and *Fate*, and tends (under pretence of making God a *Supramundane Intelligence*) to exclude *Providence* and *God's government* in reality out of the world'.

he would lack either wisdom to *foresee* things or power to *provide for* them. He would be like the God of the Socinians, who lives from day to day, as M. Jurieu said.[b] It is true that God, according to the Socinians, fails even to foresee defects, whereas, according to these gentlemen who force him to correct himself, he fails to provide for them. But this seems to me to be still a very great lack; he would have to lack either power or good will.

I do not think I can be justly rebuked for having said that God is *Intelligentia Supramundana*. Will those who disapprove of it say he is *Intelligentia Mundana*, that is to say the Soul of the World? I hope not. However, they would do well to take care not to slip into this unintentionally.

The comparison with a king in whose kingdom everything went on without his interference is not to the point, since God preserves things continually, and since they cannot subsist without him: thus his kingdom is not a nominal one. To say this would be like saying that a king who had his subjects so well educated, and by his care in providing for their subsistence, preserved them so well in their fitness for their several stations and in their good affection towards him,[c] that he had no occasion ever to be amending anything amongst them, was only a nominal king.

Finally, if God is obliged to correct natural things from time to time, this must occur either supernaturally or naturally. If it occurs supernaturally, recourse is had to miracles to explain natural things; which is in effect a *reductio ad absurdum* of a hypothesis. For by miracles, anything can easily be accounted for. But if it occurs naturally, God will not be *Intelligentia Supramundana*, he will be included in the nature of things, that is to say, he will be the Soul of the World.

LEIBNIZ'S THIRD PAPER[1]

1. According to the usual way of speaking, *mathematical principles*[2] are those which consist in pure mathematics, for

---

[1] Written in answer to Clarke's reply to the *Second Paper*. It is given here complete.

[2] Clarke had argued that the *Mathematical Principles of Philosophy* (i.e.

instance numbers, figures, arithmetic, geometry. But *metaphysical principles* concern more general notions, as for example cause and effect.

2. I am granted this important *principle, that nothing happens without a sufficient reason why it should be thus rather than otherwise*. But it is granted me in words and refused me in fact; which shows that the full force of it has not been properly understood; and in this connexion the author makes use of an example which exactly falls in with one of my demonstrations against real absolute space, the *idol* of some modern Englishman. I call it 'idol' not in a theological sense, but in the philosophical sense in which Chancellor Bacon used the word[d] when he said, a long time ago, that there are *idola tribus, idola specus*.[1]

3. These gentlemen maintain, then, that space is a real absolute being; but this leads them into great difficulties. For it appears that this being must be eternal and infinite. This is why there have been some who believed that it was God himself, or else his attribute, his immensity. But as it has parts, it is not a thing which can be appropriate to God.

4. As for me, I have more than once stated that I held *space* to be something purely relative, like *time*; space being an order of co-existences as time is an order of successions. For space denotes in terms of possibility an order of things which exist at the same time, in so far as they exist together, and is not concerned with their particular ways of existing: and when we see several things together we perceive this order of things among themselves.

5. I have several proofs for refuting the conception of those who take *space* to be a substance, or at least an absolute being of some kind. But here I only wish to make use of the one which the present occasion requires. I say then that

---

Newton's philosophical doctrines) are opposed to *Materialism* because they demonstrate that the existing state of things can only have arisen from an Intelligent and Free Cause. As regards the propriety of the name, he says: 'So far as metaphysical consequences follow demonstratively from mathematical principles, so far the mathematical principles may (if it be thought fit) be called metaphysical principles'.

[1] 'idols of the tribe, idols of the cave'.

if space were an absolute being, there would happen something for which it would be impossible that there should be a
sufficient reason, and this is contrary to our axiom. This is
how I prove it. Space is something absolutely uniform, and
without the things situated in it one point of space does not
differ absolutely in any respect from another point of space.
Now from this it follows that if we suppose that space is
something in itself, other than the order of bodies among
themselves, it is impossible that there should be a reason why
God, preserving the same positions for bodies among themselves, should have arranged bodies in space thus and not
otherwise, and why everything was not put the other way
round (for instance) by changing east and west. But if space
is nothing other than this order or relation, and is nothing
whatever without bodies but the possibility of placing them
in it, these two conditions, the one as things are, the other
supposed the other way round, would not differ from one
another: their difference exists only in our chimerical supposition of the reality of space in itself. But in truth the one
would be just the same as the other, as they are absolutely
indiscernible; and consequently there is no occasion to
search after a reason for the preference of the one to the
other.

6. The same is true of *time*. Suppose someone asks why
God did not create everything a year sooner; and that the
same person wants to infer from that that God did something
for which there cannot possibly be a reason why he did it
thus rather than otherwise, we should reply that his inference would be sound if time were something apart from
temporal things, for it would be impossible that there should
be reasons why things should have been applied to certain
instants rather than to others, when their succession remained
the same. But this itself proves that instants apart from
things are nothing, and that they only consist in the successive order of things; and if this remains the same, the one of
the two states (for instance that in which the creation was
imagined to have occurred a year earlier) would be nowise
different and could not be distinguished from the other which
now exists.

7. It will be seen from everything I have said that my axiom has not been fully understood, and that the author, while appearing to grant it, has really denied it. *It is true,* he says, *that nothing exists without a sufficient reason why it exists, and why it exists in this way rather than in some other,*[e] but he adds that this sufficient reason is often the *simple* or *mere will* of God, as when it is asked why matter was not placed elsewhere in space, the positions as between bodies being preserved. But this is simply maintaining that God wills something without there being a sufficient reason for his will, contrary to the axiom or general rule governing everything which happens. This is to relapse into the loose indifference which I have amply refuted, and which I have shown to be absolutely chimerical, even in created beings, and contrary to the wisdom of God, as if he could operate without acting reasonably.

8. I am met with the objection that not to admit this *simple and mere will* would be to remove from God the power of choice, and that this would be to fall into fatalism. But quite the reverse is true. I maintain that God has the power of choice, since I base it on the reason for the choice which is in conformity with his wisdom. And it is not this fatalism (which is nothing but the order of the highest wisdom or of providence) but a brute fatalism or necessity, in which there is neither wisdom nor choice, that we ought to avoid.

9. I had observed that if we diminish the quantity of matter, the quantity of objects on which God can exercise his goodness is diminished. The author answers that instead of matter there are other things in the void on which he does not fail to exercise it. Be it so; though I do not agree, for I hold that all created substance is accompanied by matter. But be it so. I answer that more matter was compatible with those same things, and consequently the said object will still be lessened. The example of a greater number of men or animals[f] is not to the purpose, for they would occupy the room of other things.

10. It will be difficult to make me believe that, in its ordinary use, *sensorium* does not mean the organ of sensation. Here are the words of Rudolphus Goclenius, in his *Philosophical Dictionary*:[g] *Sensiterium: barbarum Scholasticorum* (he says)

qui interdum sunt simiae Graecorum. Hi dicunt αἰσθητήριον, *ex quo ille facerunt Sensiterium pro Sensorio, id est, organo sensationis.*[1]

11. The simple presence of a substance, even an animated one, is not enough for perception: a blind man does not see, nor even does an absent-minded one. It is necessary to explain how the soul perceives what is outside itself.

12. God is not present in things by situation but by essence; his presence is manifested by his immediate operation. The presence of the soul is of quite another nature. To say that it is diffused throughout the body is to make it extended and divisible; to say that the whole of it exists in each part of each body is to make it divisible from itself. To attach it to one point, to spread it over several points are only improper expressions, *idola tribus.*[2]

13. If active force were lost in the universe by the natural laws which God has established in it, so that he needed a new impression to restore this force, like a workman setting right the imperfection of his machine, the disorder would occur not only with regard to us, but with regard to God himself. He could have prevented it and have taken better steps to avoid such an untoward occurrence. Actually, indeed, he has done so.

14. When I said that God has prepared actual remedies against these disorders in advance, I do not mean that God lets the disorders come and then finds remedies for them; but that he has found means in advance to prevent disorders from happening.

15. Our author attempts without success to criticise my expression, that God is *Intelligentia Supramundana*. To say that he is above the world is not to deny that he is in the world.

16. I have never given occasion for doubt whether God's conservation is an actual preservation and continuation of beings, powers, orders, dispositions, and motions; and I

[1] '*Sensiterium*: a barbarism of the Scholastics, who sometimes ape the Greeks. The latter say αἰσθητήριον, from which the former have manufactured the word *sensiterium* in place of *sensorium*, i.e. the organ of sensation.'

[2] Cf. note, p. 211.

think I have perhaps explained it better than many others. But, says our author, *this is all that I contended for: herein consists the whole dispute.* To this I answer: Your most humble servant. Our dispute consists in quite different things. The question is whether God does not act in the most regular and perfect manner; whether his machine is liable to disorders which he will be obliged to set right by extraordinary means; whether the will of God is capable of acting without reason; whether space is an absolute being; wherein consists the nature of miracles: and many similar questions which set a great gulf between us.

17. Theologians will not agree with the thesis advanced against me, that there is no difference in relation to God between the natural and the supernatural. The majority of philosophers will approve it even less. There is an infinite difference, but it certainly seems not to have been given proper consideration. The supernatural surpasses all the powers of created things. We must take an example. Here is one which I have often made use of with success. If God wished to cause a free body to circle in the ether round about a given fixed centre, without any other created thing acting on it, this, I say, could only occur by miracle, not being explicable by the nature of bodies. For a free body naturally departs from a curve along the tangent. It is in this sense that I maintain that the attraction of bodies, properly so called, is a miraculous thing, since it cannot be explained by their nature.

LEIBNIZ'S FOURTH PAPER[1]

1. In things which are absolutely indifferent there is no choice and consequently no election or will, since choice must have some reason or principle.

2. A simple will without any motive (*a mere will*) is a fiction which is not only contrary to the perfection of God, but also chimerical and contradictory, incompatible with the definition of will and sufficiently refuted in my *Theodicy.*

[1] Written in answer to Clarke's reply to the *Third Paper.* As will be seen, some paragraphs have been omitted here.

3. It is indifferent whether three bodies which are equal and alike in every respect be placed in any order whatsoever, and consequently they never would be placed in order by Him who does nothing without wisdom. But also, being the Author of things, He will not produce any such; and consequently there are none in nature.

4. There are no two individuals indiscernible from one another. A clever gentleman, a friend of mine, when conversing with me in the presence of Her Electoral Highness[1] in the garden at Herrenhausen, thought he would certainly find two leaves exactly alike. Her Electoral Highness challenged him to do so, and he spent a long time running about looking for them, but in vain. Two drops of water or milk looked at under the microscope will be found to be discernible. This is an argument against atoms, which, like the void, are opposed to the principles of a true metaphysic.

5. These great principles of a Sufficient Reason and of the Identity of Indiscernibles change the state of metaphysics, which by their means becomes real and demonstrative; whereas formerly it practically consisted of nothing but empty terms.

6. To suppose two things indiscernible is to suppose the same thing under two names. Thus the hypothesis that the universe should have originally had another position in time and place from that which it actually had, and yet all the parts of the universe should have had the same position with regard to one another as that which they have in fact received, is an impossible fiction.

7. The same reason which shows that space outside the world is imaginary proves that all empty space is something imaginary; for they differ only as the great from the small.

8. If space is a property or an attribute, it must be the property of some substance. Of what substance is the bounded empty space, which the supporters of this view suppose to exist between two bodies, the property or affection?

9. If infinite space is immensity, finite space will be the opposite of immensity, that is to say mensurability or bounded extension. Now extension must be the affection of something

[1] Sophia, Electress of Hanover, mother of George I of England.

extended. But if this space is empty, it will be an attribute without a subject, an extension of no extended thing. This is why in making space a property the author is accepting my position, according to which it is an order of things and not something absolute.

10. If space is an absolute reality, far from being a property or accident opposed to substance, it will have more subsistence than substances; God will be unable to destroy it, or even to change it in any respect. It will be not only immense in the whole, but also immutable and eternal in each of its parts. There will be an infinity of eternal things besides God.

11. To say that infinite space is without parts, is to say that it is not made up of finite spaces, and that infinite space might continue to exist though all finite spaces were reduced to nothing. It would be as if we were to say, on the Cartesian supposition of a corporeal extended universe without limits, that this universe might continue to exist though all the bodies which make it up were reduced to nothing.

13. To say that God could cause the universe to move forward in a straight line or otherwise without changing it in any other way is another chimerical supposition. For two indiscernible states are the same state, and consequently it is a change which changes nothing. Further, there is no rhyme nor reason in it. Now God does nothing without a reason, and it is impossible that there should be one here. Besides, it would be *agendo nihil agere*,[1] as I have just said, because of the indiscernibility.

14. These are *idola tribus*,[2] the purest chimeras and superficial imaginings. It is all founded merely on the supposition that imaginary space is real.

15. It is a similar, that is to say an impossible, fiction to suppose that God had created the world several million years sooner. Those who incline towards such kinds of fiction will be unable to reply to those who argue in favour of the eternity of the world. For since God does nothing without a reason,

[1] 'acting without doing anything'.
[2] Cf. p. 211, note.

and since there is no reason assignable why he did not create the world sooner, it will follow either that he created nothing at all, or that he produced the world before any assignable time, which is to say that the world is eternal. But when we show that the beginning, whatever it was, is always the same thing, the question why it was not otherwise ceases to arise.

16. If space and time were something absolute, that is to say if they were something other than certain orders of things, what I am saying would be a contradiction. But since this is not the case, the hypothesis is contradictory, that is to say it is an impossible fiction.

17. It is very like what happens in geometry where, by the very supposition that a figure is greater, we sometimes prove that in fact it is not greater. It is a contradiction; but the contradiction is in the hypothesis, which for this very reason is shown to be false.

18. The uniformity of space means that there is neither *internal nor external reason* for discerning its parts, and for choosing between them. For such external reason for discerning could only be founded in the internal one; otherwise it would be discerning the indiscernible, or choosing without discerning. Will without reason would be the 'chance' of the Epicureans.[h] A God who acted by such a will would be a God only in name. The source of these errors is want of care to avoid what is derogatory to the Divine perfections.

19. When two incompatible things are equally good, and when one has no advantage over the other either in itself or in its combination with others, God will produce neither.

20. God is never determined by external things, but always by what is in himself, that is to say by his knowledge, before anything exists outside him.

21. There is no possible reason which could limit the quantity of matter. Therefore there cannot in fact be any such limitation.

22. And suppose such an arbitrary limitation did exist, it would always be possible to add something without derogating from the perfection of those things which already exist: and consequently it would always be necessary to add something,

in order to accord with the principle of the perfection of Divine operations.

23. Thus it could not be said that the present quantity of matter is the most fitting for the present constitution of things. And even if this were the case, it would follow that this present constitution of things would not be the most fitting absolutely, if it prevents the employment of more matter; it would therefore be necessary to choose another constitution of things, capable of something more.

29. God perceives things in himself. Space is the place of things, and not the place of the ideas of God: unless we consider space as something which causes the union of God and things, in imitation of the imagined union of the soul and the body; which would still make God the Soul of the World.

32. Those who imagine that souls can give a new force to bodies, and that God does the same in the world so as to correct the imperfections of his machine, make God too like the soul, by attributing too much to the soul and too little to God.

33. For it is only God that can give nature new forces, and he does it supernaturally only. If he needed to do it in the natural course of things he would have made a very imperfect work. He would be, in the world, like what the soul is commonly held to be in the body.

38. Those who imagine that active forces[1] diminish of themselves in the world, do not properly understand the principal laws of nature, and the beauty of the works of God.

41. The author says that space does not depend on the

---

[1] Clarke says that when he spoke of active forces diminishing, he meant by active force 'nothing but motion, and the impetus or relative impulsive force of bodies, arising from and being proportional to their motion'. He quotes from Newton's *Optics*: 'Since therefore all the various motions that are in the world are perpetually *decreasing*, 'tis absolutely necessary, in order to preserve and renew those motions, that we have recourse to some *active* principles'. (*Optics*, Query 31. Clarke, Paper 3, 13–14.)

situation of bodies. I answer that it is true that it does not depend on such and such a particular situation of bodies; but it is the order which makes bodies capable of having situation, and through which they have a situation with regard to one another when existing together; just as time is this order in relation to their successive position. But if there were no created beings space and time would only exist in the ideas of God.[1]

PS.

All those who believe in the void allow themselves to be guided more by imagination than by reason. When I was a young man, I also fell into the snare of the void and of atoms; but reason brought me back. The imagination was a pleasing one. On this theory a limit is set to our researches; reflexion is fixed and as it were pinned down; we suppose ourselves to have found the first elements—a *non plus ultra*. We should like nature to go no further; we should like it to be finite, like our mind; but this is to ignore the greatness and majesty of the Author of things. The least corpuscle is actually subdivided *ad infinitum* and contains a world of new created things, which the universe would lack if this corpuscle were an atom, that is a body all of a piece and not subdivided. In the same way, to want to put a void in nature is to attribute to God a very imperfect production; it is to violate the great principle of the necessity of a *sufficient reason*, of which many people speak with their lips without at all recognising its force, as I showed recently when I made it clear by means of this principle that space is only an order of things, like time, and in no sense an absolute being. Not to mention many other reasons against the void and atoms, here are those which I derive from the perfection of God and from *sufficient reason*. I assume that any perfection which God could put in things, without derogating from the other perfections in them, has been put there. Now let us imagine a space entirely empty; God could put in it some matter without in any way derogating from anything else whatever; therefore he did put some matter therein; therefore there is no

[1] Several sections containing a further discussion of the nature of *miracles* are omitted here.

space entirely empty; therefore everything is full. The same argument proves that there is no corpuscle which is not subdivided. Here also is the reason taken from the necessity of a *sufficient reason*. It is not possible that there should be a principle determining the proportion of matter, or what is filled, to the void, or of the void to the plenum. It will perhaps be said that one must be equal to the other; but as matter has more perfection than empty space, reason demands that a geometrical proportion be observed, and that there should be more plenum in proportion as it is worthy of preference. But then there would be no void at all, for the perfection of matter is to the perfection of the void as something is to nothing. The same argument applies to atoms. What reason can be assigned for limiting nature in the process of subdivision? Purely arbitrary fictions, and unworthy of true philosophy. The reasons alleged in favour of the void are but sophisms.

LEIBNIZ'S FIFTH PAPER[1]

8.[2] But the good, whether true or apparent, in a word the motive, inclines without necessitating, that is to say without imposing an absolute necessity. For when God (for instance) chooses the best, that which he does not choose and which is inferior in perfection is none the less possible. If what God chooses were necessary,[1] everything else would be impossible, which would be contrary to our hypothesis, for God chooses between possibles, that is to say between several courses, not one of which implies a contradiction.

9. To say that God can only choose the best, and to infer from this that what he does not choose is impossible, is to confuse terms: namely, power and will, metaphysical necessity and moral necessity, essences and existences. For what is necessary is so by its essence, because the opposite implies a

---

[1] Written in answer to Clarke's reply to the *Fourth Paper*. Here Leibniz takes up the points at much greater length. It will be seen that much of this paper has been omitted here.

[2] §§ 1–7 contain further answers to the charge of *fatalism*. Cf. p. 209.

contradiction; but the contingent which exists owes its existence to the principle of what is best, the sufficient reason for things. And this is why I say that motives incline without necessitating; and that there is a certainty and infallibility, but not an absolute necessity, in contingent things.

10. And I have sufficiently shown in my *Theodicy* that this moral necessity is good, and in conformity with Divine perfection, and in conformity with the *great principle of existences*, which is that of the need of a sufficient reason; whereas absolute and metaphysical necessity depends on the other great principle of our reasonings, the principle of *essences*, that is to say that of identity or contradiction: for what is absolutely necessary is the only possible course, and its contrary implies a contradiction.

11. I have shown also that our will does not always precisely follow the practical understanding, because it may have or find reasons for suspending its resolution until a further discussion.

14. . . . I now come to the objection made against my comparison between the weights of a balance and the motives of the will. The author objects that the balance is purely passive and weighed down by the weights, whereas agents which are intelligent and endowed with will are active. To this I reply, that the principle of the necessity of a sufficient reason is common both to active and to passive things. They need a sufficient reason for their activity as well as for their passivity. Not only does the balance not act when it is weighed down equally on both sides, but equal weights do not act either, when they are in equilibrium in such a way that one cannot go down without the other going up to the same extent.

15. It must also be considered that, strictly speaking, motives do not act on the mind like weights on a balance; it is rather the mind which acts by virtue of the motives, which are its dispositions to act. Thus to maintain, as it is here maintained, that the mind sometimes prefers weak motives above stronger ones, and even sometimes what is indifferent above motives, is to separate the mind from its motives, as if they were outside of it, as the weight is distinct from the

balance; and as if there were in the mind other dispositions to action besides motives, by virtue of which the mind rejected or accepted the motives. Whereas the truth is that motives comprise all the dispositions which the mind can have to act voluntarily, for they comprise not only reasons but also inclinations, which come from the passions or from other preceding impressions. Thus if the mind preferred a weak above a strong inclination it would be acting against itself and otherwise than it is disposed to act. This shows that notions which differ on this point from mine are superficial and turn out to have nothing in them, when they are properly considered.

16. To say also that *the mind may have good reasons for acting* when it has no motives, and *when things are absolutely indifferent,* as is explained here, is a manifest contradiction. For if there are good reasons for the course it adopts, the things are not indifferent to it.

17. And to say that a man will act when he has reasons for acting, *even though the ways of acting may be absolutely indifferent,* is again to speak most superficially, and in a very unjustifiable manner. For in this case there is no sufficient reason for acting when there is not a sufficient reason for acting *in a particular manner,* since every action is individual, and not general or abstracted from its circumstances, and it needs some way of being carried out. Thus when there is a sufficient reason for doing a particular action, there is a sufficient reason also for acting in a particular way, and consequently the ways of acting are not indifferent. On every occasion that a man has sufficient reasons for a given particular action, he has sufficient reasons also for doing everything which is requisite for that action.

21. It must be admitted that this great principle,[1] although it has been recognised, has not been sufficiently made use of. And this is to a great extent why *First Philosophy*[2] has been so little productive and demonstrative hitherto. I infer from this principle, among other consequences, that there are not

[1] i.e. the principle of sufficient reason.
[2] i.e. metaphysics.

in nature two real absolute beings which are indiscernible from one another; because if there were, God and nature would be acting without reason in treating one differently from the other; and thus that God does not produce two portions of matter which are perfectly equal and alike, The author replies to this conclusion without refuting the reason for it, and he replies by a very feeble objection. *That argument*, he says, *if it was good would prove that it would be impossible for God to create any matter at all. For the perfectly solid parts of matter, if we take them of equal figure and dimensions (which is always possible in supposition) would be exactly alike.* But it is an obvious *petitio principii* to suppose this perfect agreement which, on my view, cannot be admitted. This supposition of two indiscernibles, as of two portions of matter which perfectly agree with one another, seems possible in the abstract, but it is not compatible with the order of things, nor with Divine wisdom, by which nothing is admitted without a reason. The vulgar imagine such things because they are satisfied with incomplete notions. And this is one of the faults of the Atomists.

22. Besides, I do not allow that there are in matter parts which are perfectly solid, or which are all of a piece, without any variety or particular motion in their parts, as the pretended atoms are conceived to be. To suppose that there are such bodies is another popular and ill-founded opinion. According to my demonstrations, each portion of matter is actually subdivided into parts differently affected, and no one altogether resembles another.

23. I had maintained that two indiscernibles can never be found among sensible things, and that, for example, we should never find two leaves in a garden, nor two drops of water, which were perfectly alike. The author admits this with regard to leaves and 'perhaps' with regard to drops of water. But it might be admitted without question, or without the 'perhaps', of the drops of water too.

24. I hold that these general observations which apply to sensible things apply also in proportion to insensible things. And that in this respect it may be said, as Harlequin says in the *Emperor of the Moon*, ''tis there as 'tis here'. And it is a

great argument against indiscernibles that no instance of them can be found. But the author objects to this consequence on the ground that sensible bodies are compounded, whereas there are alleged to be insensible bodies which are simple. I answer again that I do not admit of any. According to me, there is nothing simple except true monads, which have no parts and no extension. Simple bodies and even perfectly similar ones are a consequence of the false doctrine of a void and of atoms, or else of lazy philosophy, which does not press far enough the analysis of things, and thinks it can arrive at the primary corporeal elements of nature, since they would satisfy our imagination.

25. When I deny that there are two drops of water perfectly alike, or two other bodies indiscernible from one another, I do not mean that it is absolutely impossible to suppose them, but that it is a thing contrary to Divine wisdom and consequently that it does not exist.

26. I admit that if two perfectly indiscernible things did exist, they would be two. But the supposition is false, and contrary to the great principle of reason. The vulgar philosophers were mistaken when they thought that there existed things which differed *solo numero*,[1] or only because they were *two*: and it is from this error that their perplexities about what they called the *principle of individuation* arose. Metaphysics has ordinarily been treated as a mere doctrine of terms, like a philosophical dictionary, without ever coming to a discussion of things. *Superficial philosophy*, like that of the Atomists and Vacuists, fabricates for itself things which higher reasons render inadmissible. I hope that my proofs will change the face of philosophy, in spite of feeble contradictions such as I meet with here.

27. The parts of time and of place, taken in themselves, are ideal things: thus they are perfectly alike, like two abstract units. But this is not the case with two concrete unities, nor with two actual times, nor with two occupied, that is to say truly actual, spaces.

28. I do not say that two points of space are one and the same point, nor that two instants of time are one and the

---

[1] 'numerically only'.

same instant, as seems to be imputed to me. But it may be imagined through lack of knowledge that there are two different instants when there is one only, as I observed in § 17 of my foregoing reply that often in geometry we suppose there to be two, so as to show up an opponent's error, and find but one. If someone supposed that one straight line cut another at two points he would ultimately find out that these two pretended points must coincide and can only make one. This also happens when a straight line, which in all other instances cuts a given curve, becomes a tangent.[k]

29. I have proved that space is nothing other than an order of the existence of things, which is observed when they exist simultaneously. Thus the fiction of a finite material universe, the whole of which moves about in an infinite empty space, cannot be admitted. It is altogether unreasonable and impracticable. For besides the fact that there is no real space outside the material universe, such an action would be without purpose; it would be working without doing anything, *agendo nihil agere*. No change which could be observed by any one whatever would be occurring. Such things are the imaginings of *philosophers with incomplete notions*, who make of space an absolute reality. Mere mathematicians who do but concern themselves with the play of the imagination are capable of fabricating to themselves such notions; but they are destroyed by higher reasons.

30. Absolutely speaking, it appears that God is able to make the material universe finite in extension; but the contrary seems better to conform with his wisdom.

31. I do not allow that everything finite is mobile. Indeed, according to the hypothesis of my opponents, a part of space, though finite, is not mobile. What is mobile must be able to change its position in relation to something else, and it must be possible for a new state discernible from the first state to arise: otherwise the change is a fiction. Thus a mobile finite thing must be part of some other finite thing, so that a change that can be observed can take place.

32. Descartes maintained that matter has no limits,[1] and I do not think he has been sufficiently refuted. And even if this is granted him,[1] it does not follow that matter would be

necessary, nor that it should have existed from all eternity, since the unlimited diffusion of matter would but be an effect of the choice of God, who held it to be better so.

33. Since space is itself a thing ideal, like time, space outside the world must certainly be imaginary, as the Schoolmen themselves recognised well enough. The same is true of empty space in the world, which I also hold to be imaginary for the reasons I have given.

34. The author brings forward as an objection against me the vacuum discovered by M. Guericke of Magdeburg:[m] this was made by pumping the air out of a container. It is claimed that there genuinely is a perfect void, or space empty of matter, in part at least, in the container. The Aristotelians and the Cartesians, who do not admit the existence of a true void, replied to this experiment of M. Guericke's as well as to the experiment made by M. Torricelli[n] of Florence (who emptied the air out of a glass tube by means of mercury), by saying that there is no vacuum at all in the tube or in the container since the glass has small pores, through which rays of light, magnetic rays, and other very fine sorts of matter can pass. And I am of their opinion. For I hold that the container may be compared to a box full of holes placed in water, in which there are fish or other gross bodies, which being removed, their room would not fail to be filled with water. There is this difference only, that water, though it is fluid and more yielding than these gross bodies, is yet as heavy and as massive as they are, or even more so; whereas the matter which enters the container in the room of the air is much finer. The new supporters of the void reply in this instance that it is not the grossness of matter, but simply its quantity, which produces resistance, and that consequently there is necessarily more void where there is less resistance. They add that thinness has nothing to do with it, and that the parts of quicksilver are as rarefied and as fine as those of water, and that yet quicksilver has more than ten times the resistance. To this I answer, that it is not so much the quantity

[1] Clarke had said: 'To say that God could not have altered the *time* or *place* of the existence of matter, is making it to be *necessarily infinite* and *eternal*, and reducing all things to *Necessity* and *Fate*'. (Clarke, Paper 4, 5–6.)

of matter as the difficulties it makes in giving way which causes the resistance. For example, floating timber contains less weight of matter than water of equal volume, and yet it resists a boat more than the water does.

35. And as to quicksilver, it contains in truth about fourteen times as much weight of matter as an equal volume of water; but it does not follow that it contains fourteen times more matter absolutely. On the contrary, water contains as much, if we take together both its own matter which has weight and a foreign matter of no weight which passes through its pores. For both quicksilver and water are masses of heavy matter pierced with holes, through which there passes a great deal of matter which has no weight and which does not resist sensibly. Such, it appears, is the matter which composes rays of light, and other insensible fluids; such above all is that fluid which itself causes the gravity of gross bodies, by withdrawing itself from the centre where it forces them to go. For it is a strange fiction to regard all matter as having gravity, and even to regard it as gravitating towards all other matter, as if every body had an equal attraction for every other body in proportion to mass and distance; and this by means of attraction properly so called, and not derived from an occult impulsion of the bodies. Whereas in truth the gravitation of sensible bodies towards the centre of the earth must be produced by the movement of some fluid. And the same is true of other gravitations such as those of the planets towards the sun or towards one another. A body is never moved naturally except by another body which impels it by touching it; and after this it goes on until it is hindered by another body touching it. Any other operation on bodies is either miraculous or imaginary.

36. As I objected that space, taken as something real and absolute without bodies, would be a thing eternal, impassible, and independent of God, our author has tried to elude this difficulty by saying that space is a property of God. In my previous paper I opposed this by saying that the property of God is immensity; but that space, which is often commensurate with bodies, and the immensity of God are not the same thing.

37. I further objected that if space is a property, and if infinite space is the immensity of God, then finite space will be the extension or mensurability of something finite. Thus the space occupied by a body will be the extension of that body: which is absurd, since a body can change space, but cannot leave its extension.

38. I also asked: If space is a property, of what thing will a limited empty space, such as is imagined in the container emptied of air, be the property? It does not seem reasonable to say that this round or square empty space is a property of God. Is it perhaps the property of some immaterial, extended, imaginary substance which (it seems) our author pictures to himself in the imaginary spaces?

39. If space is the property or affection of the substance which is in space, the same space would be the affection now of one body, now of another body, now of an immaterial substance, now perhaps of God, when it is empty of every other substance, material or immaterial. But it must be a very strange property or affection to pass like this from subject to subject. Subjects would thus put off their accidents like garments, so that other subjects could put them on. After that, how would one distinguish accidents and substances?

40. If limited spaces are the affections of limited substances which are in them, and if infinite space is the property of God, it must follow (strange though it may seem) that a property of God is composed of the affections of created things; for all the finite spaces, taken together, make up infinite space.

41. If it is denied that limited space is an affection of limited things, it will not be reasonable either for infinite space to be the affection or property of an infinite thing. I have touched on all these difficulties in my previous paper, but it does not look as though any attempt has been made to answer them.

42. I have yet other reasons against this strange fancy that space is a property of God. If it is, space enters into the essence of God. Now space has parts, so there would be parts in the essence of God. *Spectatum admissi.*[1]

---

[1] *Spectatum admissi risum teneatis, amici?* 'If you saw such a thing, my friends, could you restrain your laughter?' (Horace, *De Arte Poetica*, l.5.)

43. Moreover, spaces are sometimes empty, sometimes full: thus there would be in the essence of God parts which are sometimes empty, sometimes full, and consequently subject to a perpetual change. The bodies which fill space would fill a part of the essence of God, and would be commensurate with it; and, on the supposition of a vacuum, a part of the essence of God would be in the container. This *God with parts* will be very like the Stoic God, who was the whole universe, considered as a divine animal.

44. If infinite space is God's immensity, infinite time will be God's eternity. We must say, then, that what is in space is in God's immensity, and consequently in his essence; and that what is in time is in the essence of God also. Strange phrases, which plainly show that our author is misusing terms.

45. Here is another instance: God's immensity makes him present in all spaces. But if God is in space, how can it be said that space is in God, or that it is his property? We have heard of the property being in the subject, but never of the subject being in its property. In the same way God exists in every time; how then is time in God, and how can it be a property of God? These are perpetual ἀλλογλωσσίαι.[1]

46. It looks as though the immensity or extension of things were being confused with the space according to which that extension is taken. Infinite space is not the immensity of God, finite space is not the extension of bodies, just as time is not their duration. Things keep their extension, but they do not always keep their space. Each thing has its own extension, its own duration; but it does not have its own time, and it does not keep its own space.

47. This is how men come to form the notion of space. They consider that several things exist at the same time, and they find in them a certain order of co-existence, in accordance with which the relation of one thing to another is more or less simple. This is their situation or distance. When it happens that one of these co-existent things changes its relation to a number of others without their changing with regard to one another, and when another thing makes its appearance and acquires the same relation to the others as the first one

[1] 'misuses of words'.

had, we say that it has taken its *place*, and we call this change a *motion* in that body wherein is the immediate cause of the change. And when several or even all of these co-existent things change in accordance with certain known rules of direction and speed, we can always determine the relation of situation which any given body acquires with regard to every other; and even the relation which any other would have,⁰ or which the given body would have to any other, if it had not changed, or if it had changed in a different way. If we suppose or pretend that among these co-existents there were a sufficient number which suffered no change in themselves, then we may say that those which have the same relation to these fixed existents as others had before, occupy the same *place* as those others occupied. That which includes all these places is called *space*. This shows that in order to have the idea of place, and consequently of space, it is enough to consider these relations and the rules of their changes, without needing to picture any absolute reality beyond the things whose situation is being considered. To give a kind of definition: *Place* is that which is said to be the same for *A* and for *B*, when the relation of co-existence between *B* and *C, E, F, G*, etc., entirely agrees with the relation of co-existence which *A* previously had with those bodies, supposing there has been no cause of change in *C, E, F, G*, etc. It may also be said (without ἔκθεσις¹) that *place* is that which is the same at different moments for certain existents when they, although different, have relations of co-existence with other existents (these latter being supposed to be fixed from the one of these moments to the other) which agree entirely. And *fixed existents* are those in which there has been no cause for a change of the order of co-existence with others, or (which is the same thing) in which there has been no motion. Lastly, *space* is that which results from places taken together. And it is well here to consider the difference between place and the relation of situation of the body which occupies the place. For the place of *A* and *B* is the same, whereas the relation of *A* to fixed bodies is not precisely and individually the same as the relation that *B* (which is to take its place) will have to the same fixed bodies;

---

¹ i.e. without reference to particulars.

these relations only agree. For two different subjects, such as
A and *B*, cannot have exactly the same individual affection,
since one and the same individual accident cannot occur in
two subjects, nor pass from one subject to another. But the
mind, not content with agreement, seeks an identity, a thing
which is truly the same, and conceives it as outside these
subjects; and this is what is here called *place* and *space*. This,
however, can only be ideal, comprising a certain order
wherein the mind conceives the application of the relations:
just as the mind can imagine an order consisting of genealogical lines, whose length would consist only in the number of
generations, in which each person would have his place. And
if we added the fiction of metempsychosis, and made the
same human souls come in again, the persons might change
their places in these lines. He who had been father or grand-
father might become son or grandson, etc. And yet those
genealogical places, lines, and spaces, although they expressed real truths, would only be ideal things. I will give
another example of the mind's habit of creating for itself,
upon occasion of accidents existing in subjects, something
which corresponds to those accidents outside the subjects.
The ratio or proportion of two lines *L* and *M* can be conceived in three ways: as a ratio of the greater *L* to the smaller
M, as a ratio of the smaller *M* to the greater *L*, and lastly as
scmething abstracted from both of them, that is to say as the
ratio between *L* and *M*, without considering which is the
anterior and which the posterior, which the subject and which
the object. It is in this way that proportions are considered in
music. In the first way of considering them, *L* the greater is
the subject; in the second, *M* the smaller is the subject of this
accident which philosophers call relation. But which will be
the subject in the third way of considering them? We cannot
say that the two, *L* and *M* together, are the subject of such an
accident, for in that case we should have an accident in two
subjects, with one leg in one and the other leg in the other,
which is contrary to the notion of accidents. Thus we are
bound to say that the relation in this third way of considering
it is indeed outside the subjects; but that being neither substance nor accident, it must be a purely ideal thing, the con-

sideration of which is none the less useful. For the rest, I have acted rather like Euclid, who, when he could not make it absolutely understood what is meant by *ratio*, in the geometricians' sense, defined properly what is meant by *the same ratios*. In the same way, in order to explain what *place* is, I have tried to define *the same place*. Finally I remark that the traces which mobile things sometimes leave on the immobile things on which they exercise their motion, have afforded to men's imagination occasion to form this idea, as if there still remained some trace even when there is nothing immobile: but this is ideal merely, and only means that *if there were something immobile actually there, the trace might be pointed out on it.* And it is this analogy which causes us to imagine places, traces, and spaces, although these things only consist in the truth of relations, and nowise in any absolute reality.

49. We cannot say that a certain duration is eternal, but we can say that the things which last for ever are eternal, because they are always acquiring a new duration. Whatever of time and of duration does exist, since it is successive, continually perishes. And how could a thing exist eternally which properly speaking never exists? And how could a thing exist, no part of which ever exists? In the case of time nothing exists but instants, and an instant is not even a part of time. Whoever gives proper consideration to these observations will easily understand that time can only be an ideal thing. And the analogy of time and space will indeed make us judge that the one is as ideal as the other. Still, if, when it is said that the duration of a thing is eternal, this only means that the thing endures eternally, I have nothing further to say.

52. In order to prove that space without bodies is an absolute reality, the author raised it as an objection to my view that a finite material universe might move about in space. I answered, that it does not seem reasonable that the material universe should be finite; and even if it were supposed to be so, it is unreasonable that it should have any movement except in so far as its parts change their situation among themselves: because a movement of this kind would produce

no observable change and would be without purpose. It is a different thing when its parts change their situation among themselves, for then we recognise a movement in space; but it consists in the order of the relations, which are changed. The author now answers that the truth of the movement is independent of its being observed, and that a ship can go forward without a man who is in it perceiving the motion. I answer that motion is independent of being observed, but it is not independent of being observable. There is no motion when there is no observable change. Moreover, when there is no observable change, there is no change at all. The contrary view is based on the supposition of a real absolute space, which I demonstratively refuted by the principle of the necessity of a sufficient reason of things.

53. I find nothing in the eighth definition of the *Mathematical Principles of Nature*,ᵖ nor in the *Scholium* of this definition, which proves or can prove the reality of space in itself. But I grant that there is a difference between a genuine absolute movement of a body and a simple relative change of its situation with respect to another body. For when the immediate cause of the change is in the body, it is genuinely in motion and then the situation of the rest with respect to it will be changed in consequence, although the cause of this change is not in them. It is true that, to speak exactly, there is no body which is perfectly and entirely at rest; it is an abstraction which we make when we consider the thing mathematically. Thus I have left unanswered nothing of all the arguments alleged in favour of the absolute reality of space. And I have proved the falsity of this reality by one of the most reasonable and well founded of fundamental principles, against which no exception nor example can be brought. For the rest, it may be seen from all that I have just said, that I cannot admit a movable universe, nor any place outside the material universe.

54. I know of no objection which I do not think I have adequately answered. And as to this objection that space and time are quantities, or rather things having quantity, and that situation and order are not such, I reply that order also has its quantity: there is that which precedes and that which follows,

there is distance or interval. Relative things have their quantity as well as absolutes: for example, ratios or proportions in mathematics have their quantity and are measured by logarithms, and yet they are relations. Thus although time and space consist in relations, they have their quantity none the less.

57. This enables us to see how to interpret the assertion that God created things at the time which was pleasing to him, for this depends on the things which he resolves to create. Once the things have been resolved upon with their relations, there remains no further choice of time or place; for these considered apart have nothing real in them, nothing to determine them, and indeed nothing that is discernible.

58. So it cannot be said, as is said here, that the wisdom of God may have *good reasons* for creating this world at a given particular time; for this particular time, taken apart from things, is an impossible fiction, and there can be no *good reasons* for a choice there where everything is indiscernible.

60. It should not then be said, as is said here, that God created things in a particular space, or at a particular time, *which was pleasing to him*, for since all times and all spaces are in themselves perfectly uniform and indiscernible, one cannot *please* more than another.

63. But it nowise follows that matter is eternal and necessary, unless we suppose that space is eternal and necessary: an altogether ill-founded supposition.

67. The parts of space are determined and distinguished only by the things which are in them, and the diversity of the things in space determines God to act differently on different parts of space. But space, taken apart from things, has nothing in itself to distinguish it, and indeed it has nothing actual about it.

68. If God has decided to place a certain cube of matter, he thereby also becomes determined on the place of the cube: but this is with respect to other particles of matter, and not with respect to detached space which has nothing in it to distinguish it.

93. I do not admit that every action gives a new force to the thing acted upon. It often happens at the meeting of bodies that each keeps its force, as when two hard bodies of equal size meet directly. Then the direction alone is changed, without there being any change in the force, each body taking the direction of the other, and turning back with the same speed it had before.

94. I am, however, careful not to say that it is supernatural to give a body a new force, for I recognise that one body often receives a new force from another body, which loses as much of its own. But I say merely that it is supernatural for the whole universe of bodies to receive a new force; and thus that one body should gain force without others losing the same amount. This is why I say also that it cannot be maintained that the soul gives force to the body; for then the whole universe of bodies would receive a new force.

99. I do not here undertake to establish my *Dynamics*, or my doctrine of forces. This would not be the proper place. But I can reply very well to the objection raised here. I had maintained that active forces are preserved in the world. The objection is that two soft or non-elastic bodies meeting together lose some of their force. I answer that this is not so. It is true that the wholes lose it in relation to their total movement, but the parts receive it, being internally agitated by the force of the meeting or shock.[q] Thus this loss occurs in appearance only. The forces are not destroyed, but dissipated among the small parts. There is here no loss of forces, but the same thing happens as takes place when big money is turned into small change. I agree, however, that the quantity of motion does not remain the same, and in this matter I approve what is said on page 341 of Mr. Newton's *Optics* which the author here quotes. But I have shown elsewhere that there is a difference between the quantity of motion and the quantity of force.[r]

104. I do not say that space is an *order* or *situation* which makes things situable. That would be talking nonsense. It is only necessary to consider my own words and to join them

with what I have said above (§ 47), to show how the mind comes to form the idea of space, without its being necessary for there to be a real and absolute being, corresponding to that idea, outside of the mind and outside of relations. I do not say then that space is an order or situation, but an *order of situations*, or an order according to which situations are arranged; and that abstract space is this order of situations which are conceived as possible. Thus it is something ideal, but the author appears not to want to understand me. I have already replied (§ 54) to the objection that an order is not capable of quantity.

105. The author objects that time could not be an order of successive things, because the quantity of time can become greater or smaller, while the order of successions remains the same. I answer that this is not so; for if the time is greater there will be more similar successive states interposed, and if it is less there will be fewer, because there is no void nor condensation nor penetration (so to speak) in times any more than in places.

106. I maintain that if there were no created things, the immensity and eternity of God would none the less subsist, but without any dependence on times or places. If there were no created things there would be no time or place, and consequently no actual space. The immensity of God is independent of space, as the eternity of God is independent of time. They only signify with regard to these two orders of things that God would be present and co-existent with everything which existed. Thus I do not admit what is here advanced, that if God alone existed time and space would exist as at present. On the contrary, on my view, they would exist in ideas only, as mere possibilities. The immensity and eternity of God are something more eminent than the duration and extension of created beings, not only in relation to the greatness, but also to the nature of the thing. These Divine attributes are not dependent upon things outside God, as are actual places and times. These truths have been sufficiently recognised by theologians and philosophers.

124. The natural forces of bodies are all subject to *mechanical*

laws; and the natural forces of minds are all subject to *moral laws*. The former follow the order of *efficient causes*; and the latter follow the order of *final causes*. The former operate without liberty, like a watch; the latter are exercised with liberty, although they agree exactly with that kind of watch which another, superior, free cause has set beforehand to fit in with them. I have already spoken of this in the present paper (§ 92).[8]

Notes

ABBREVIATIONS

A   Leibniz: *Sämtliche Schriften und Briefe*, Academy edition. (References to series, volume and page)

C   Couturat: *Opuscules et fragments inédits de Leibniz*

CL   Couturat: *La Logique de Leibniz*

GM *Leibnizens mathematische Schriften*, ed. Gerhardt

GP   *Die philosophischen Schriften von G. W. Leibniz*, ed. Gerhardt

SL   *Studia Leibnitiana*

OF AN ORGANUM OR ARS MAGNA OF THINKING

From the Latin, C 429–32. Couturat (CL, p. 128) argues that the work is closely related to a paper entitled 'A plan for a new encyclopaedia, to be written by a method of discovery' (C 30 ff), dated June 15–25 1679, and suggests that it belongs to the same period.

[a] 'Organum'—literally 'instrument'—is a reference to Aristotle's logical works, known collectively as the *Organon*. Leibniz, like Francis Bacon before him, is proposing a new 'instrument' of thought. 'Ars Magna' is a reference to the work of the same title by the Spanish theologian Raymond Lull, 1235–1315 (on whom see CL, pp. 36 ff, 541 ff; J. N. Hillgarth, *Ramon Lull and Lullism in Fourteenth-Century France* [Oxford, 1972]). Lull distinguished six groups of categories, with nine in each group, and he explored the ways in which terms from these groups can be combined. Leibniz criticised this scheme severely in his early work, *On the Art of Combinations* (1666), A VI.1, 192–4; GP IV, 61–4.

ᵇ Leibniz is referring to what he calls elsewhere an 'alpha-bet of human thoughts'; indeed, he wrote after this sentence (but then deleted): '*The alphabet of human thoughts* is a catalogue of those things which are conceived through themselves, and by whose combination the rest of our ideas arise'. See also *Of Universal Synthesis and Analysis*, p. 10.

ᶜ Although Leibniz was not the first mathematician to use a binary system (he was preceded, for example, by Thomas Harriot, who died in 1621) he appears to have discovered it independently during his stay in Paris, 1672–6 (J. E. Hof-mann, SL II [1970], pp. 232–3), and he wrote many studies of it, the first extensive one being dated 15 March 1679 (C 574. Cf. GM VII, 223 ff, 228 ff). The binary system is now well known because of its use in digital computers; the calculating machine invented by Leibniz, however, used the decimal system (cf. L. von Mackensen: 'Zur Vorgeschichte und Entstehung der ersten digitalen 4-Spezies-Rechen-maschine von G. W. Leibniz'. *Studia Leibnitiana Supplementa* II [Wiesbaden, 1969], pp. 34 ff).

ᵈ Leibniz often returns to this point, saying that definitions must be 'real' and not merely 'nominal': e.g. *Of Universal Synthesis and Analysis*, p. 12; *Discourse on Metaphysics*, art. 24; *A Specimen of Discoveries*, p. 76.

AN INTRODUCTION TO A SECRET ENCYCLO-PAEDIA

From the Latin, C 511–15. The paper is placed by Müller and Krönert (*Leben und Werk von G. W. Leibniz*, p. 58) at the end of 1679; cf. CL, p. 133.

ᵃ A similar account of the types of concept is to be found in *Of Universal Synthesis and Analysis*, pp. 11–12, 14; *Discourse on Metaphysics*, art. 24. Leibniz published his account of these distinctions in *Meditations on Knowledge, Truth and Ideas*, 1684 (GP IV, 422 ff).

ᵇ The work in question is *On the Equilibrium of Planes*.

ᶜ Cf. *Of Universal Synthesis and Analysis*, p. 15.

ᵈ A reference to Aristotle's *Topics*, which deals with arguments involving premises which are only probable (*Topics*, 100 a 18).

OF UNIVERSAL SYNTHESIS AND ANALYSIS

From the Latin, GP VII, 292–8. Müller and Krönert (op. cit., p. 64) date the work as 1680–4 (?); cf. CL, p. 189 n. 1, p. 323 n. 1. The work seems much more mature than the two preceding works, and a date near the end of this period— say, 1683—seems most probable (cf. D. J. Schulz, SL III [1971], p. 120 n. 16).

ᵃ 'notiones'. 'Notio' (and 'la notion') are normally translated in these selections as 'notion', and 'conceptus' as 'concept'. Leibniz draws no distinction between the two, and in the present context 'concept' seems a better translation for 'notio', since categories are traditionally associated with concepts.

ᵇ The reference is to *Ars Magna Sciendi, sive Combinatoria*, by Athanasius Kircher, published in 1669.

ᶜ Leibniz is referring to Euclid III 21: 'The angles in the same segment of a circle are equal to one another'.

ᵈ Probably Nicolas Malebranche (1638–1715) (see Leibniz's letter to him of 22 June 1679, GP I, 331–2) and Arnold Eckhard (d. 1685), a Cartesian professor of mathematics (conversation with Eckhard, 5 April 1677, GP I, 212–13).

ᵉ Leibniz is referring to St. Anselm (1033–1109), whose ontological argument was first expounded in the *Proslogion*. Gaunilo replied to this in his *Liber pro Insipiente* ('Book on behalf of the fool'); it is Anselm's reply to this which Leibniz mentions above.

ᶠ *Summa Theologica*, I, Qu. 2, Art. 1, ad 2.

ᵍ Leibniz offers such a proof in a paper submitted to Spinoza in 1676 (A II.1, 271–2; GP VII, 261–2). Essentially the same argument is contained in an abbreviated form in *Monadology*, par. 45.

ʰ *De corpore*, Book I, Chap. 3, secs. 7–9.

ʲ Literally 'ostensive and apagogic demonstration'. Indirect or apagogic proof is proof by means of a reduction to the impossible, 'apagōgē eis to adunaton'.

^k The reference is to St. Augustine's treatise, *De utilitate credendi*. See Augustine: *Earlier Writings*, trans. J. S. Burleigh (London, 1953), pp. 284 ff.

^l 'aphorismi ac praenotiones'. The term 'praenotio' was coined by Cicero to render the Epicurean term 'prolepsis' (*De natura deorum*, 1.17.44), and means roughly 'prior notion', 'innate idea'.

^m Cf. Leibniz's *Elementa Nova Matheseos Universalis*, C 351: analysis 'through a leap' is when 'we begin to solve the problem itself, making no other presuppositions. . . . Analysis by degrees (per gradum) is when we reduce the given problem to one which is easier, and this in turn to one which is easier still, and so on until we come to one which is within our power'. See also C 557: 'Analysis reduces a given problem to what is simpler; this occurs either by a leap, as in algebra, or by intermediate problems, in topics or reduction'.

ⁿ Cf. Descartes, *Reply to Second Objections* (*Œuvres*, ed. Adam and Tannery, Paris, 1896–1910, VII, 155–6; *Philosophical Works*, trans. E. S. Haldane and G. R. T. Ross, Cambridge 1934, II, 48–9).

^o 'Characteristica sive *speciosa*'.

^p Leibniz is here putting forward the idea of a purely formal science. He cannot be said ever to have completed such a science, but in the later years of his life he did something towards it, by constructing (after 1690) an abstract logical calculus which is capable of more than one interpretation (GP VII, 236 ff).

DISCOURSE ON METAPHYSICS

From the French. There are two main sources for the text: Leibniz's original manuscript, and a copy made by a secretary and corrected by Leibniz. The former was published by H. Lestienne in his edition of 1907 (2nd ed., Paris, 1952), and the latter is the basis of Gerhardt's text, GP IV, 427–63. The edition by H. Schmalenbach, in *G. W. Leibniz: Ausgewählte philosophische Schriften*, Vol. I (Leipzig, 1914), pp. 1–50, is a useful guide to the various editions, but is itself not without mistakes. Gerhardt's edition has been used as the basis of this translation, but some errors in the text have been corrected from Lestienne. The translation also includes the article headings, which are not in the copy but are in the original manuscript, and which were sent to Arnauld (see below).

The 'Discourse on Metaphysics'—Leibniz did not give the work a title, but it is referred to as such in a letter of 11 February 1686 (GP II, 11)—was written early in 1686. Its strongly theological tone is explained by the fact that Leibniz had the Catholic theologian Antoine Arnauld in mind as a recipient; the intermediary between them was Ernst, Duke of Hessen-Rheinfels, who was himself a Catholic convert and who wished to convert Leibniz. Leibniz sent Arnauld a summary of the Discourse, but never in fact sent him the complete work. (On the reasons for this, see E. Hochstetter, 'Leibniz als geistesgeschichtliches Problem' in SL, Sonderheft 1, *Systemprinzip und Vielheit der Wissenschaften* [1969], pp. 101–2.)

a The headings of the first seven articles are as follows: 1. Of the divine perfection, and that God does everything in the most desirable way. 2. Against those who maintain that there is no goodness in the works of God, or that the rules of goodness and beauty are arbitrary. 3. Against those who believe that God could have done better. 4. That the love of God demands a complete satisfaction and acquiescence with regard to what he does. 5. In what the rules of the perfection of the divine conduct consist, and that the simplicity of the ways is in equilibrium with the richness of the effects. 6. That God does nothing that is without order, and that it is not even possible to imagine events which are not regular. 7. That miracles conform to the general order, though they are contrary to subordinate maxims. Of what God wishes or permits, and of general or particular will.

b Leibniz is referring to the occasionalists and the Cartesians respectively. 'Occasionalist' philosophers, such as Malebranche and Geulincx (1624–69), argued that it is not really the case that one body causes another to move by hitting it; really, God causes the one to move *on the occasion of* its being hit by the other. A similar account was given of mind-matter interaction. Leibniz was always careful to distinguish his account of the pre-established harmony from occasionalism; see, e.g. *A Specimen of Discoveries*, p. 80, *New System*, pp. 121–2.

ᶜ This is closely related to the definition given by Aristotle, *Categories*, 2 a 11 ff: substance, in the primary sense of the word, is that 'which is neither predicated of a subject nor is in a subject'.

ᵈ Literally, 'being-in'. This term was used by Scholastic translators of Aristotle to render the Greek 'huparchei' ('belongs to').

ᵉ Literally, 'thisness'. The term is borrowed from Duns Scotus (*c.* 1270–1308), whose views on the principle of individuation were discussed by Leibniz in his earliest published philosophical work, *De principio individui* (1663).

ᶠ *Summa Theologica*, I, Qu. 50, Art. 4; *Summa contra Gentiles*, II, 93. St. Thomas argued that in the case of angels the principle of individuation comes, not from matter, but from form; Leibniz argues that this applies to all substances. Another way of putting Leibniz's point is to say (to Clarke, 4.6 p. 216) that 'to suppose two things indiscernible' (sc. exactly alike) 'is to suppose the same thing under two names'. Hence the name 'the identity of indiscernibles' (to Clarke, 4.5), usually given to the proposition that no two substances are different in number alone.

ᵍ Leibniz takes the phrase from a book by Libert Froidmont, *Labyrinthus, sive de compositione continui* (1631). Elsewhere Leibniz says that there is another labyrinth of the human mind—the problem of the nature of freedom (*On Freedom, c.* 1689, p. 107; *Theodicy*, Preface, GP VI, 29).

ʰ A reference to the occasionalism of Malebranche. Cf. note b above.

ʲ The term 'archaeus' is associated by Leibniz with J. B. van Helmont (*Ortus medicinae*, 1648), who meant by it a kind of vital principle which produces chemical reactions [A VI.2, 255]. The notion of the archaeus was also used to explain mind-matter relations. See *Metaphysical Consequences of the Principle of Reason*, sec. 4, p. 173.

ᵏ 'il extravague'.

[1] The distinction between 'absolute necessity' (also called 'logical', 'metaphysical' or 'mathematical' necessity) and 'hypothetical necessity' (also called 'moral' or 'consequential' necessity) is fundamental to Leibniz's account of freedom. The term 'hypothetically necessary' is derived from Aristotle, *Physics*, 200 a 13–14.

m 'So that it can be in the subject'.

n 'S'en aperçoivent'. Later (e.g. *Monadology*, par. 23) Leibniz uses the word 'apperception' to refer to conscious perception, as distinct from the perception which absolutely all substances have. The phrase could therefore be rendered, 'or whether others are conscious of them too'.

o Leibniz follows Scholastic usage in distinguishing between God's 'ordinary' and 'extraordinary' concourse. God's 'ordinary concourse' (for which see *Discourse on Metaphysics*, arts. 28 and 30; to Arnauld, 30 April 1687, p. 65) is the action by which God conserves the world with its laws, independently of his miraculous intervention; the latter is the work of his 'extraordinary concourse'. Descartes also used the terminology: see, e.g., *Discourse on Method*, Part V, Adam and Tannery VI, p. 42.

p The reference is to *Discourse on Metaphysics*, article 7. This begins: 'Now, since nothing can be done which is not orderly, it can be said that miracles are as orderly as natural operations, which are called 'natural' because they conform to certain subordinate maxims which we call the 'nature' of things. For one could say that this 'nature' is merely a custom of God, which he could dispense with because of a reason which is stronger than that which moved him to make use of these maxims'.

q The reference is to the Cartesians. Leibniz constantly returns to this point: e.g. to Arnauld, 8 December 1686, GP II, 78 ff; to Bayle, 1687, GP III, 42 ff; Observations on Descartes' *Principles*, GP IV, 370 ff; Explanation of the New System, par. 20, pp. 129–30.

r The headings of the next five articles are: 18. The distinction between force and quantity of motion is important, amongst other things, in that it makes one judge it necessary to have recourse to metaphysical considerations, distinct

from extension, in order to explain bodily phenomena. 19.
The usefulness of final causes in physics. 20. A memorable
passage of Socrates, in Plato's *Phaedo*, against philosophers
who are too materialist. 21. If the rules of mechanics de-
pended on geometry alone, without metaphysics, phenomena
would be entirely different. 22. A reconciliation of the way
which goes by final causes and the way which goes by
efficient causes, to satisfy both those who explain nature
mechanically and those who have recourse to incorporeal
natures.

   s Roughly, a 'being in itself', an independent being. Cf. *A
Specimen of Discoveries*, p. 76.

   t The reference is to Hobbes. Cf. *Of Universal Synthesis and
Analysis*, note h.

   u Perhaps a reference to the Scholastic theory of 'impressed species'—qualities sent out by the object and impressed on the faculty of knowledge. Alternatively, Leibniz
may have in mind the Scholastic theory of 'intentional
species', received from the object in the case of sensation—a
theory referred to, and rejected, in the Preface to the *New
Essays*, p. 63.

   v *Meno*, 81e–86b.

   w *De Anima*, 430 a1.

   x 'Ces sortes de doxologies ou practicologies'.

   y Gospel according to St. John, 1, 9.

   z Leibniz touches on the Scholastic and Aristotelian distinction between the active and the passive intellect. The
'bad sense' which Averroes (Ibn Roschd, 1126–98) and his
followers gave to the former was one which verged on the
idea of a world-mind; according to them, the active intellect
in each man is a part of a single active intellect.

   aa Taught at the University of Paris, *c.* 1250.

   ab The reference is to Malebranche.

   ac Romans, 11.33.

   ad A Calvinist sect. 'There are some authors who claim
that God, wishing to manifest his mercy and his justice in
accordance with reasons which are worthy of him but are
unknown to us, has chosen the blessed, and consequently
rejected the damned, before all consideration of sin, even that

of Adam . . . and it is because of this that these authors are called "Supralapsarians"' (*Theodicy*, par. 82; GP IV, 146).

ae See, e.g. Augustine, *Confessions*, III, Chap. 7, VII, Chap. 16. The 'others' referred to by Leibniz include Aquinas: *Summa Theologica*, I, Qu. 48, Art. 1; *Summa contra Gentiles*, III, 7–9.

af Article 31 is theological rather than philosophical. The heading of the article is: 'Of the motives of election, of faith foreseen, of mediate knowledge, of the absolute decree, and that everything is reduced to the reason why God chose for existence such and such a possible person, whose notion includes such and such a succession of graces and free actions; this ends the difficulties at a stroke.'

On 'mediate knowledge' see below, *Necessary and Contingent Truths*, note j.

ag St. Teresa. The reference is to Chap. 13 of the *Life*.

ah 'Eminently' in the Scholastic sense—i.e. in a higher or more perfect degree.

aj This ends the philosophical argument of the *Discourse on Metaphysics*. There is one more article, no. 37, headed: 'Jesus Christ has disclosed to men the mystery and the admirable laws of the heavenly kingdom, and the grandeur of the supreme happiness that God prepares for those who love him'. The article is little more than a string of quotations from the New Testament.

CORRESPONDENCE WITH ARNAULD

From the French, GP III, 17 ff. Gerhardt's text is based on the copy of the correspondence retained by Leibniz in Hanover; errors in this text can sometimes be corrected from copies of the letters that Arnauld actually received, preserved among his papers. (See *Lettres de Leibniz à Arnauld*, ed. by Geneviève Lewis, Paris, 1952.)

a It was mentioned in the notes to the *Discourse on Metaphysics* that Leibniz sent Arnauld only a summary of the *Discourse*. Arnauld replied (GP II, 15–16) by criticising article 13; the present letter is a reply to this.

ᵇ This sentence was omitted from Gerhardt's text.

ᶜ The Socinians (followers of Lelio and Fausto Sozini, 16th-century theologians) disbelieved in the Trinity.

ᵈ 'these circumstances'—i.e. all human events.

ᵉ The 'knowledge of vision' (scientia visionis) is concerned with what was, is or will be actual; 'simple knowledge' (scientia simplicis intelligentiae) is the knowledge of possibles. See the appendix to the *Theodicy, Causa Dei*, pars. 14, 16, GP VI, 440–1; also *Necessary and Contingent Truths*, pp. 96 and 103.

ᶠ Cf., e.g. *Primary Truths*, p. 90.

ᵍ That is, relations.

ʰ Leibniz is referring to Arnauld's book, *Des vraies et des fausses idées* (1683).

ʲ That is, the physicist does not concern himself with the theory of occasionalism, or the problems it was intended to solve.

ᵏ Cordemoy (d. 1684), a Cartesian occasionalist, differed from Descartes in holding that there are indivisible corpuscles and a vacuum in which they moved. His argument was that unless something indivisible is assured, it will be impossible to explain the unity and individuality of a complex body. (Cf. S. V. Keeling, *Descartes* [Oxford, 1934], pp. 207–9.)

ˡ Probably a reference to Democritus, fragment 9: 'By convention are sweet and bitter, hot and cold, by convention is colour; in truth are atoms and the void'. (Trans. by G. S. Kirk and J. E. Raven: *The Pre-Socratic Philosophers*, Cambridge, 1957, p. 422.)

ᵐ Gerhardt (GP II, 102) reads 'parties', but G. Lewis (op. cit., p. 75) suggests that the reading should be 'parélies' (parhelia, mock-suns), which gives better sense. The same phrase occurs in a work of about the same period, *Primary Truths*, p. 92.

ⁿ Leibniz refers to his letter of 30 April 1687; GP II, 91 (not translated here). Cf. *Discourse on Metaphysics*, art. 33.

A SPECIMEN OF DISCOVERIES

From the Latin, GP VII, 309–18. The many references to topics discussed in the *Discourse on Metaphysics* and the correspondence with Arnauld make it probable that the paper was written in about 1686.

ᵃ These points are made in greater detail in the first two paragraphs of *Primary Truths*, p. 87.

ᵇ *a se.* Cf. *Discourse on Metaphysics*, art. 23.

ᶜ A criticism of Descartes. Cf. *Discourse on Metaphysics*, art. 2; Remarks on a letter of Arnauld, May 1686, p. 52; *Monadology*, par. 46.

ᵈ *Concerning Diet*, par. 23.

ᵉ A German scholastic philosopher, 1096–1141.

ᶠ By 'universal substances' Leibniz seems to mean Aristotle's 'secondary substances' (deuterai ousiai; *Categories*, 2 a 14–19); that is, genera and species.

ᵍ Cf. *Discourse on Metaphysics*, art. 6.

ʰ Cf. a draft of a letter to Arnauld, 8 December 1686, p. 64.

ʲ Cf. *Specimen Dynamicum*, GM VI, 251: the 'common motion' of a number of bodies is that which can be ascribed to their common centre of gravity.

ᵏ No more is heard about the former alternative. When writing the *Discourse on Metaphysics*, Leibniz seems to have toyed with phenomenalism, suggesting that to talk about physical things is really to talk about perceptions. However, he deleted these passages from his manuscript (see Lestienne ed., pp. 40–1, 87, 89).

ˡ Cf. *Discourse on Metaphysics*, art. 18; to Clarke, 5.53.

ᵐ Albertus Magnus (*c.* 1207–80) was a Scholastic philosopher and theologian, who was also an important figure in mediaeval science (see, e.g. A. C. Crombie, *From Augustine to Galileo* [London, 1952], especially pp. 41–2, 92–7, 116–28). The Bacon referred to is John of Baconthorp (d. 1348), a Scholastic philosopher with Averroist leanings. Cf. to Arnauld, 8 December 1686, GP II, 75; *New System*, p. 117.

ⁿ Cf. to Arnauld, 30 April 1687, p. 67: 'That which is not truly *one* entity . . .'.

ᵒ Cf. *Discourse on Metaphysics*, art. 10; to Arnauld, 14 July 1686, p. 63, 30 April 1687, p. 68; *New System*, p. 117.

ᵖ Gerhardt's transcription of the manuscript ends here. Leibniz added to the last page a number of rough notes, in which he discussed the nature of firmness and fluidity, and added to his list of 'laws of corporeal nature'. Cf. G. H. R. Parkinson, 'Science and Metaphysics in Leibniz's *Specimen Inventorum*', *Proceedings of the 2nd International Leibniz Congress, Hanover 1972*.

PRIMARY TRUTHS

From the Latin, C 518–23. The work is untitled, but is usually referred to by its opening words, 'Primary truths' (Primae veritates). Like the *Specimen of Discoveries*, it is closely connected with the *Discourse on Metaphysics* and the correspondence with Arnauld.

a Cf. GP VII, 300, and to J. Bernoulli, August 1696, GM III, 321–2.

b Cf. *Generales Inquisitiones* (1686), pars. 16, 132 (C 366, 388). This definition of truth does not seem like Aristotle's, which is, 'To say of what is, that it is, and of what is not, that it is not, is true' (*Metaphysics*, 1011b 27, trans. W. D. Ross). Perhaps Leibniz understood him to mean that to say truly that S is P is to say that P is contained in S when P *is* contained in S.

c In *Primary Truths*, Leibniz does not reveal this secret, but he clearly has in mind his view that in the case of a contingent truth, to show the inclusion of the concept of the predicate in that of the subject would require an infinite analysis. Cf. *A Specimen of Discoveries*, p. 75; *Necessary and Contingent Truths*, p. 97; *On Freedom*, p. 109; *Generales Inquisitiones*, C 388–9.

d This principle is termed by Couturat the 'principle of symmetry' (CL, pp. 227–8). In the *Generales Inquisitiones* it is formulated as: 'If all things are alike on each side in our hypotheses, there can be no difference in the conclusions' (C 389).

e Cf. to Clarke, 4.4, p. 216.

f The text has 'sub notione possibilitatis'; but 'sub ratione possibilitatis' seems to be meant.

g Leibniz means that it is wrong to say that a body is really an aggregate of smaller, corporeal substances, for each of these smaller substances is really an aggregate of unextended substances.

THE NATURE OF TRUTH

From the Latin, C 401–3. The title is that supplied by Couturat. In content, the paper is close to the works of 1686.

ᵃ Leibniz adds a diagram, but since it adds nothing to the understanding of the text it is not reproduced here.

ᵇ This may be expressed more clearly as follows.

(i) (In terms of subject-predicate propositions.) If all A is B, and all C is A, then all C is B. (This is the mood *Barbara* in the first figure of the syllogism.)

(ii) (In terms of antecedent and consequent.) If A implies B, and C implies A, then C implies B.

ᶜ The term 'reduplicative proposition' refers to such propositions as 'Man, in so far as he is an object of the senses, is perishable' (Aristotle, *Analytica Priora*, 49 a 11 ff; Jungius, *Logica Hamburgensis* [1st ed., 1638], Bk. II, Chap. 11). An example is to be found in one of Leibniz's logical papers, C 261: 'Though a triangle and a trilateral are the same, yet if you say "A triangle, as such, has 180 degrees", "trilateral" cannot be substituted. There is in it something material'. The implication seems to be that it cannot be said that a trilateral, as such, has 180 degrees, because the term 'trilateral' contains no reference to angles.

ᵈ Leibniz seems to have in mind what the Scholastics termed 'suppositio materialis', where reference is made to a word itself rather than to what it stands for: e.g. the word 'gold' in '"Gold" is a word'. When the thing meant by the word is considered, the supposition is said to be 'formal'; e.g. the word 'gold' in 'Gold is a metal'.

NECESSARY AND CONTINGENT TRUTHS

From the Latin, C 16–24. The title was provided by Couturat. The topics discussed and the arguments brought are typical of the period of the *Discourse on Metaphysics*.

ᵃ That is, the knowledge of propositions depends on the

understanding of concepts. On 'the simple' and 'the complex' in this sense, cf. *An Introduction to a Secret Encyclopaedia*, p. 6.

ᵇ A 'duodenary' is a number divisible by 12: a 'senary' (used in the proof which follows) is a number divisible by 6. Cf. a similar argument in *On Freedom*, p. 109.

ᶜ Couturat's text does not mark a new sentence at this point. In the manuscript, however, not only a new sentence but a new paragraph begins with 'In Contingenti Veritate'.

ᵈ Literally, 'most universally true'. Similarly, the phrase 'absolutely universal laws' used below renders what is literally 'most universal laws'.

ᵉ Leibniz uses the Greek word 'kardiognōstes'. This adjective is used of God in the *Acts of the Apostles* (1.24; 15.8), but Leibniz can hardly be referring to God here.

ᶠ The two sentences which follow are a digression, relating to God's knowledge. In the passage beginning 'And although it is not true ...' Leibniz returns to his main point—that no created being can know in advance how a mind will act.

ᵍ This is in fact Leibniz's view. He argues that, because of the identity of indiscernibles, there cannot be two courses of action which are exactly alike. So the case of Buridan's ass— assumed to be placed midway between two equally attractive bundles of hay—is one which cannot arise (*Theodicy*, Par. 49, GP VI, 129–30).

ʰ Leibniz's argument may be made clearer by empha- sising that by 'physical necessity' he means the determination which holds when something *becomes* such and such. The truth of future contingents is not a matter of physical neces- sity; for although their truth is determined, this determination never *began*—it always existed.

ʲ For 'knowledge of vision' cf. *Correspondence with Arnauld*, note e. The term 'mediate knowledge' (scientia media) was introduced by the Spanish Jesuits Molina and Fonseca. By this they meant, according to Leibniz, knowledge *de futuris sub conditione*; that is, knowedge of what will happen if certain conditions are fulfilled. (*Causa Dei*, par. 17, GP VI, 411.) Cf. *On Freedom*, p. 111, and see the account given in G. Grua *Jurisprudence universelle et théodicée selon Leibniz* (Paris, 1953), pp. 288–93.

ON FREEDOM

From the Latin. Foucher de Careil, *Nouvelles Lettres et opuscules inédits de Leibniz* (Paris, 1857), pp. 178–85. A number of corrections to this text have been listed by G. Grua, *G. W. Leibniz: Textes inédits* (Paris, 1948), p. 236. Grua suggests 1689 as the date.

[a] A 'requisite' (*requisitum*) of a thing is 'that without the assumption of which the thing does not exist' (*Demonstratio Propositionum Primarum*, 1671–2?, A VI.2, 483).

[b] This appears to be a reference to Spinoza, who holds that there is a distinction between necessity and compulsion. A thing is called 'free' by Spinoza if it exists 'merely from the necessity of its own nature, and is determined to action by itself alone'; such a thing is distinguished from what is 'compelled' (coacta), which is determined by another (*Ethics*, I, Def. 7).

[c] Descartes.

[d] Cf. *Primary Truths*, p. 87.

[e] Cf. *Necessary and Contingent Truths*, p. 96.

A LETTER ON FREEDOM

From the French. E. Bodemann: *Die Leibniz-Handschriften der Königlichen öffentlichen Bibliothek zu Hannover* (Hanover, 1889), pp. 115–17. This was described by Bodemann as a letter without address or date. However, the reference towards the end of the letter to a 'recent' distinction between philosophical and theological sin dates the letter to Leibniz's journey in Italy, 1689–90. A collection of documents relating to the controversy concerning this distinction can be found in Grua, *G. W. Leibniz: Textes inédits*, pp. 235 ff.

NEW SYSTEM, AND EXPLANATION OF THE NEW SYSTEM

From the French, GP IV, 477–87, 493–8, 498–500. The first two articles were published initially in the *Journal des Savants*,

June 1695 and April 1696; the PS. comes from a letter to Henri Basnage de Beauval (1657–1710), editor of the *Histoire des Ouvrages des Savants*.

(The paragraph numbers found in some editions of the *New System* were added by the 19th-century editor Erdmann.)

a A reference to Descartes. Cf. Preface to *New Essays*, p. 170.

b *De Anima*, 412 a 27, b 5; the soul is 'the first entelechy of a natural body'.

c Perhaps a reference to *Summa contra Gentiles*, II, 58, 5, which states that there must be only one soul in one man or one animal.

d Pierre Gassendi (1592–1655) advanced a physical theory roughly similar to that of the classical Greek atomists, Democritus and Epicurus, and argued that such a theory was compatible with Christianity.

e Swammerdam (1637–80) was a Dutch biologist, author of *Historia insectorum generalis*; Malpighi (1628–94) and Leeuwenhoek (1632–1723) were early microscopists.

f Pierre Regis (1656–1726) was a French physician, author of *Cours entier de philosophie ou système général d'après les principes de Descartes*; Nicholas Hartsoeker (1656–1725) was a Dutch microscopist, who corresponded with Leibniz (GP III, 488–535).

g Pliny the Elder, *Natural History*, VII, 189. Cf. Kathleen Freeman, *The Pre-Socratic Philosophers* (Oxford, 1949), p. 314 n.

h *De caelo*, 298 b 17.

j St. Teresa. Cf. *Discourse on Metaphysics*, note ag.

k A reference to the Scholastics; cf. *Discourse on Metaphysics*, note u.

l Leibniz does not have in mind, say, a clockwork machine; the soul is not a kind of mechanism. (Cf. *Explanation of the New System*, p. 126.) Rather, he has in mind the literal sense of 'automaton'—'self-moved'.

m Leibniz means that, if we pay no attention to force, we cannot say that body *A* is in motion and body *B* is at rest (e.g. in astronomy, it would be as justifiable to say that the sun moves round the earth as that the earth moves round the sun; this is Leibniz's 'equivalence of hypotheses'). But we can say that *A* really moves if *A* possesses a motive *force*. (Cf. *A Specimen of Discoveries*, note l.)

n The phrase 'to save phenomena' (cf. *New Essays*, Preface, p. 171) is derived from the neo-Platonist Proclus (410–85; *Hypotyposis astronomicarum positionum*, 5.10). Proclus' view was that the astronomer should 'save the empirical phenomena exhibited by the planets from the verdict of unreality that seems to be invited by their irregularity' by discovering the orderly reality that lies behind appearances. (E. J. Dijksterhuis, *The Mechanization of the World-Picture*, English translation, Oxford, 1961, pp. 15–16.) Leibniz seems to use the phrase to mean taking care that one's hypotheses are consistent with empirical observations.

o i.e. activity which passes from the agent to some other; distinct from 'immanent' activity.

p Cf. *Discourse on Metaphysics*, art. 17, and note q.

q The *Histoire des Ouvrages des Savants*.

ON THE PRINCIPLE OF INDISCERNIBLES

From the Latin, C 8–10. The use of the term 'monad' indicates that the work was written after 1695 (Leibniz's first dated use of this word as a philosophical term is in a letter to the Marquis de l'Hospital, 22 July 1695; GM II, 295). The reference to Arnauld at the end may indicate that the paper was written during the period 1695–7, when Leibniz was thinking of publishing his correspondence with Arnauld; though it should be added that Leibniz was again planning to publish the correspondence in 1707–8. (Evidence summarised in the Introduction to *The Leibniz-Arnauld Correspondence*, trans. Mason, pp. xiii–xiv.)

a Compare the definition of existence in *Generales Inquisitiones*, par. 73 (C 376).

b Arnauld to Leibniz, 28 Sept. 1686; GP II, 64.

ON THE ULTIMATE ORIGINATION OF THINGS

From the Latin, GP VII, 302–8.

a Cf. a similar example used by Spinoza, Letter 40 (*Opera*, ed. Gebhardt, Heidelberg, 1925, Vol. IV, 198–9).

ᵇ Reading '*a priori* fingeretur' in place of Gerhardt's '*a priore* fingeretur'. Cf. W. Kabitz, quoted by L. Prenant, *G. W. Leibniz: Œuvres Choisies* (Paris, 1940), p. 458; cf. also P. Schrecker, *Leibniz: Monadology and other Philosophical Essays* (N.Y., 1965), p. 85, n. 2.

ᶜ Gerhardt's text has 'essentiam', but it is clear that 'existentiam' is meant.

ᵈ Cf. *A Specimen of Discoveries*, p. 75¹, and *A Résumé of Metaphysics*, par. 10 (p. 146).

ᵉ Leibniz is referring to his early work, *Hypothesis physica nova* (1671), and to his criticism of this in his *Specimen Dynamicum* of 1695 (GM VI, 240–1).

ᶠ Cf. p. 143 below; also *Discourse on Metaphysics*, art. 36; *Monadology*, pars. 85–6; *Metaphysical Consequences of the Principle of Reason*, par. 12, p. 177.

ᵍ Cf. Gospel according to St. John, 12.24.

ʰ Cf. *Principles of Nature and of Grace*, par. 18; to Bourguet, 5 Aug. 1715, GP III, 582–3.

RÉSUMÉ OF METAPHYSICS

From the Latin, GP VII, 289–91, C 533–5. The work seems to summarise the main theses of *On the Ultimate Origination of Things*.

ᵃ 'Existentificare'.

ᵇ 'Existiturire'.

NEW ESSAYS

From the French. Mrs. Morris' translation was made from GP V, 41–61; this text has been checked against the Academy edition, A VI, 6, 43–68. The *New Essays* were written between 1703 and 1705 (A VI, 6, xxiii–xxvi), but were substantially complete by 1704 (Müller and Krönert, op. cit., p. 190).

ᵃ Cf. *Discourse on Metaphysics*, note w; Locke, *Essay concerning Human Understanding*, II.1.2.

[b] Cf. *Of Universal Synthesis and Analysis*, note l.

[c] The name given by Euclid to his axioms.

[d] J. C. Scaliger (1484–1558): *Electa Scaligerea*, 1634.

[e] The edict of a praetor (a Roman magistrate concerned with justice) was written on white tablets (alba) posted up in some public place.

[f] Cf. to Arnauld, 9 Oct. 1687, p. 72, and note n.

[g] *New Essays*, 2.20.6.

[h] *Extrait d'une Lettre de M.L. sur un Principe General.* July 1687, GP III, 51 ff. Cf. Observations on Descartes' *Principles*, GP IV, 375–6.

[j] The reference is to Descartes and his followers.

[k] Cf. *Metaphysical Consequences of the Principle of Reason*, par. 13, p. 177.

[l] *Metaphysics*, 1073 a 26-b1; *De caelo*, 292 a 20 ff.

[m] Cf. to Hessen-Rheinfels, 14 March 1685: 'The Socinians, it seems to me, deny that the soul is naturally immortal, and maintain that it is conserved only by a special grace of God' (A I, 4, 353–4).

[n] For Leibniz, the cause of cohesion is 'conspiring motion' (GP IV, 388).

[o] With this attack on the Newtonian concept of gravity, compare *Metaphysical Consequences of the Principle of Reason*, par. 2, p. 177, and to Clarke, 5.35, p. 228.

[p] This sentence is omitted from Gerhardt's text (GP V, 57).

[q] 17th-century philosophers and scientists generally condemned explanations by means of 'occult qualities'—that is, explaining the observed behaviour, *B*, of a thing *X* by saying that there is in *X* a hidden *B*-producing quality. See, e.g., Descartes, Regula IX, ad fin., Adam and Tannery X, p. 403; Spinoza, Letter 56, *Opera*, ed. Gebhardt IV, p. 261; see also Leibniz, *Metaphysical Consequences of the Principle of Reason*, par. 2 (p. 172).

[r] *Du royaume de Siam*, 1691.

[s] Perhaps an echo of Spinoza's phrase 'asylum of ignorance' (ignorantiae asylum): *Ethics*, I Appendix (*Opera*, ed. Gebhardt, II, p. 81). See also to Clarke, paper 2, ad fin. p. 210.

[t] Bellarmin, *Disputationes de controversiis christianae fidei* (1619–20), Controversy VI, bk. 2, ch. 11.

ᵘ Robert Fludd, *Philosophia mosaica* (1638). Cf. Leibniz, *Specimen Dynamicum*, GM VI, 242.

ᵛ Cf. *Discourse on Metaphysics*, art. 10.

METAPHYSICAL CONSEQUENCES OF THE PRINCIPLE OF REASON

From the Latin, C 11–16. The use of the term 'monad' indicates that the work is later than 1695 (cf. notes to *On the Principle of Indiscernibles*); A. Robinet (SL I [1969], p. 87) relates the work to the correspondence with des Bosses, 1712.

[a] Cf. *Discourse on Metaphysics*, note j.

[b] See, e.g. *Unicum Opticae, Catoptricae et Dioptricae Principium*, 1682; *Tentamen Anagogicum*, GP VII, 273–8; *New Essays*, 4.7.15. Leibniz uses the principle that 'nature acts by the shortest paths, or at least by the most determinate' (*New Essays*, loc. cit.). Cf. Couturat, CL pp. 229 ff; G. Buchdahl, *Metaphysics and the Philosophy of Science* (Oxford, 1969, pp. 425 ff).

[c] 'Antitypia'. Cf. Leibniz, *On Nizolius*, A VI.2, 435.

[d] Cf. to des Bosses, 20 Sept. 1712 (GP II, 459 and note); see also GP II, 439.

[e] Cf. the account of 'expression' in the letter to Arnauld, 9 Oct. 1687, p. 71; also a letter to Foucher, 1686, GP I, 383.

[f] Cf. *Monadology*, par. 87; *Principles of Nature and of Grace*, par. 15.

MONADOLOGY

From the French, GP VI, 607–23. Cf. the edition by A. Robinet, *Principes de la Nature et de la Grace; Principes de la Philosophie ou Monadologie* (Paris, 1954). The work was written in 1714 for Nicolas Remond, an admirer of Leibniz's *Theodicy* (GP III, 599; Robinet, op. cit., p. 13). The title 'Monadology' was supplied by H. Köhler, who published a German translation in 1720.

[a] This presupposes Leibniz's definition of extension as a plurality of co-existing parts. See, e.g. *Generales Inquisitiones*, C 361; *Observations on Descartes' 'Principles'*, GP IV, 364.

ᵇ Cf. *Discourse on Metaphysics*, note u.

ᶜ 'un detail de ce qui change'.

ᵈ The term is defined below, par. 18.

ᵉ Rorario, a Papal legate (1485–1556) held that animals have rational minds; in his article 'Rorarius' Bayle attacked Leibniz's views. The passage in question comes from note h (see Bayle: *Historical and Critical Dictionary, Selections*, trans. R. H. Popkin, N.Y., 1965, p. 239).

ᶠ Cf. par. 64 below, and *New System*, note l.

ᵍ Pierre Poiret (1646–1719), a follower of Descartes.

ʰ Hermolaus Barbarus (1545–95) was an Italian interpreter of Aristotle. Cf. *Theodicy*, par. 87, GP VI, 150: 'This word "entelechy" apparently derives its origin from the Greek work which means "perfect", and it is for that reason that the celebrated Hermolaus Barbarus expressed it in Latin literally as "perfectihabia"'.

ʲ 'Et les composés symbolisent en cela avec les simples'. The term 'symboliser' here means 'agree with, tally with'. This was noted by E. Boutroux (*Leibniz: La Monadologie*, Paris, 1881, p. 176, n. 2), who quotes the surgeon Ambroise Paré on the subject of alchemical doctrine: 'Les éléments symbolisent tellement les uns avec les autres, qu'ils se transmuent l'un en l'autre'.

ᵏ Cf. *New Essays*, Preface, p. 156.

ˡ Cf. *Explanation of the New System*, par. 20, p. 130.

ᵐ The distinction between antecedent and consequent will is clearly explained in *Causa Dei*, par. 24, GP VI, 442. According to Leibniz, it is God's antecedent will that all men shall be saved; it is his consequent will that some shall be damned. 'Consequent will' refers to God's decisions (hence it is called 'decisive' in the *Monadology*), whereas the antecedent will only inclines.

PRINCIPLES OF NATURE AND OF GRACE

From the French, GP VI, 598–606. Cf. the edition by Robinet, cited in the notes to the *Monadology*. The work was written in 1714 for Prince Eugene of Savoy.

ᵃ Cf. *Monadology*, par. 64.

ᵇ Cf. *Monadology*, par. 74, and *New System*, p. 118.

ᶜ Cf. *Discourse on Metaphysics*, note ah.

ᵈ Cf. *Explanation of the New System*, par. 20, and note p.

ᵉ L. E. Loemker (*G. W. Leibniz: Philosophical Papers and Letters*, Chicago, 1956, p. 1203) suggests that this symbol—that of the infinite sphere—could have been derived from Pascal (*Pensées*, Brunschvicg ed., par. 72), or from the German Rosicrucians and theosophists.

CORRESPONDENCE WITH CLARKE

From the French, GP VII, 352 ff. Some editors of Leibniz are content to reproduce the English translation made by Clarke himself (London, 1717); Mrs. Morris, however, translated from the original French. The edition of the correspondence by A. Robinet (*Correspondance Leibniz-Clarke*) was subsequently published, in 1957. Gerhardt's edition, however, remains the basis. This was based on a copy of the correspondence which Leibniz retained; it sometimes differs from the text which Clarke received, as Leibniz revised his text slightly after sending the letters.

ᵃ The phrase 'either of the things . . . common cause' was added by Leibniz later, and is not in Clarke's version.

ᵇ Pierre Jurieu (1637–1713) was a French Protestant theologian. On the Socinians, cf. *Correspondence with Arnauld*, note c.

ᶜ This is Clarke's translation of 'les maintiendroit si bien dans leur capacité et bonne volonté'.

ᵈ Bacon's 'idols', described in the *Novum Organum*, are false notions which hinder the progress of science. The 'idola tribus', to which further reference is made below, have their basis in human nature—e.g. a tendency to rashness in judgement, to over-estimate arguments which support one's own views, etc. (cf. to Clarke, 3.12; 4.14). The 'idola specus' are due to man's individuality, in which he is enclosed like Plato's prisoners in their cave.

[e] Gerhardt's text is defective at this point. The correct reading (which was known to Clarke) is given in Robinet's edition.

[f] Clarke had objected (to Leibniz, 2.2), 'By the same argument it might just as well have been proved that men, or any other particular species of beings, must be infinite in number, lest God should want subjects, on which to exercise his power and wisdom'.

[g] Goclenius' *Lexicon Philosophicum* was published in 1613.

[h] To explain free will, the Epicureans postulated that the atoms made a chance swerve ('clinamen') from their natural movements.

[j] Clarke's version reads 'absolutely necessary' (i.e. the opposite of hypothetically necessary) which is clearer. Cf. to Clarke, 5.9 ad fin.

[k] This sentence is not in Clarke's version.

[l] Descartes, *Principles of Philosophy*, II, 21.

[m] Otto von Guericke (1602–86) performed in 1654 a spectacular experiment involving hemispheres from which air was pumped out.

[n] Torricelli's barometric experiment was performed in 1643.

[o] Sc. 'to the given body'. Clarke translates as 'which any other co-existent would have to this'.

[p] i.e. Newton's *Principia.*

[q] 'or shock' is not in Clarke's version.

[r] Cf. *Discourse on Metaphysics*, art. 17, and note q.

[s] Leibniz argues in par. 92 that 'Every agent which acts with choice, in accordance with final causes, is free, even though it happens to agree with that which acts only by efficient causes and without knowledge, or mechanically; for God, foreseeing what the free cause would do, has regulated its machine in such a way that it could not fail to agree with the free cause'.

Index of Names

263

Index of Subjects